D1066453

PR
2400
.A2
1975

1-22365

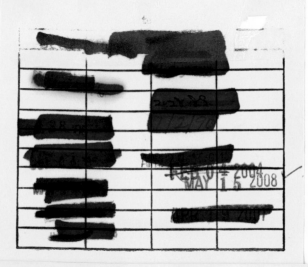

FEB 0 1 2004
MAY 1 5 2008

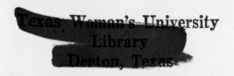

Texas Woman's University
Library
Denton, Texas

BRO
DART   PRINTED IN U.S.A.   23-364-002

WYATT

Collected Poems

Oxford University Press, Ely House, London W.1

GLASGOW   NEW YORK   TORONTO   MELBOURNE   WELLINGTON
CAPE TOWN   SALISBURY   IBADAN   NAIROBI   DAR ES SALAAM   LUSAKA   ADDIS ABABA
BOMBAY   CALCUTTA   MADRAS   KARACHI   LAHORE   DACCA
KUALA LUMPUR   SINGAPORE   HONG KONG   TOKYO

SIR THOMAS WYATT

Collected Poems

EDITED BY
JOOST DAALDER

LONDON
OXFORD UNIVERSITY PRESS
NEW YORK TORONTO
1975

SIR THOMAS WYATT
Born, Allington Castle, Kent, 1503
Died, Sherborne, Dorset, October 1542

ISBN 0 19 254167 6

© Oxford University Press 1975

This Oxford Standard Authors edition of
the *Collected Poems* of Sir Thomas Wyatt was
first published in 1975

Printed in Great Britain by
The Camelot Press Ltd, Southampton

PR
2400
.A2
1975

TEXAS WOMAN'S UNIVERSITY LIBRARY

PREFACE

An edition offering correct and annotated transcripts of the primary sources containing Wyatt's and other early Tudor verse is badly needed; meanwhile it is hoped that the present volume will provide the general reader with as accurate a modernized text as can at this stage be constructed, and that the annotation[1] will help him to understand and to enjoy Wyatt's poems, which are increasingly attracting attention for their intrinsic significance and appeal.

Much of the work on this edition was done in England in 1972, when the Council of the University of Otago and my colleagues kindly allowed me a year's leave of absence. However, textual problems in Wyatt have preoccupied me since my student days, when I first worked on them under Professor J. Swart, of the University of Amsterdam.

Since there was no reliable edition of Wyatt on which I could base my text, it has been necessary to re-edit it entirely. All the primary sources from which the text derives have been re-examined for this purpose. I have found that manuscripts, particularly, need to be investigated at first hand.

It will be observed that the text differs significantly from that in Kenneth Muir and Patricia Thomson, eds., *Collected Poems of Sir Thomas Wyatt* (Liverpool, 1969), which I have reviewed, together with other editions, in 'Editing Wyatt', *Essays in Criticism* XXIII (1973), pp. 399–413. It has been impossible to draw attention to the numerous errors throughout MT. A list of them would take up many pages. Mr. H. A. Mason attempts to correct MT from cover to cover in *Editing Wyatt* (Cambridge, 1972). Unfortunately the task is not carried out adequately. But I have avoided one or two mistakes as a result of Mr. Mason's efforts, and despite our disagreement on several matters we agree on others.

A good point about MT is that its Commentary gathers so much of the work done by other scholars, or at least references

---

[1] In accordance with O.U.P. practice, words explained in *The Concise Oxford Dictionary* have not been glossed.

1-22365

to it. This has saved me much time. I have also greatly benefited from the discussions of Wyatt's foreign sources, and I am indebted to the labours of the editors in some other respects; more so than I have been able to indicate in detail.

Since MT is readily available, it has seemed unnecessary to take over specific acknowledgements recorded there; however, I have attempted to correct several mistaken ones. My debt to Nott (the best editor of Wyatt), Rollins, and to a lesser extent Hughey, Padelford, and Foxwell, goes well beyond my specific references to their editions. For biographical information, I am particularly indebted to Nott, E. K. Chambers, Foxwell, Muir, and William H. Wiatt. But my least adequately acknowledged debt is to Raymond Southall, formerly of the University of Sheffield, now Professor of English at Wollongong University College, who has generously allowed me the use of his unpublished Ph.D. thesis (Birmingham University, 1961), which amongst other useful material includes the best complete transcripts of E and D which I have seen; and who not only offered me special transcripts of the H, C, and P poems, but also checked those in B, and rechecked several in E and D. An editor must make up his own mind about the primary sources, but I have greatly appreciated Professor Southall's help.

I am also very grateful to Mr. John Buxton, Fellow of New College, Oxford, for all the work he has put into supervising this edition.

My thanks are further due to the following for permission to consult and print from material in their possession: the Trustees of the British Museum; His Grace the Duke of Norfolk, E.M., K.G.; the Librarian of Trinity College, Dublin; and the Master and Fellows of Corpus Christi College, Cambridge. My task has been much eased by permission to consult material in the Bodleian Library and the English Faculty Library in Oxford.

While I have received generous help from many (I apologize to those I have overlooked), I alone am responsible for my inaccuracies. I should be grateful if they were pointed out to me.

Dunedin, May 1974   J. D.

CONTENTS

CHRONOLOGICAL TABLE

1503 Born Allington Castle, Kent. Son of Sir Henry Wyatt and Anne Skinner.

1516 Sewer Extraordinary at Court. Perhaps a student at Cambridge.

c. 1520 Married Elizabeth Brooke, daughter of Thomas, Lord Cobham.

1521 His son, Thomas, born. A daughter, Frances, born 1521 or 1522. W later (in 1526?) left his wife, apparently because she was adulterous.

1523 W, who became an Esquire of the Royal Body, twice carried royal funds to St. Mary's Abbey, York.

1524 Clerk of the King's Jewels.

1524 At Christmastide, participated in a feat of arms before Henry VIII, with Brian (cf. CVII), Poyntz (CV), and Norris (CXLIX).

1526 On a diplomatic mission to France with Sir Thomas Cheney. Carried messages from France to England and *vice versa*.

1527 On a mission to the papal court in Italy, with Sir John Russell. Also to Venice. Taken prisoner by the Spaniards; escaped, or set free.

1527 Translated Plutarch's *The Quyete of Mynde*.

1528 (or 1529) Marshal of Calais; again in 1530.

1532 Justice of the Peace in Essex.

1532 Accompanied Henry VIII and Anne Boleyn to France (cf. LIX).

1533 Deputized for his father as Chief Ewer at the wedding of Henry VIII and Anne Boleyn.

1534 May: committed to the Fleet after an affray with the sergeants of London. June: licensed to have twenty men in livery, and to command Kentish soldiers.

1535 High Steward of the Abbey of Malling. Knighted. Received grant of the lease of Aryngden Park, Yorkshire.

1536 May: put in the Tower, apparently in connection with the downfall of Anne Boleyn and her supposed lovers. Cf. CXLIII and CXLIX. Soon released, on parole to his father at Allington. Steward of Conysborowe Castle; aided King against Northern rebels with supply of men; Sheriff of Kent.

1537 Given the livery of his deceased father's lands. Sent to Spain as Ambassador, to improve strained relations between Henry VIII and Charles V—an impossible mission. Spent next few years mostly abroad.

1537 April: wrote letters to his son (cf. ML, 38–44).

1537 October: wrote letter at Barbastra, near Monçon, and poem LXXXI.

1538 April: Bonner (later Bishop of London) joined W as special ambassador. Thomas Cromwell, the Lord Privy Seal and W's patron, ensured that B.'s slanderous accusations against W (cf. ML, 64–69) came to nothing.

1538   June: in England with proposals from Charles V, who meanwhile agreed on a truce with Francis I. Visited Elizabeth Darrell (cf. e.g. XCVIII), the mistress of his later years. She bore him a son.

1539   Left Spain (early June) to return to England. Cf. XCIX.

1539   November: sent to Charles V in France, again as Ambassador.

1540   January: followed Charles V to Flanders. May: returned to England. June: an exchange of property arranged between Henry VIII and W. July: Cromwell arrested and put in the Tower.

1540   28 July: Cromwell beheaded. Cf. CLX.

1541   17 January: arrested and put in the Tower. Bonner's charges had been found amongst Cromwell's papers, and were revived. W instructed to answer the charges in writing (cf. his Declaration, ML 178–84); prepared his Defence (ML, 187–209). Soon released. Perhaps 'confessed', or was ordered to take back his wife.

1541   April: sent to Calais as captain of 300 light cavalry. Later M.P. for Kent.

1542   February: given some offices which had belonged to Katherine Howard's lover. March: again exchanged property with the King; made Chief Steward of the manor of Maidstone. August: captain of a number of vessels, and Vice-Admiral of the Fleet. October: conducted Irish leaders to do duty to Prince Edward.

1542   October: sent out to meet the Spanish Envoy at Falmouth. On his way, fell ill with a violent fever, and died in the house of a friend at Sherborne, Dorset. Buried there on 11 October, in the Great Church.

INTRODUCTION

As several scholars have recently observed, Wyatt's poems now enjoy greater critical esteem than at almost any time since his death. By and large, the poems in this edition will need no defence. The purpose of this Introduction will be to remove some possible obstacles to a just appreciation of them, and to present the poet himself to his readers.

In the past, Wyatt has been severely attacked for his supposed lack of prosodic skill. This criticism is now generally coming to be seen as largely unwarranted. The song-like poems, it is true, have on the whole given pleasure rather than offence to those who like flowing verse, but such readers have been inclined to disapprove of many poems (often, but certainly not always, 'translations') which they expected to be iambic, and then proceeded to condemn as irregular. The expectation is hardly justified. There is no doubt that the iambic pentameter became normative after Wyatt's death. It is clear, for instance, that the editor of Tottel's *Songes and Sonettes* (1557), which for the first time presented a sizeable proportion of Wyatt's poems to the general public, persistently attempted to eliminate what were felt to be undesirable metrical irregularities in them. However, when Wyatt himself came to write poetry, he naturally turned to such English traditions as were available to him. One of these traditions was that of native but rhythmically smooth lyrics, but 'side by side with this line of metrical form there existed the discursive poetry of the fifteenth century in which regular flowing rhythms played little or no part. This seems to have been part of the rhythmical tradition of the language that went back to the alliterative line with its well-marked pause separating two distinct rhythmical units.'[1] It is evident from more than one of Wyatt's revisions

[1] D. W. Harding, 'The Poetry of Wyatt', in *The Age of Chaucer*, ed. Boris Ford, Vol. I of *The Pelican Guide to English Literature* (1954; rev. impr. 1959), pp. 197–212. I quote from p. 203, but am indebted to the whole article.

that he had no consistent desire to make his lines iambic, and any attempt to read all of his verse as though he had is doomed to frustration, or forces one to record so many departures from the norm that the very existence of such a norm becomes questionable.

None the less, it is possible that Wyatt was to some extent working towards iambic pentameter verse. There are moments when it is difficult to escape this feeling—for instance the opening of Psalm 130 (CVIII). Where we can study his practice rather than that of his scribes, we can observe that he carefully varies his forms (e.g. in CVIII, *provokt* in line 89, but *provokyd* in line 396) so as to secure syllabic regularity.[2] But his accentual patterning is highly varied.

Much work has gone into the question of the relation between Wyatt's poems and his sources. This, however, is a matter for the specialist rather than the general reader, who need not feel that he cannot enjoy the poems without prolonged attention to it. Wyatt does build on traditional materials, both native and foreign, but it is the result which matters. As has been shown, the extent of his debt to foreign models has been much exaggerated. Many of his poems have been virtually ignored because they could not be compared with Petrarch and other continental authors. Those that can be are often quite different from their sources, and even when Wyatt is close to them, he works as a poet whose style bears the stamp of his own personality. He selects and shapes materials *he* can use. Much that he could find in Petrarch already existed in English literature anyway, and thus a Petrarchan sonnet is to him often no more than 'the occasion for a lover's complaint'.[3]

Of late, some of the 'translations' have been highly praised, the Psalms (CVIII) in particular, for the originality which they contain. This praise was much overdue, but it should not obscure two important points. The first is that originality is

---

[2] Accentuation and syllabification in Wyatt's time differed from modern English. Even with this fact in mind, however, we cannot read the verse as consistently iambic in the sense that, e.g., Pope's is.

[3] Raymond Southall, *The Courtly Maker* (Oxford, 1964), p. 35.

perhaps overvalued in our age. It is a quality that we are no doubt justified to esteem, but we must remember that Wyatt did not set himself up as an original poet in the way a later one might, so that if we treasure the original aspects of his work at the expense of the traditional ones, we are in danger of using an anachronistic yardstick. The second point is closely connected with the first. There has been a tendency amongst recent critics to reject the lyrics because these poems contain much conventional phrasing. This verdict does not seem valid. In art, we should not admire something because it is new or old, but because it is intrinsically important or appealing. It is, in any case, perfectly possible for a poet to share the feelings which a traditional phrase expresses; his use of such a phrase is no sign of insincerity on his part. But the real test of a poem's merit is not whether or not the poet uses conventional elements or really feels what he says; it is whether or not the poem is in its own right a successful artefact. Judged as such, many of Wyatt's lyrics are entirely satisfying, and it will be noticed that they reveal much the same *poetic* personality as do his other poems.

Even so, there are unmistakable signs that at least a number of Wyatt's poems did spring from his own experience, and we should probably see his life and his poems as an integrated whole. There is no space here for a detailed biography (which works by Nott, Chambers, and Muir go some way towards providing), and Southall, in *The Courtly Maker*, has already related much of Wyatt's verse to his life at Court. A brief sketch of the man and his poems may nevertheless be useful.

A Hans Holbein drawing of Wyatt is in the possession of the Queen. It is described (and dated about 1537 or later) by K. T. Parker, who also reproduces it, in *The Drawings of Hans Holbein in the Collection of His Majesty the King at Windsor Castle* (Oxford & London, 1945). According to Parker's account (pp. 54–55), three other portraits of Wyatt are based on a Holbein original which is now lost. One of these, a painting in the National Portrait Gallery, is reproduced on the cover of this book. Cf. also Kenneth Muir's *Life and Letters* (ML).

Contemporaries thought of Wyatt as strikingly handsome.

Surrey says that his form was one where force and beauty met, and that when he died Nature lost the mould of perfect manhood. Leland also comments on his beauty and physical strength. His all-round ability has often been remarked. He seems to have been skilled in arms, in sports, in diplomacy, in poetry, and in letters generally. About his learning there can be no doubt. According to the erudite Camden, Wyatt was 'splendide doctus'. He knew several languages, as is evident from his work as an Ambassador and from his poems. He was not only interested in politics and literature, however, but also in other activities of the mind—for instance, astronomy (cf. CIV). His intelligence is apparent from his diplomatic work and his poetry; perhaps particularly from his observations of Charles V, whose mind he seems to have gauged even where it hardly showed itself, from his Defence (1541; cf. ML, 187–209), and from his handling of difficult theological material in the Penitential Psalms (CVIII). It is often thought that he was an accomplished musician, but of this there is even less evidence than that he wrote poems to be sung.[4]

Wyatt was held in high regard by Henry VIII, Thomas Cromwell, and Charles V. There are several poems in his praise by people who knew him (cf. Nott and ML). Surrey's tributes (cf. ed. Emrys Jones, poems 28–31) are well worth reading for their perceptive comments on Wyatt's character and attributes. Quite rightly, Surrey sees Wyatt as restless, profound, moral, a generally excellent poet and particularly a Christian one, possessed of sharp judgement, and free from deceit himself, though the innocent victim of deceit practised by others.

A good deal has been written about Wyatt's supposed relationship with Anne Boleyn. It is doubtful whether we shall ever get at the exact truth about this, and even if we do, we should not see the matter as the chief thing behind Wyatt's verse. None the less, there are indications that Wyatt was at one time emotionally involved with Anne; the issue is of interest in itself; and to some extent it does affect our view of the poems.

[4] Despite, e.g., Winifred Maynard, *RES*, 1965, pp. 1–13 and 245–57.

Poem XCVII demonstrates that Wyatt had been in love with Anne Boleyn; line 8, before Wyatt revised it, read 'Her that did set our country in a rore'. However, poem VII, which quite likely also alludes to Anne, seems to suggest that he courted her rather than that he succeeded in becoming her lover. Obviously, we would read the poem differently if he was. The problem is to decide whether the contemporary documents which suggest a sexual relationship should be trusted (cf. ML, 19 ff.). Some of them may be Roman Catholic slander. But the account by William H. Wiatt (*ELN*, 1968, 94–102) would seem to lend quite plausible support to the tradition that Wyatt was Anne's lover, and confessed this to Henry VIII when the King set his mind on her.

According to Wiatt, the intimacy between the poet and Anne Boleyn probably began in 1525 or 1526. When he discovered that he had a rival in the King himself, and when in the late summer of 1527 the Court knew that Henry intended to marry Anne, Wyatt presumably confessed his former illicit affair to the King. Wyatt was sent to Calais, perhaps because it was convenient to have him away from Court for some time. In 1530, back at Court, Wyatt may unguardedly have talked about his earlier relationship, upon which the Duke of Suffolk possibly passed this on to the King, for which he was banished. Anne, safeguarding her interests, may have had a hand in Wyatt's second departure for Calais, in 1530.

This interpretation of events depends heavily on a letter written on 10 May 1530 by Chapuys, Charles V's ambassador in England, to the Emperor. In this letter Wyatt is not actually mentioned by name, and in any case we need not regard the problems as permanently solved. But Wiatt's account tallies well with the known facts, with the various sixteenth-century reports, and with the circumstance that the poet in his Defence of 1541 refers to the persistent hostility shown to him by the Duke of Suffolk, whom he blames for his imprisonment in 1536.

Whatever the precise circumstances alluded to in poem VII, the reference to Caesar makes little sense if it does not hint at Henry VIII, and Wyatt's attitude may carry more weight with us if we realize that it probably arises from the pressure of actual experience. Typically, he speaks as though he gives up the chase of his own accord while yet he reveals (as our view of the historical situation tends to confirm) that the situation leaves him little choice. Allusions to Anne Boleyn seem to be not infrequent in his poems, and not only in those written in or before 1527. Poem XCVII is probably much later, and poem LIX was almost certainly written in 1532 when Wyatt, accompanying Anne en route to France, reflected on his changed feelings towards her. We should not try to find hints where there are none, but in several places they offer themselves quite plainly (poem L is another example). The notes will deal with this matter in more detail. The allusions are the more remarkable if one remembers the constant dangers, often mentioned by Wyatt, of treachery, slander, and death in Henry VIII's court. It would have been less surprising if there were no allusions at all than if there had been many more.

It is a reasonable assumption that we are to imagine a real situation behind poems which less obviously refer to a particular, known woman. Of course we cannot be certain of this; many poems embody situations which may look real, but which had in fact been conventional in English verse for a long time. Nevertheless, what the poems express often fits in strikingly with the events in Wyatt's life. Wyatt frequently complains about the fickleness of women and their refusal to give him the protection of permanent love. In poem VII the woman is no doubt Anne Boleyn. At other times he may or does refer to other courtly ladies, but it is also notable that Wyatt appears to have repudiated his wife, Elizabeth Brooke, because she was adulterous. In a letter to his son (ML, 38 ff.), Wyatt characteristically says that the result of strife between man and wife is unrest, and equally characteristically he blames in his own case the woman rather than himself. (He seems to have been reluctant to help his wife financially, cf. ML, 37.) Not much is known about Wyatt's life with the mistress of his later years, Elizabeth Darrell, but there is sufficient evidence to show that he loved her, and his affection

for her is plain in poem XCVII, while XCVIII almost certainly
expresses his longing for her while he is in Spain (we should
note that lines 79–80 are Wyatt's addition to his source). If
Wyatt appears anxious, this is not in the least surprising: we
know for certain that his relations with Elizabeth Brooke and
Anne Boleyn were not permanent.

Wyatt's poems often deal with courtly love in a very literal
sense; but courtly love was closely tied up with courtly politics
(as in Anne Boleyn's case), and Wyatt's reactions in both
spheres show consistency. The death of Thomas Cromwell, for
instance, is described in much the same language in poem CLX
as Wyatt uses elsewhere in his love poems. The editor of
Tottel's *Songes and Sonettes* actually thought that the poem was
about 'the death of his loue'. Clearly Wyatt thought of
Cromwell as offering the security which at other times he
expected from women. This time, his grief is on record outside
the poem; and we find Wyatt writing (ML, 142) that his *only
trust* is in Cromwell and the King. Much of his verse is about
the loss of, or betrayal of, trust. It is often impossible to decide
whether he is referring to a treacherous mistress or to a
deceitful enemy at Court. Certainly his courtly experiences
account for his fear and hatred of slander, the more dangerous
because it is concealed. We need only think of the malicious
Bonner, a persistent enemy, to whom Wyatt owed his
imprisonment in 1541. Poems that refer to a sudden,
unhinging shift in the favours of Fortune can be seen as related
to this confinement, or for example to Wyatt's spell in the
Tower in 1536, when he witnessed the fall of others besides.
This event is specifically alluded to in poems CXLIII and
CXLIX.

It is true that on the whole Wyatt's life was not unsuccessful,
given the circumstances of Henry's regime, but he suffered
enough misfortune to explain the melancholy tone in much of
his work, and his condemnation of the vices which he saw
around him or was the victim of. He encountered a good deal
of frustration in his diplomatic work, and he witnessed the
duplicity of Charles V, on which he comments in his letters,
and perhaps in poem CV. In his first letter to his son, he

speaks as though he has gone through 'a thousand dangers and hazards, enmities, hatreds, prisonments, despites and indignations' (cf. ML, 40). He blames his own 'folly and unthriftiness' for this, as he does more than once in his verse; but it is significant, and fully consistent with what we find in the poems, that already in 1537 he saw his life as made up of these depressing experiences. It is only natural that in several poems we see Wyatt turn away from the courtly life (outwardly alluring, but perilous and nauseating underneath), and express a preference for a quiet, humble, and anonymous life.

This may sound as though he tended to indulge in easy escapism, but such is not the case. He remained involved in the courtly life until his sudden death, but tried to steel his nerves by enduring suffering patiently. He instructed his son to read Seneca, the Roman Stoic philosopher, who left his stamp on some of Wyatt's verse, and he was influenced, too, by Boethius and by Plutarch's *Quyete of Mynde* (Wyatt's title), which he translated. Quiet of mind is indeed what Wyatt in several poems professes to be his aim. But even when we see him in poem CV at Allington, the family's castle in Kent, we must remember (no matter whether the poem was written in 1536 or 1541) that Wyatt in all probability had been released from prison shortly before, and that, besides, his chief interest is in attacking courtly vices, not in the countryside. He shows a tough kind of wit here, too.

In not a few poems, he sets himself against desire for materials things (CVI) and against lust (CVI and CLXXXIV), because they lead man astray and into unhappiness. In CVI he does not see lust as a bad thing merely because it makes man unhappy, but also because it is God's way that it does, and God's wish that man seek virtue. Against man's vice, whether it springs from others or from himself, Wyatt seeks support in God. The Penitential Psalms (CVIII) reveal how David turns to God partly because he is in danger from his enemies (as Wyatt was in 1536 and 1541), but particularly because of his own sexual sin. David must show repentance if his relationship with God is to be harmonious. Unfortunately we do not know precisely when the poem was written or what autobiographical events Wyatt may allude to. But we do know from Wyatt's letters to his son (ML, 38 ff.) that in 1537 he was much concerned with his own sins, God's chastising him, God's favour 'purchased' for him by his father, and the need for repentance. There is a striking resemblance to David's concerns within the poem. And it is interesting that Wyatt's father writes, with reference to the cause of Wyatt's imprisonment in 1536, that Wyatt has been indiscreet and needs to be disciplined; he is to learn to 'fly vice and serve God better than he hath done' (cf. ML, 31). The poet, in his first letter to his son, states as plainly why one is to give God the helm of the ship of one's life, and what the disastrous consequences are if one does not, as he does in several of his poems (cf., e.g., CXLIII). Wyatt relates his religious message to events in his own life in this letter; presumably the relationship is implied in his poems.

It should also be pointed out that Mr. Mason finds Protestantism in the Psalms. Again, there are several indications outside the poem that Wyatt did have Protestant sympathies. There is the testimony of Wallop (ML, 176–7), also that of the Swiss reformer Heinrich Bullinger (1545). Wyatt himself admits in his Defence (ML, 195) that he was thought of as a Lutheran rather than a 'Papist'. He showed great zeal in attacking the Inquisition, from which he was in danger. And his anti-Roman feelings are obvious in poem CV. But, as Mr. Mason explains, Wyatt was not a sectarian. In one letter to Henry VIII, he describes himself as a good papist (ML, 72). This was a time when the best and most earnest minds struggled with their religious and ethical problems in an independent way, and Wyatt is no exception. We should not call the Psalms 'Lutheran' or 'Protestant' and then conveniently leave them unread; they have plenty of life, and this is because we see in them a mind reforming itself—in a true and significant sense—in contact with God.

Wyatt's loyalty to Henry VIII is apparent throughout his career. His father had been as loyal to Henry VII. We need not, as modern readers, question Wyatt's sincerity in this. He was a patriot, and anti-papal. His patriotism is evident from his diplomatic work, but also, for instance, from poem XCIX. His loyalty to King and Country is in character. He felt threatened by and disapproved of man's treachery and instability. He is sorrowful; he attacks; he tries to attain quiet of mind in the face of danger; but above all he values a strong *rapport*—with women and friends, with Cromwell and Henry, and with God.

NOTE ON THE TEXT

Full, accurate descriptions and transcripts of most of the primary sources are yet to appear; only a few brief comments can be offered here. (Cf. also the somewhat more detailed account of the textual situation in *EinC*, 1973, 399–413.)

The following are the most important manuscripts containing poems supposedly by Wyatt (I use Muir and Thomson's abbreviations):

1. Egerton MS. 2711 (British Museum)	E
2. Devonshire MS. Add. 17492 (B.M.)	D
3. The 'Blage' MS.D.2.7. (Trinity College, Dublin)	B
4. Arundel (Arundel Castle)	A
5. Harleian MS. 78 (B.M.)	H
6. Parker MS. 168 (Corpus Christi College, Cambridge)	C
7. Hill MS.Add. 36529 (B.M.)	P
8. Royal MS. 17^A, xxii (B.M.)	R

The following are the chief printed sources:

1. Richard Tottel's *Songes and Sonettes* (1557)	T
2. *The Court of Venus* (*c.* 1538 and 1563)	V
3. *A Boke of Balettes* (*c.* 1548)	BB
4. *Certayne Psalmes* (1550)	Q
5. *Nugae Antiquae* (1769, 1775, 1804)	N

So far, the most thorough descriptions of E and D are those by Southall in SCM. Hughey, in her edition of A, discusses that MS. fully, and contributes much material on P, N, T, and E also.

E is the most authoritative MS. It contains a number of poems in Wyatt's hand (cf. Appendix). From this it is often inferred that W owned the MS., but the assumption is without foundation, even though several other poems are corrected by W. It is not always possible to be sure whether a correction is

W's or someone else's (certainly more than one hand undertook revisions), but where I feel that corrections are by W I have recorded that impression. Poems in W's hand are probably his (particularly because he was in the habit of revising them), and poems in someone else's hand but corrected by W may well be, though corrections are not confined to him.

Many poems, particularly at the beginning of the MS., are not in W's hand, and several of these are not corrected by him. Their authorship is more doubtful, though such evidence as we have points in W's direction. There are poems bearing the ascription 'Tho', almost certainly for 'Thomas'. The poet himself may have been responsible for these ascriptions, or else, quite likely, someone close to him. If these ascriptions are to be trusted, the authorial status of the remaining poems is somewhat ambiguous. A group is ascribed 'Wyat'; Southall thinks by the poet Nicholas Grimald (who also appears in T), but I rather tend to doubt this. (Certainly Grimald is responsible for some of the revisions and punctuation marks.) Some of the poems are unascribed. It is nevertheless possible that all the E poems are W's, and I think that the evidence favours those who think that they are. Apart from the facts mentioned, it should be pointed out that E differs significantly from, say, D, in that D contains many poems, at various points, known to be not by W; that some other sources (D, H, T) ascribe E poems to W (T, particularly, of course need not be reliable, though it is significant that in T2 a 'W' poem was transferred to the section 'Uncertain Authors'); and that E contains many 'translations' of the kind known to be W's.

Since the order of the poems in E may to some extent be important chronologically, it has been retained, except that I follow MT in detaching CV–CVIII.

D is presumably the second most important MS. Several poems in it are ascribed to W, either in D itself, or elsewhere (E, T). The D poems that occur also in E in most cases can be shown or assumed to be versions earlier than E's final ones. There are several readings in D which correspond to E readings later rejected by W. D is thus likely to offer readings which do not represent W's final intentions, but which are at least close to what he once wrote. However, poem XCVIII is an exception, the E version being textually earlier than D's.

D shows the typical history of a court album. The MS. went from one hand to another, from scribe to scribe and from reader to reader. For this reason, and because D (like other MSS. but unlike E) contains many poems not by W, there is no particularly good reason for assuming that unascribed poems which happen to look like W's, in some or many respects, are his. Until they can be shown to be, they are strictly anonymous. If all such poems, from D and other MSS., had been included in this edition, it would have been much too big (one might have included even more poems than previous editors), and this volume is to present Wyatt's poems rather than a collection of anonymous ones. I have nevertheless included a number of unascribed poems, chiefly for their interest, but also because some, at least, might be W's. Except in the case of E, unascribed poems are printed separately.

Very little is known about B, which in MT is preferred to D. The MS. was at some stage in the hands of Sir George Blage, a friend of W's who was with him in Spain, but this by itself lends little special authority to B, and it is quite possible that Blage did not first own the MS. but got possession of it sometime in the 1540s and realized that it was not a collection of Wyatt poems (cf. Richard Harrier, *RenQ*, 1970, 471–4). There are in fact very few poems in B which by any scholarly criterion can safely be attributed to W. Comparison with E shows that B is reasonably close to it, but there are many important departures. Nothing is known about the authority of readings unique to B, and though one or two of them may look superior to D's, we appear to be on safer ground with D.

Ruth Hughey has shown that A almost certainly derives from E, and that its variants represent later, editorial tampering. Several of them are identical to T's, and there must be a fairly direct connection between A and T, but it is not clear of what kind.

H provides only few poems not found elsewhere. However,

comparison with E indicates that it is highly reliable if E is. It usefully ascribes poems to W.

C contains a good version of CV, and a superior one of a T poem (CLXVII).

P has roughly speaking as much or as little authority as A, with which it has much in common (cf., e.g., MEW, 31 ff.), though it provides few poems.

R contains only a very good version of CVIII; it is helpful in the reconstruction of lines 100–53.

The printed sources are generally of less value. T provides some poems not found elsewhere, and many that are. Collation with E and other MSS. reveals that T derives from one or more excellent sources, but contains many variants that are the product of an editorial process characterized by a taste very different from W's own. The lyrics have been least affected. The second edition (T2) shows independence of the first and may sometimes be better, but little is known about its authority. Later editions of T are increasingly degenerate. T has been superbly edited by H. E. Rollins. Cf. also the facsimile reprint of T1, *Songes and Sonettes (Tottel's Miscellany) 1557*, by The Scolar Press Ltd. (Menston, 1967).

The fragments of V and BB have little to recommend themselves to the editor of W. The texts of the poems, unlike those in T1, are printed very badly, and they appear to be unreliable. Fortunately we need almost never use them. They have been thoroughly edited by Russell A. Fraser under the title *The Court of Venus* (Durham, N.C., 1955). (However, the relationship with B and other primary sources needs to be reconsidered, and cf. Charles A. Huttar, *SB*, 1966, 181–95.)

Like R, Q need only be used in the reconstruction of lines 100–53 of CVIII. However, it is inferior to A and especially R, as comparison with E shows (cf. MEW, 149). It was brought out by Thomas Raynald and John Harrington.

The N poems may have been set up from leaves now missing in A (cf. Hughey, I, 375 ff.).

There is a good deal of important Wyatt material missing. Even for this reason alone the text we construct must needs be tentative. On the other hand, it is plain that we have some very good manuscript material (part of it in the poet's hand), and other texts which we can be reasonably sure are less reliable. Although the hierarchy of texts is not entirely certain, instances where two or more versions seriously compete with each other for our attention are in practice rare.

In almost all instances it has not been difficult to decide which version should be selected as the copy text for a poem. In one or two cases (cf. Appendix), the text produced here is the result of conflation. In a number of instances, I have had to depart from the copy text. Obvious scribal errors have been silently corrected, but where the copy text might be right, where I have felt that a variant should be considered, and where I have not been able to make up my mind, I have presented the relevant facts—the most important of them in the footnotes, others in the Selected Textual Notes. An effort has been made to record all significant departures; however, most of them are readings supplied by other primary sources where the copy text is clearly defective, and the few editorial emendations are generally neither new, nor, I imagine, controversial. As far as substantial readings are concerned, the primary sources have been conservatively treated.

However, the text has been modernized, and consistently so, since otherwise it would have looked like a curious mixture of modern English and archaisms.[1] A few old forms have been retained for, e.g., prosodic reasons. Final -e has not been, since there are strong indications that it was not sounded (but in XI, 4, MS. *nede* represents our *needy*).[2] Final -es has been selectively preserved.

Thorough account has been taken of the punctuation in the primary sources, but the punctuation here provided, though sometimes a translation of that in the MSS., is editorial, and modern. It differs drastically from what is found in previous editions of W, though it seems to me that Nott often interprets

---

[1] For convenience, quotations from ML have also been modernized.

[2] Once or twice (cf., e.g., CVII, 24) MS. *withoute* is perhaps an error for *withouten*.

W's syntax correctly where subsequent editors do not.[1]

To distinguish authentic titles from editorial ones, the former have been printed in italics.

In general, the aim has been to make W accessible to today's readers by modernizing the text and punctuating it, but otherwise to be faithful to the best primary sources.

---

[1] Except, occasionally, Gerald Bullett, ed., *Silver Poets of the Sixteenth Century* (London, 1947; repr. 1962).

Postscript: since the above was written, and after this edition had already gone to the press, R. L. Greene's note (*RES*, 1974, pp. 437–9) about MT's CCXX has reached me. Greene's valuable information does not persuade me that the anonymous poem is by W; on the contrary, the writer is more likely to be Anne Boleyn or her brother George.

LIST OF ABBREVIATIONS

For abbreviations of the chief primary sources, see Note on the Text, p. xxi.

Baldi	Sergio Baldi, *La Poesia di Sir Thomas Wyatt* (Florence, 1953).
Camp.	Ioannis Campensis; cf. Appendix, CVIII.
Chambers	E. K. Chambers, *Sir Thomas Wyatt and Some Collected Studies* (London, 1933; repr. New York, 1965).
CC	Cambridge Univ. MS., ff. 5, 14. (Cf. F. D. Hoeniger, *N & Q*, 1957, 103–4.)
CT	Chaucer, *Canterbury Tales*. (Cf. Robinson.)
EinC	*Essays in Criticism.*
ELN	*English Language Notes.*
EM	*English Miscellany.*
F	A. K. Foxwell, ed., *The Poems of Sir Thomas Wiat*, 2 vols. (London, 1913; repr. New York, 1964).
Flügel	Ewald Flügel, ed., 'Die Handschriftliche Überlieferung der Gedichte Von Sir Thomas Wyatt', *Anglia*, 18 (1896), 263–90, 455–516; 19 (1897), 175–210.
FMLS	*Forum for Modern Language Studies.*
FS	A. K. Foxwell, *A Study of Sir Thomas Wyatt's Poems* (London, 1911; repr. New York, 1964).
GG	H. E. Rollins, ed., *A Gorgeous Gallery of Gallant Inventions* (Cambridge, Mass., 1926).
Grimald	Nicholas Grimald; cf. Note on the Text, p. xxii.
Hughey	Ruth Hughey, ed., *The Arundel Harington Manuscript of Tudor Poetry*, 2 vols. (Columbus, Ohio, 1960).
JEGP	*Journal of English and Germanic Philology.*
Jones, Emrys, ed.	*Henry Howard, Earl of Surrey, Poems* (Oxford, 1964).
Kökeritz	Helge Kökeritz, 'Dialectal Traits in Sir Thomas Wyatt's Poetry', in *Franciplegius*, ed. J. B. Bessinger Jr. and R. P. Creed (London, 1965).
LGW	Chaucer, *The Legend of Good Women*. (Cf. Robinson.)
M	Kenneth Muir, ed., *Collected Poems of Sir Thomas Wyatt* (London, 1949; 4th impr., 1963).
Mason	H. A. Mason, *Humanism and Poetry in the Early Tudor Period* (London, 1959).
Maxwell	J. C. Maxwell, review of MT, *N & Q*, 1969, 465–7.
MEW	H. A. Mason, *Editing Wyatt* (Cambridge, 1972).

ML   Kenneth Muir, *The Life and Letters of Sir Thomas Wyatt* (Liverpool, 1963).

MT   Kenneth Muir and Patricia Thomson, eds., *Collected Poems of Sir Thomas Wyatt* (Liverpool, 1969).

N.E.D.   See *OED*.

Nott   G. F. Nott, ed., *The Works of Henry Howard, Earl of Surrey, and of Sir Thomas Wyatt, the Elder*, 2 vols. (London, 1815–16; repr. New York, 1965).

N & Q   *Notes and Queries*.

ODEP   *The Oxford Dictionary of English Proverbs*, 3rd ed. (Oxford, 1970).

OED   *Oxford English Dictionary*.

Padelford   F. M. Padelford, ed., *Early Sixteenth Century Lyrics* (Boston, 1907).

Petrarch, *Rime* Francesco Petrarca, *Le Rime*, ed. G. Carducci and S. Ferrari (Florence, 1899; repr. 1957).

PF   Chaucer, *The Parliament of Fowls*. (Cf. Robinson.)

QM   W's *The Quyete of Mynde* (MT, 440–63). Cf. also fac. ed. Charles R. Baskervill (Cambridge, 1931).

RenQ   *Renaissance Quarterly*.

RES   *The Review of English Studies*.

Robbins   R. H. Robbins, ed., *Secular Lyrics of the XIVth and XVth Centuries* (Oxford, 2nd ed. 1955; repr. 1968).

Robinson   F. N. Robinson, ed., *The Works of Geoffrey Chaucer* (2nd ed., London, 1957).

Rollins   H. E. Rollins, ed., *Tottel's Miscellany* (1557–1587), 2 vols. (Cambridge, Mass., 1928 and 1929; rev. ed. 1965).

RR   Chaucer, *The Romaunt of the Rose*. (Cf. Robinson.)

S   Raymond Southall (see SCM below); also in private communications.

SB   *Studies in Bibliography*.

SCM   Raymond Southall, *The Courtly Maker* (Oxford, 1964).

Serafino, *Opere* *Opere dello Elegantissimo Poeta Seraphino Aquilano* (Florence, 1516). Cf. also Barbara Bauer-Formiconi, ed., *Die Strambotti des Serafino dall' Aquila* (München, 1967).

ST   Raymond Southall, transcripts of E and D in his unpublished Ph.D. thesis (Birmingham University, 1961).

Stevens   John Stevens, *Music and Poetry in the Early Tudor Court* (London, 1961).

T & C   Chaucer, *Troilus and Criseyde*. (Cf. Robinson.)

Thomson   Patricia Thomson, *Sir Thomas Wyatt and his Background* (London and Stanford, 1964).

Tilley   M. P. Tilley, *A Dictionary of the Proverbs in England in the Sixteenth and Seventeenth Centuries* (Ann Arbor, 1950).

Tillyard   E. M. W. Tillyard, ed., *The Poetry of Sir Thomas Wyatt: a Selection and a Study* (London, 1929; rev. ed. 1949).

TLS	*Times Literary Supplement.*
TSSL	*Texas Studies in Literature and Language.*
W	Wyatt.
Whiting	B. J. Whiting, *Proverbs, Sentences and Proverbial Phrases from English Writings Mainly before 1500* (Cambridge, Mass., 1968).
WMT	William Tydeman, ed., *English Poetry 1400–1580* (London, 1970).
Z	British Museum Add. MS. 18752. Cf. Appendix, CLXXXII.

I

POEMS FROM
THE EGERTON
MANUSCRIPT

3

I

Behold, Love, thy power how she despiseth!
My great pain how little she regardeth!
The holy oath, whereof she taketh no cure,
Broken she hath, and yet she bideth sure,
Right at her ease, and little she dreadeth.   5
Weaponed thou art, and she unarmed sitteth;
To thee disdainful her life she leadeth,
To me spiteful without cause or measure:
    Behold, Love!

I am in hold: if pity thee moveth,   10
Go bend thy bow, that stony hearts breaketh,
And with some stroke revenge the displeasure
Of thee and him that sorrow doth endure,
And as his lord thee lowly entreateth:
    Behold, Love!   15

II

What 'vaileth truth? Or by it to take pain?
To strive by steadfastness for to attain
To be just, true, and flee from doubleness?
Sithens all alike where ruleth craftiness:
Rewarded is both false and plain,   5
Soonest he speedeth that most can feign,
True meaning heart is had in disdain.
Against deceit and doubleness
    What 'vaileth truth?

Deceived is he by crafty train   10
That meaneth no guile, and doth remain

---

3 *oath*: of loyalty in a 'mistress'–'servant' relationship.
3 *cure*: care, heed.   4 *bideth sure*: remains unconcerned.
10 *in hold*: in prison (fig.). Cf., e.g., Robbins, poem 136, 37; poem 160, 5.
11 *hearts*: MS *hertes*; possibly disyllabic.   12 *displeasure*: injury; wrong.

---

10 *train*: deceit.

Within the trap without redress.
But for to love, lo, such a mistress,
Whose cruelty nothing can refrain,
    What 'vaileth truth?   15

III

Caesar when that the traitor of Egypt
With the honourable head did him present,
Covering his gladness, did represent
Plaint with his tears outward, as it is writ;
And Hannibal eke when fortune him shut   5
Clean from his reign, and from all his intent,
Laughed to his folk whom sorrow did torment,
His cruel despite for to disgorge and quit.
So chanceth it oft: that every passion
The mind hideth by colour contrary,   10
With feigned visage now sad now merry.
Whereby if I laughed any time or season,
It is for because I have no other way
To cloak my care but under sport and play.

IV

The long love that in my thought doth harbour
And in mine heart doth keep his residence,
Into my face presseth with bold pretence,
And therein campeth, spreading his banner.

12 *redress*: remedy.
13 *But*: T and Nott seem to agree that this is independent of *redress* (12), which in E is followed by a point. However, it is possible to read 10–14 as one sentence.

---

1 *the . . . Egypt*: Ptolemy XII (r. 51–47 B.C.).
2 *the . . . head*: Pompey's. After losing the civil war between him and Caesar, P. fled to Egypt, where, however, he was killed.   3 *represent*: show.
5 *shut*: MS. *shitt*, rhyming with *writ* (4).   14 *care*: grief.

---

1 *harbour*: lodge, encamp (in hiding). Or perhaps a metaphor from hunting: a stag is said to harbour in its regular retreat, cf. *OED*. II. 8 (Buxton).

She that me learneth to love and suffer 5
And will that my trust and lust's negligence
Be reined by reason, shame and reverence,
With his hardiness taketh displeasure.
Wherewithal unto the heart's forest he fleeth,
Leaving his enterprise with pain and cry, 10
And there him hideth, and not appeareth.
What may I do, when my master feareth,
But in the field with him to live and die?
For good is the life ending faithfully.

V

Alas the grief and deadly woeful smart,
The careful chance, shapen afore my shirt,
The sorrowful tears, the sighes hot as fire,
That cruel love hath long soaked from mine heart!
And for reward of over-great desire 5
Disdainful doubleness have I for my hire!

O lost service! O pain ill rewarded!
O pitiful heart, with pain enlarged!
O faithful mind, too suddenly assented!
Return, alas, sithens thou art not regarded; 10
Too great a proof of true faith presented
Causeth by right such faith to be repented.

O cruel causer of undeserved change!
By great desire unconstantly to range—
Is this your way for proof of steadfastness? 15
Perdie you know (the thing was not so strange)
By former proof too much my faithfulness:
What needeth then such coloured doubleness?

6 *will*: wishes (It. *vòl*).
6 *lust's negligence*: 'the careless confidence (Padelford) caused by my lust'; MS.
may have *lustie*. 8 *displeasure*: umbrage. 9 *fleeth*: MS. *fleith* (disyllabic).
14 'For the life which ends with faithful service is good.'

2 *careful*: sorrowful. 2 *shapen . . . shirt*: 'created before my shirt was';
proverbial, cf., e.g., Chaucer, *CT*, A1566.

I have wailed thus weeping in nightly pain,
In sobs and sighs, alas, and all in vain,   20
In inward plaint, and heart's woeful torment,
And yet alas, lo, cruelty and disdain
Have set at nought a faithful true intent,
And price hath privilege truth to prevent.

But though I starve, and to my death still mourn,   25
And piecemeal in pieces though I be torn,
And though I die, yielding my wearied ghost,
Shall never thing again make me return:
I quit the enterprise of that that I have lost
To whomsoever lust for to proffer most.   30

VI

(fragment)

But sithens you it essay to kill
By cruelty and doubleness,
That that was yours you seek to spill
Against all right and gentleness,
And sithens you will, even so I will.   5

And then alas when no redress
Can be, too late, ye shall repent,
And say yourself with words express:
'Alas, an heart of true intent
Slain have I by unfaithfulness.'   10

23 *intent*: endeavour.
24 *price*: probably Henry VIII's wealth, which gives him the privilege of
purchasing Anne Boleyn's affection, to the injury of W's true love (Nott). Cf.
30, but also F and MT.
25 *starve*: die (from lack of love).
29 *enterprise*: management.
30 *lust*: likes (subjunctive).

---

3 *spill*: destroy, kill.

VII

Whoso list to hunt: I know where is an hind.
But as for me, alas I may no more:
The vain travail hath wearied me so sore,
I am of them that farthest cometh behind.
Yet may I by no means my wearied mind   5
Draw from the deer, but as she fleeth afore
Fainting I follow. I leave off therefore,
Sithens in a net I seek to hold the wind.
Who list her hunt, I put him out of doubt,
As well as I may spend his time in vain,   10
And graven with diamonds in letters plain
There is written her fair neck round about:
'*Noli me tangere*, for Caesar's I am,
And wild for to hold, though I seem tame.'

VIII

Mine old dear enemy, my froward master,
Afore that Queen I caused to be accited

This, as Nott and others have remarked, seems an unmistakable reference to Henry VIII's capture of Anne Boleyn, and was probably written in 1527 or before.
2 *may*: can. Cf. ML, 87, 'I can no more'.
8: Proverbial, cf. Tilley, W416.
9 *I . . . doubt*: 'I can assure him' (*put out of*=remove); cf. *RR*, 2102 (WMT).
11–12: Cf. Hawes, *Passetyme of Pleasure*, 169–71.
11 *diamonds*: in Petrarch symbolic of chastity, but in W perhaps of hardness.
13: *Noli me tangere* was said by Christ to Mary Magdalene after his resurrection; the motto was held 'to be inscribed on the collars of Caesar's hinds so that they were were left alone' (MT), and had become traditional. *Caesar's*: presumably here Henry VIII (the 'price' of V, 24?). Petrarch means that Laura will return to God after a short earthly life. Cf. also Matthew 22:21.
14: Nott finds this line (not in Petrarch) an appropriate comment on Anne Boleyn.

This may have been written at the same time as V and VII, if 'price' (140) refers to Henry VIII. Cf. V, 24.   1: Cupid.
2 *that Queen*: Reason.
2 *accited*: summoned.

Which holdeth the divine part of nature,
That like as gold in fire he might be tried.
Charged with dolour, there I me presented   5
With horrible fear, as one that greatly dreadeth
A wrongful death, and justice alway seeketh.

And thus I said: 'Once my left foot, Madame,
When I was young I set within his reign,
Whereby other than firely burning flame   10
I never felt, but many a grievous pain;
Torment I suffered, anger and disdain,
That mine oppressed patience was passed,
And I mine own life hated at the last.

Thus hitherto have I my time passed   15
In pain and smart. What ways profitable,
How many pleasant days, have me escaped
In serving this false liar so deceivable?
What wit hath words so prest and forcible
That may contain my great mishappiness   20
And just complaints of his ungentleness?

O, small honey, much aloes and gall!
In bitterness hath my blind life tasted
His false sweetness that turneth as a ball,
With the amorous dance hath made me traced.   25
And where I had my thought and mind araced
From all earthly frailness and vain pleasure,
He took me from rest, and set me in error.

3 *the . . . nature*: reason (T: 'of *our* nature').   4 *tried*: refined.
8 *my left foot*: acc. to Vellutello the left foot is sense or appetite (cf. MT).
9 *reign*: kingdom. 10 *firely*: fierily, ardently.   18 *deceivable*: deceitful.
19–20: 'What talent has words so prompt and powerful that it can contain my
great unhappiness?' Cf. Petrarch, and 36–39.
23–25: '"In bitterness has my blind life tasted his [the lord of Love's] false
sweetness which has drawn me into (or with) the amorous dance." W adds the
proverbial phrase *that torneth as a ball* (cf. Tilley, W901)' (MT). *Dance*: cf. 'loves
daunce' (*T & C*, II, 1106), and Stevens, 360, 'thowe I do fere to trace
[=participate in] that dawnce'.
26 *araced*: lifted forcefully; cf. It. *sollevarmi*.   28, 123 *error*: wandering (lit.).

He hath made me regard God much less than I ought,
And to myself to take right little heed,   30
And for a woman have I set at nought
All other thoughts, in this only to speed.
And he was only counsellor of this deed,
Always whetting my youthly desire
On the cruel whetstone, tempered with fire.   35

But alas where now had I ever wit,
Or else any other gift given me of nature,
That soon shall change my wearied sprite
Than the obstinate will that is my ruler?
So robbeth my liberty with displeasure   40
This wicked traitor, whom I thus accuse,
That bitter life hath turned me in pleasant use.

He hath chased me thorough divers regions,
Thorough desert woods, and sharp high mountains,
Thorough froward people, and strait pressions,   45
Thorough rocky seas, over hills and plains,
With weary travail and laborious pains,
Always in trouble and in tediousness,
In all error and dangerous distress.

But neither he nor she, my t'other foe,   50
For all my flight did ever me forsake:
That though timely death hath been too slow,
That as yet it hath me not overtake
The heavenly goodness of pity do it slake,
And not this cruel extreme tyranny   55
That feedeth him with my care and misery.

40 *displeasure*: sorrow.
42: 'That my bitter life has, out of habit, become pleasant.'
45 *strait pressions*: tight pressures (MT). *Pressions* is a French borrowing.
48 *trouble*: grief, affliction.   48 *tediousness*: pain.
53–55: 'If death have not already overtaken me, this is owing to the pity of
[heavenly goodness], and not to any abatement of cruelty on the part of Love'
(Nott).   56 *care*: grief.

Since I was his, hour rested I never,
Nor look for to do, and eke the waky nights
The banished sleep may nowise recover.
By deceit and by force over my sprites   60
He is ruler, and since there never bell strikes,
Where I am, that I hear not, my plaints to renew.
And he himself he knoweth that that I say is true.

For never worms have an old stock eaten
As he my heart, where he is alway resident   65
And doth the same with death daily threaten.
Thence come the tears, and the bitter torment,
The sighs, the words, and eke the languishment,
That annoy both me and peradventure other:
Judge thou, that knowest the one and the other.'   70

Mine adversary with grievous reproof
Thus he began: 'Hear, lady, the other part,
That the plain truth from which he draweth aloof,
This unkind man, shall show ere that I part.
In young age I took him from that art   75
That selleth words and maketh a clattering knight,
And of my wealth I gave him the delight.

Now shameth he not on me for to complain
That held him evermore in pleasant game
From his desire, that might have been his pain.   80
Yet only thereby I brought him to some frame
Which as wretchedness he doth greatly blame,
And toward honour I quickened his wit,
Where else as a daskard he might have sit.

70 *the . . . other*: i.e. both Love and me.
73–74: 'Which shall, before I leave, reveal the plain truth from which he, this ungrateful man, deviates.'
76 *selleth*: 'palms off false words as true' (Rollins).
77, 136 *wealth*: well-being.
81 *frame*: state of order; profit.
84 *daskard*: (i.e. *dastard*) dullard, sot.

He knoweth that Atrides, that made Troy fret,   85
And Hannibal, to Rome so troublous,
Whom Homer honoured, Achilles that great,
And the African Scipion the famous,
And many other by much virtue glorious
Whose fame and honour did bring them above,   90
I did let fall in base dishonest love.

And unto him, though he no deals worthy were,
I chose right the best of many a million,
That under the moon was never her peer
Of wisdom, womanhood, and discretion;   95
And of my grace I gave her such a fashion,
And eke such a way I taught her for to teach,
That never base thought his heart might have reach.

Evermore thus to content his mistress,
That was his only frame of honesty.   100
I stirred him still toward gentleness,
And caused him to regard fidelity;
Patience I taught him in adversity.
Such virtues he learned in my great school,
Whereof he repenteth, the ignorant fool.   105

These were the deceits and the bitter gall
That I have used, the torment and the anger,
Sweeter than for to enjoy any other in all.

85 *Atrides*: Agamemnon, son of Atreus.
86 *troublous*: causing grief. MS. *trobelous*, trisyllabic.
87 *Whom . . . honoured*: i.e. Achilles.
88: Scipio Africanus Major, the conqueror of Hannibal (86).
91 *dishonest*: dishonourable; unchaste.   92 *no deals*: not at all.
94 *under the moon*: in this sublunary sphere, on earth.
98 *reach*: the syntax is obscure, and hardly explained by the It. As T implies,
base thought seems to be the subject. Perhaps: '*to* his heart might have reach'?
Or *reach=reached*. The idea is the frequent one that the courtly lover is purified
morally by serving a superior mistress.
100 *frame of honesty*: form of decency. Cf. ML, 38.   101 *gentleness*: courtesy.
108: 'Sweeter than whatever else could be enjoyed in any other woman.'

Of right good seed ill fruit I gather,
And so hath he that the unkind doth further.   110
I nourish a serpent under my wing,
And of his nature now 'ginneth he to sting.

And for to tell at last my great service,
From thousand dishonesties I have him drawn,
That by my means in no manner of wise   115
Never vile pleasure hath him overthrown,
Where in his deed shame hath him always gnawn,
Doubting report that should come to her ear:
Whom now he accuseth, he wonted to fear.

Whatsoever he hath of any honest custom,   120
Of her and me that holdeth he every whit.
But lo, there was never nightly phantom
So far in error as he is from his wit
To plain on us: he striveth with the bit
Which may rule him, and do him pleasure and pain,   125
And in one hour make all his grief remain.

But one thing there is above all other:
I gave him wings, wherewith he might fly
To honour and fame, and if he would farther,
By mortal things, above the starry sky: 130
Considering the pleasure that an eye
Might give in earth, by reason of his love,
What should that be that lasteth still above?

109: Cf. XXIX, 14.
111 *a serpent*: i.e. an ungrateful and treacherous being. Proverbial expression,
cf. XLIX, 5.
118 *Doubting*: fearing.
123 *wit*: 'right mind'.
124 *striveth . . . bit*: cf. Tilley, B424.
130 *By*: through (It. *Per*).
131–3: 'Considering the pleasure which an eye, by virtue of its love, can instil
into others even here on earth, what must everlasting pleasure in Heaven be
like?'

And he the same himself hath said or this,
But now forgotten is both that and I,   135
That gave her him, his only wealth and bliss.'
And at this word, with deadly shright and cry,
'Thou gave her me,' quod I, 'but by and by
Thou took her straight from me, that woe worth thee!'
'Not I,' quod he, 'but price that is well worthy.'   140

At last both each for himself concluded,
I trembling, but he with small reverence:
'Lo thus as we have now each other accused,
Dear lady, we wait only thy sentence.'
She smiling, after this said audience,   145
'It liketh me,' quod she, 'to have heard your question.
But longer time doth ask resolution.'

IX

Was I never yet of your love grieved,
Nor never shall, while that my life doth last,
But of hating myself that date is past,
And tears continual sore have me wearied.
I will not yet in my grave be buried,   5
Nor on my tomb your name yfixed fast,
As cruel cause that did the spirit soon haste
From the unhappy bones, by great sighs stirred.

137 *shright*: shriek.   139 *worth*: befall. Cf., e.g., WMT, 41.
140 *price*: cf. V, 24. Nott hesitated between Petrarch's 'He (God) who willed to
take her to himself' and 'a richer rival'. The second suggestion is supported by
H. Howarth (*Italica*, 1964, 80–81), who argues that the rival is Henry VIII
taking Anne Boleyn.
145 *after . . . audience*: as Nott saw, this phrase is not part of Petrarch's quoted
matter, and fits well into 145.
147: 'But finding an answer requires more time.'

1 *of your love*: by loving you.   1 *grieved*: cf. CXVII, 5.
6 *yfixed*: fixed. The *y* is a past participle prefix, rare in Wyatt (Kökeritz notes
only four instances of its use), perhaps taken from Chaucer, apparently
archaic, and probably a metrical filler.

Then if an heart of amorous faith and will
May content you, without doing grief,   10
Please it you so to this to do relief.
If other wise ye seek for to fulfil
Your disdain, ye err, and shall not as ye ween:
And ye yourself the cause thereof hath been.

X

Each man me telleth I change most my device,
And on my faith me think it good reason
To change propose like after the season,
For in every case to keep still one guise
Is meet for them that would be taken wise: 5
And I am not of such manner condition,
But treated after a diverse fashion,
And thereupon my diverseness doth rise.
But you that blame this diverseness most,
Change you no more, but still after one rate   10
Treat ye me well, and keep ye in the same state:
And while with me doth dwell this wearied ghost,
My word nor I shall not be variable,
But always one, your own both firm and stable.

XI

Farewell, the reign of cruelty!
Though that with pain my liberty
Dear have I bought, yet shall surety
Conduct my thought of joys needy.

---

12 *other wise*: another manner (object of *seek*); cf. Baldi, 220.

---

1 *device*: purpose (but see *OED*).
2-3: Proverbial, cf. *ODEP*, p. 900 (Tilley, M431), particularly *Precepts of Cato*
(1545), 'In a wyse man it is no maner of cryme, His maners to chaunge,
accordynge to the tyme.'   3 *propose*: i.e. purpose.
4-5: Cf. *ODEP*, p. 900 (Tilley, M420), 'A wise man changes his mind, a fool
never.'   4 *guise*: 'course of life' (Hughey).
14 *always one*: always one and the same; cf. *semper idem*.

---

1 *reign*: MS. *rayn*, possibly=*rein*, cf. IV, 7 and XCV, 7.
3 *surety*: security (from danger, an enemy).
4 *needy*: i.e. *thought* (cf. Baldi, 220).

Of force I must forsake pleasure,   5
A good cause just, since I endure
Thereby my woe, which be ye sure
Shall therewith go, me to recure.

I fare as one escaped that fleeth,
Glad that is gone, yet still feareth   10
Spied to be caught, and so dreadeth
That he for nought his pain leseth.

In joyful pain rejoice, mine heart,
Thus to sustain of each a part.
Let not this song from thee astart: 15
Welcome among my pleasant smart.

XII

If amorous faith, in heart unfeigned,
A sweet languor, a great lovely desire,
If honest will, kindled in gentle fire,
If long error, in a blind maze chained,
If in my visage each thought depainted,   5
Or else in my sparkling voice lower or higher
Which now fear, now shame woefully doth tire,
If a pale colour, which love hath stained,
If to have another than myself more dear,
If wailing or sighing continually,   10
With sorrowful anger feeding busily,
If burning afar off, and freezing near,
Are cause that by love myself I destroy:
Yours is the fault, and mine the great annoy.

---

8 *recure*: cure.
9–11 *I . . . caught*: 'I go like one who is fleeing after having escaped, glad that he's gone, but always afraid that he's spied on in order to be caught.'
9 *fleeth*: MS. *fleith*, disyllabic.   12 *leseth*: loses.
14 *each*: i.e. joy and pain.   15 *astart*: escape.

---

2 *lovely*: loving.   4 *error*: wandering.
6 *sparkling*: producing scattered sounds (It. *interrotte*).
14 *annoy*: injury; sadness. Cf. It. *danno*, and Chaucer.

XIII

Farewell Love, and all thy laws for ever!
Thy baited hooks shall tangle me no more:
Senec and Plato call me from thy lore,
To perfect wealth my wit for to endeavour.
In blind error when I did persever,   5
Thy sharp repulse, that pricketh aye so sore,
Hath taught me to set in trifles no store,
And 'scape forth, since liberty is liever.
Therefore farewell! Go trouble younger hearts,
And in me claim no more authority;   10
With idle youth go use thy property,
And thereon spend thy many brittle darts:
For hitherto though I have lost all my time,
Me lusteth no longer rotten boughs to climb.

XIV

My heart I gave thee, not to do it pain,
But to preserve it was to thee taken.
I served thee, not to be forsaken,
But that I should be rewarded again.
I was content thy servant to remain,   5
But not to be paid under this fashion.
Now since in thee is none other reason,
Displease thee not if that I do refrain:

3 *Senec*: Seneca, the Roman stoic philosopher (*c.* 4 B.C.–A.D. 65). W's poems are sometimes influenced by him, and W recommended him to the attention of his son (Nott; cf. ML, 43).
4: 'To apply my intelligence to achieving perfect happiness' (WMT).
8 *liever*: dearer.
11 *property*: instrument (i.e. the bow).
14 *no . . . climb*: proverbial (Nott), cf. Tilley, B557. *Me lusteth*: I like.

2 *taken*: entrusted.
8 *refrain*: give up; withdraw.

Unsatiate of my woe and thy desire,
Assured by craft to excuse thy fault!   10
But since it please thee to feign a default,
Farewell I say, parting from the fire:
For he that believeth bearing in hand
Plougheth in water, and soweth in the sand.

XV

For to love her for her looks lovely
My heart was set in thought right firmly,
Trusting by truth to have had redress.
But she hath made another promise,
And hath given me leave full honestly.   5
Yet I do not rejoice it greatly,
For on my faith I loved too surely.
But reason will that I do cease
        For to love her.

Since that in love the pains been deadly,   10
Me think it best that readily
I do return to my first address,
For at this time too great is the press,
And perils appear too abundantly
        For to love her.   15

10: 'Presumptuous enough to excuse your fault with deceitful cunning.'
11 *feign*: conceal.
13: 'For he who believes in being deluded by false promises . . .' Cf. CXXXVI, 23.
14: Proverbial (F; cf. Rollins). See also Tilley, S87, S184.

---

4 *another*: to another. I.e. Henry VIII?
5 *given me leave*: permitted me to go. Cf. XXXVII, 18.
7 *surely*: confidently.
8 *will*: demands. Cf. Marot's 'la raison *ordonne*'.
12 *my first address*: 'the attitude I adopted towards her at first'.
13 *press*: either 'throng (of rivals)' (but cf. *another*, 4), or 'pressure, distress', or 'exertion' (cf. LXXI, 9).

XVI

There was never file half so well filed
To file a file for every smith's intent,
As I was made a filing instrument
To frame other, while I was beguiled.
But reason hath at my folly smiled,   5
And pardons me, since that I me repent
Of my lost years and time misspent,
For youth did me lead, and falsehood guided.
Yet this trust I have of full great appearance:
Since that deceit is aye returnable,   10
Of very force it is agreeable
That therewithal be done the recompense.
Then guile beguiled plained should be never,
And the reward little trust for ever.

XVII

Help me to seek, for I lost it there,
And if that ye have found it, ye that be here,
And seek to convey it secretly,
Handle it soft, and treat it tenderly,
Or else it will plain and then appair.   5
But rather restore it mannerly,
Since that I do ask it thus honestly.
For to lose it, it sitteth me too near:
    Help me to seek.

Alas, and is there no remedy,   10
But have I thus lost it wilfully?

1 ff. *file*: (noun) 1 the instrument for polishing, 2 deceiver; (verb) 1 to polish, 2 deceive, 3 defile.
2 *intent*: use; scheme.   4 *frame*: 1 shape, 2 benefit, serve.
9: 'But I have one hope which looks very promising.'
11–12: 'It (deceit) is automatically suitable for one to requite deceit with it.'

3 *convey*: perhaps 'steal' (Nott).
5 *plain*: i.e. complain; *appair*: pine away.   11 *wilfully*: willingly; unwisely.

Iwis it was a thing all too dear
To be bestowed and wist not where:
It was mine heart—I pray you heartily
Help me to seek.   15

XVIII

If it be so that I forsake thee
As banished from thy company,
Yet my heart, my mind, and mine affection
Shall still remain in thy perfection,
And right as thou list so order me.   5
But some would say in their opinion
Revulsed is thy good intention:
Then may I well blame thy cruelty,
        If it be so.

But myself I say on this fashion: 10
I have her heart in my possession,
And of itself there cannot, perdie,
By no means love an heartless body,
And on my faith, good is the reason
        If it be so.   15

XIX

Thou hast no faith of him that hath none,
But thou must love him needs by reason,
For as sayeth a proverb notable,
Each thing seeketh his semblable,
And thou hast thine of thy condition.   5
Yet is it not the thing I pass on,
Nor hot nor cold of mine affection;
For since thine heart is so mutable
        Thou hast no faith.

12 *Iwis*: truly.

7 *Revulsed*: violently turned away from me.

1 *of*: in.

4: Proverbial (Rollins), cf. Tilley, L286. *His semblable*: its like (cf. MEW, 175, Lydgate ref.).   5: 'And your disposition (or: state) has found its like.'
6–9: Though likes attract each other, the lady's disposition is her own.

I thought thee true without exception,   10
But I perceive I lacked discretion
To fashion faith to words mutable:
Thy thought is too light and variable—
To change so oft without occasion
      Thou hast no faith.   15

XX

Go, burning sighs, unto the frozen heart!
Go break the ice with pity painful dart
Might never pierce, and if mortal prayer
In heaven may be heard, at last I desire
That death or mercy be end of my smart.   5
Take with thee pain whereof I have my part,
And eke the flame from which I cannot start,
And leave me then in rest, I you require:
      Go, burning sighs!

I must go work, I see, by craft and art,   10
For truth and faith in her is laid apart.
Alas, I cannot therefore assail her
With pitiful plaint and scalding fire
That out of my breast doth strainably start:
      Go, burning sighs!   15

XXI

It may be good, like it who list,
But I do doubt: who can me blame?
For oft assured yet have I missed,
And now again I fear the same:
The windy words, the eyes' quaint game,   5

2–3 Go . . . pierce: 'With an appeal to pity, go and break the ice which Cupid's painful dart has never yet been able to pierce.' Grimald reads which pites, and D with piteus, but E's reading makes excellent sense.
8 require: implore.   11 laid apart: dismissed.   12 assail: also 'woo'.
13 fire: MS. fyer, disyllabic.   14 strainably: compulsively; violently.

5 windy: i.e. 'wavering as the wind' (cf. Tilley, W412), changeable.
5 quaint: crafty.

Of sudden change maketh me aghast:
For dread to fall I stand not fast.

Alas, I tread an endless maze
That seeketh to accord two contraries
And hope still, and nothing has,   10
Imprisoned in liberties,
As one unheard and still that cries,
Always thirsty, and yet nothing I taste:
For dread to fall I stand not fast.

Assured I doubt I be not sure;   15
And should I trust to such surety
That oft hath put the proof in ure
And never hath found it trusty?
Nay, sir, in faith it were great folly.
And yet my life thus do I waste: 20
For dread to fall I stand not fast.

XXII

Resound my voice, ye woods that hear me plain,
Both hills and vales causing reflection;
And rivers eke record ye of my pain,
Which hath ye oft forced by compassion
As judges to hear mine exclamation,   5
Among whom pity I find doth remain:
Where I it seek alas there is disdain.

Oft ye rivers, to hear my woeful sound
Have stopped your course; and plainly to express
Many a tear, by moisture of the ground   10
The earth hath wept, to hear my heaviness,
Which causeless to suffer without redress
The hugy oaks have roared in the wind,
Each thing me thought complaining in their kind.

10 *has*: MS. *hase*, rhyming with *maze* (8). *Hope* (followed by 'still') perhaps
should be *hopes*. Cf. p. 248, CVIII, 4.
17 *ure*: use (i.e. he has never found the 'surety'—pledge, security—of 16
trustworthy when putting it to the test).

2 *reflection*: echo.   3 *record*: tell over (Padelford).   9 *plainly to*
express: the direct object is *Many a tear* (10), exuded and shown by the earth.

Why then alas doth not she on me rue?   15
Or is her heart so hard that no pity
May in it sink, my joy for to renew?
O stony heart, how hath this joined thee,
So cruel that art, cloaked with beauty?
No grace to me from thee there may proceed   20
But as rewarded death for to be my meed.

XXIII

In faith I not well what to say,
Thy chances been so wonderous,
Thou, fortune, with thy diverse play
That causeth joy full dolorous
And eke the same right joyous;   5
Yet though thy chain hath me enwrapped,
Spite of thy hap, hap hath well happed.

Though thou me set for a wonder,
And seekest thy change to do me pain,
Men's minds yet may thou not order,   10
And honesty, and it remain,
Shall shine for all thy cloudy rain.
In vain thou seekest to have trapped:
Spite of thy hap, hap hath well happed.

In hindering, thou diddest further,   15
And made a gap where was a stile.
Cruel wills been oft put under:

---

15 *rue*: pity.
18 *how . . . thee*: i.e. 'how has this person come to join thee?'; cf. D's *who hathe so clokid the*. W is amazed that a heart so cruel can be accompanied (and disguised) by a woman so beautiful.
20–21: 'Nothing can proceed from thee to me as a favour except death, given in reward to serve as my hire.'

---

1 *not:=ne wot*, don't know (reading conj. by Maxwell; MS. has *wot not*). Cf. XLVII, 11; LVI, 14.   5 *joyous*: trisyllabic.
9 *change*: changing (Baldi, 222). Or *thy* should be *by* (T).   11 *and it*: if it.
15 *hindering*: lit. 'keeping back'.   16: 'Where there was only a stile, you made a gap for me.' W seems to vary Tilley, H363.

Weening to lour, thou diddest smile.
Lord, how thyself thou diddest beguile,
That in thy cares wouldest me have lapped!   20
But spite of thy hap, hap hath well happed.

XXIV

Some fowls there be that have so perfect sight
Again the sun their eyes for to defend;
And some because the light doth them offend
Do never 'pear but in the dark or night.
Other rejoice, that see the fire bright,   5
And ween to play in it as they do pretend,
And find the contrary of it that they intend.
Alas, of that sort I may be by right,
For to withstand her look I am not able,
And yet can I not hide me in no dark place,   10
Remembrance so followeth me of that face;
So that with teary eyen, swollen and unstable,
My destiny to behold her doth me lead:
Yet do I know I run into the gleed.

XXV

Because I have thee still kept fro' lies and blame
And to my power always have I thee honoured,
Unkind tongue, right ill hast thou me rendered
For such desert to do me wreak and shame.

---

20 *cares*: sorrows.

1–2: W refers to the proverb 'Only the eagle can gaze at the sun' (*ODEP*, p. 210; Tilley, E3). But *fowls* may mean 'winged creatures' rather than 'birds': with 5–7, cf. CLXVI, 21 ff. (also CXIV, 10).   5 *fire*: cf. XX, 13.
14 *gleed*: fire. W is like the fowls described in 5–7. However, MS. *glede* may equally well represent *OED Glede, gled*, i.e. 'kite', proverbially the meanest of the birds of prey (see *ODEP*, p. 431). As such, the mistress would be fittingly contrasted with the noble eagle of 1–2.

---

3 *Unkind*: unnatural, perverse. Often: 'unnaturally cruel' (e.g. LV, 5).
4 *wreak*: harm.

In need of succour most when that I am   5
To ask reward, then standest thou like one afeared,
Alway most cold, and if thou speak toward,
It is as in dream, unperfect and lame.
And ye salt tears, again my will each night
That are with me when fain I would be alone,   10
Then are ye gone when I should make my moan.
And you so ready sighs to make me shright,
Then are ye slack when that ye should outstart.
And only my look declareth my heart.

XXVI

I find no peace, and all my war is done,
I fear and hope, I burn and freeze like ice,
I fly above the wind, yet can I not arise,
And nought I have, and all the world I season.
That looseth nor locketh, holdeth me in prison,   5
And holdeth me not, yet can I 'scape nowise,
Nor letteth me live, nor die at my device,
And yet of death it giveth me occasion.
Without eyen I see, and without tongue I plain,
I desire to perish, and yet I ask health,   10
I love another, and thus I hate myself,
I feed me in sorrow, and laugh in all my pain,
Likewise displeaseth me both death and life:
And my delight is causer of this strife.

---

7 *if . . . toward*: 'if you *do* speak towards her' rather than F and MT's 'if you speak to the point'.
12 *so . . . shright*: 'sighs so ready to make me shriek'. (*Shright* may be archaic in W and Spenser, and its use here is odd; cf. *OED*.)

---

4 *season*: cf. *OED season* v., 5, 'Of a bird or beast of prey: To "flesh" (its claws); hence *intr.* to seize *upon*.' (Petrarch: *abbraccio*.)
5 *That . . . locketh*: i.e. Love (Rollins).
7 *device*: will.

XXVII

Though I myself be bridled of my mind
Returning me backward by force express,
If thou seek honour to keep thy promise,
Who may thee hold, my heart, but thou thyself unbind?
Sigh then no more, since no way man may find   5
Thy virtue to let, though that frowardness
Of fortune me holdeth. And yet as I may guess,
Though other be present, thou art not all behind.
Suffice it then that thou be ready there
At all hours, still under the defence   10
Of time, truth, and love to save thee from offence,
Crying 'I burn in a lovely desire
With my dear master's, that may not follow,
Whereby his absence turneth him to sorrow.'

XXVIII

My galley charged with forgetfulness
Thorough sharp seas in winter nights doth pass
'Tween rock and rock, and eke mine enemy alas,
That is my lord, steereth with cruelness,

1–4: Cf. Hughey and MT, but the sense seems: 'Though *I* am forcefully prevented from following my inclination to return to her, if *you*, my heart, seek honour by keeping your promise to her, who can restrain you from that, unless you break your bond yourself?' While circumstances (6–7) prevent his physical return to his mistress, he wants his heart to go out to her.
8: 'Though there are rivals with her, you are not, in her thought, wholly at the end of the queue.'
11 *truth*: (cf. It. *vertute*) virtue, loyalty.
12 *lovely*: loving.
13–14: i.e. 'in keeping with the desire of my dear master, who is unable to follow me hither (to his mistress), so that his absence becomes his distress (*turneth*: cf. VIII, 42)'.

1 *charged with forgetfulness*: either 'oppressed by love so as to forget all else' (Tillyard), or 'loaded with nothing else than the feeling that she forgets me'.
3 *rock and rock*: Scylla and Charybdis in Petrarch; more general danger symbols in W.   4 *lord*: i.e. of Love (Cupid).

And every oar a thought in readiness,   5
As though that death were light in such a case.
An endless wind doth tear the sail apace,
Of forced sighs and trusty fearfulness;
A rain of tears, a cloud of dark disdain
Hath done the wearied cords great hinderance,   10
Wreathed with error, and eke with ignorance.
The stars be hid that led me to this pain,
Drowned is reason that should me comfort,
And I remain despairing of the port.

XXIX

Advising the bright beams of these fair eyes
Where he is that mine oft moisteth and washeth,
The wearied mind straight from the heart departeth
For to rest in his worldly paradise
And find the sweet bitter under this guise.   5
What webs he hath wrought well he perceiveth,
Whereby with himself on love he plaineth,
That spurreth with fire, and bridleth with ice.
Thus is it in such extremity brought:
In frozen thought now, and now it standeth in flame,   10
'Twixt misery and wealth, 'twixt earnest and game,
But few glad, and many a divers thought,
With sore repentance of his hardiness:
Of such a root cometh fruit fruitless.

5–6: Cf. Tillyard, but the sense seems 'All oars are ready thoughts, as though it
would be easy for them to row me to death in this plight.' Death is thought of
as an attractive, easy exit.   8: Dependent on *wind* (7), cf. *sighs* and Petrarch.
12 *The stars*: the lady's eyes (*that led me to this pain*, and cf. the It.; also (MT)
Petrarch, *Rime* lxxiii).
13 *comfort*: doubtful reading. Nott, M, and ST read *consort*.

1–2: 'Referring to the lady's eyes, where dwells Cupid—he who moistens and
bathes . . . the lover's own eyes with tears' (Rollins).   1 *Advising*: gazing at.
6: The first *he* is Cupid, the second the mind.   9 *it*: the mind.
11 *wealth*: well-being. 12 *divers*: adverse (cf. It. *tristi*). 14: Cf. VIII, 109. Each
statement may be a variant (MT) of 'Such is the tree such is the fruit' (cf. Tilley,
T494; also T486 and 497). But also cf. Whiting, F685, 'Evil fruit witnesses evil
root'; and with VIII, 109, compare 'He that sows good seed, shall reap
good corn' (*ODEP*, p. 758; Tilley, S209), as well as CLXVI, 28 (Tilley, G405).

XXX

Ever mine hap is slack and slow in coming,
Desire increasing, mine hope uncertain,
That leave it or wait it doth me like pain,
And tiger-like swift it is in parting.
Alas, the snow shall be black and scalding,   5
The sea waterless, fish in the mountain,
The Thames shall return back into his fountain,
And where he rose the sun shall take lodging,
Ere that I in this find peace or quietness,
In that Love or my lady righteously   10
Leave to conspire again me wrongfully.
And if that I have after such bitterness
Anything sweet, my mouth is out of taste,
That all my trust and travail is but waste.

XXXI

Love and fortune and my mind remember
Of that that is now, with that that hath been;
Do torment me so, that I very often
Envy them that be beyond all measure.
Love slaith mine heart, fortune is depriver   5
Of all my comfort, the foolish mind then
Burneth and plaineth as one that seldom
Liveth at rest, still in displeasure.
My pleasant days they fleet away and pass,
But daily yet the ill doth change into the worse,   10

---

3 *leave . . . it*: cf. 'take it or leave it' (Tilley, T28).
5–8: For reference to the use of such *impossibilia*, cf. Rollins and MT.
10 *In that*: i.e. peace will not exist unless the conspiracy of 11 ceases.

4: *beyond all measure* ('beyond all reach') translates Petrarch's *su l'altra riva* ('"on the other shore," that is, dead'—Rollins); *that be* (Buxton conj.) is not in E, but would translate P.'s *che son*, could easily have been omitted between *them* and *beyond*, and is metrically fitting. However, E has a gap before *Envy*.
8 *displeasure*: grief.

And more than the half is run of my course.
Alas, not of steel but of brickle glass
I see that from mine hand falleth my trust,
And all my thoughts are dashed into dust.

XXXII

How oft have I, my dear and cruel foe,
With those your eyes for to get peace and truce
Proffered you mine heart! But you do not use
Among so high things to cast your mind so low.
If any other look for it as ye trow,   5
Their vain weak hope doth greatly them abuse.
And thus I disdain that that ye refuse:
It was once mine—it can no more be so.
If I then it chase, nor it in you can find,
In this exile no manner of comfort,   10
Nor live alone, nor where he is called resort,
He may wander from his natural kind.
So shall it be great hurt unto us twain,
And yours the loss, and mine the deadly pain.

XXXIII

Like to these unmeasurable mountains
Is my painful life, the burden of ire,
For of great height be they, and high is my desire,
And I of tears, and they be full of fountains.
Under craggy rocks they have full barren plains,   5
Hard thoughts in me my woeful mind doth tire.
Small fruit and many leaves their tops do attire,
Small effect with great trust in me remains.

11: i.e. 'more than half of my life is gone' (therefore, W may have been 35 at this time, traditionally half a life-span—cf., e.g., Psalm 90:10).
12 *not of steel*: i.e. *my trust* (13).
12 *brickle*: brittle. Mirrors were made of glass or steel.

3 *do not use*: are not in the habit of.   9 *chase*: i.e. away.
11 *nor . . . resort*: the It. explains: 'nor apply elsewhere'.
12: Lit. 'He may stray from his natural function.' 'That is, die' (Rollins).

6 *tire*: the mind 'tears at' hard thoughts like a hawk exercising or feeding on tough flesh (*OED tire* v.²; It. *coglie*).

The boistous winds oft their high boughs do blast,
Hot sighs from me continually be shed.   10
Cattle in them, and in me love is fed.
Immovable am I, and they are full steadfast.
Of that restless birds they have the tune and note,
And I always plaints that pass thorough my throat.

XXXIV

Madame, withouten many words,
Once, I am sure, ye will or no:
And if ye will, then leave your bourds,
And use your wit, and show it so.

And with a beck ye shall me call,   5
And if of one that burneth alway
Ye have any pity at all,
Answer him fair with yea or nay.

If it be yea, I shall be fain;
If it be nay, friends as before: 10
Ye shall another man obtain,
And I mine own, and yours no more.

XXXV

Ye old mule, that think yourself so fair,
Leave off with craft your beauty to repair,

---

9 *boistous*: ferocious. (Cf. mod. *boisterous*.)
13 *that*: those. (Possibly in error for *the*, but cf. *OED* II.1.c).

---

3 *bourds*: mockery; jests.   4 *use your wit*: be sensible.
8 *yea*: E has here and in 9 [.&.]. MT suggests the & indicates a nod.
9 *fain*: willing (?). Cf. *un si criuero 'n rima*.
11 *man*: servant, lover.
12 *And . . . own*: 'and I shall be my own master' (Tillyard).

S, by restoring the text in five places (*true*, *more*, *savours*, *thayer*, *layer*) and by discussing its meaning in detail in *ELN*, 1967, 5–11, has done much to enhance the stature of this interesting poem.
1 *mule*: Anne Boleyn was called 'Mula Regina' (Sanders in Nott), but perhaps W means another woman 'of a licentious character' (Nott). Padelford compares the term *eques* as one of reproach, with examples.

For it is true without any fable
No man setteth more by riding in your saddle,
Too much travail so do your train appair,   5
    Ye old mule!
With false savours though you deceive the air,
Whoso taste you shall well perceive your lair
Savoureth somewhat of a kappur's stable,
    Ye old mule!   10

Ye must now serve to market and to fair,
All for the burden for panniers a pair,
For since grey hairs been powdered in your sable,
The thing ye seek for you must yourself enable
To purchase it by payment and by prayer,   15
    Ye old mule!

XXXVI

Such hap as I am happed in
Had never man of truth I ween.
At me fortune list to begin
To show that never hath been seen,
A new kind of unhappiness.   5
Nor I cannot the thing I mean
    Myself express.

---

5 *train*: 'course or manner of running (of a horse)' (*OED* sb.¹); deceit, trap, lure (*OED* sb.²); and perhaps other senses.
5 *do appair*: damages. Cf. XVII, 5.
7 *savours*: doubtful reading. Perhaps *favours*.
8 *taste*: (also) 'tries out'; 'handles'; 'has carnal knowledge of' (*OED* 3.b).
8 *lair*: an animal's lair, but also 'love', 'fornication'.
9 *kappur's*: MS. prob. *Kappurs*; perhaps *Kappiers* (Padelford). Cf. *Dial. Dict.*, 'kipper, adj., *light, nimble*, as *kipper* as a colt, North. Yorksh.; *amorous, fond, lascivious*, Lancashire' (Padelford). The Lancashire senses fit better, despite W's Yorkshire origin, but in any case *Kappurs* would, unsatisfyingly, be an adj. used as sb. Perhaps W's original form was a variant of *capel's*, i.e. 'nag's' (cf. Robinson, Glossary).

---

2 *of*: in.   4, 13, 20, 25 *that*: what.

Myself express my deadly pain
That can I well, if that might serve;
But why I have not help again   10
That know I not, unless I starve
For hunger still amids my food:
So granted is that I deserve
    To do me good.

To do me good what may prevail?   15
For I deserve, and not desire,
And still of cold I me bewail,
And raked am in burning fire;
For though I have, such is my lot,
In hand to help that I require,   20
    It helpeth not.

It helpeth not, but to increase
That that by proof can be no more:
That is the heat that cannot cease,
And that I have, to crave so sore.   25
What wonder is this greedy lust,
To ask and have! And yet therefore
    Refrain I must.

Refrain I must: what is the cause?
Sure as they say, 'So hawks be taught.'   30
But in my case layeth no such clause,
For with such craft I am not caught.
Wherefore I say, and good cause why,
With hapless hand no man hath raught
    Such hap as I.   35

11–12 *unless . . . food*: 'except that I know I am perpetually dying of
hunger—amidst my food'. The argument is throughout that 'food', i.e. satis-
faction of sexual appetite, contrary to expectation leads to further 'hunger'.
13, 16 *deserve*: 'earn, win', i.e. my sexual conquest—the result of 'service'.
16: Cf. Tilley, D208 'First deserve and then desire'. He does 'not desire'
conventionally, for he gets what he wanted, yet this does not satisfy.
18 *raked*: covered(?). Or perhaps=*racked*, tortured.
27: Cf. Tilley, A343, and CLXXXIII, 1.
30: Like a hawk, he must practise control of appetite by abstention.
31: 'But in my case that rule isn't appropriate.'   34 *raught*: reached.

XXXVII

They flee from me, that sometime did me seek
With naked foot stalking in my chamber.
I have seen them gentle, tame, and meek
That now are wild, and do not remember
That sometime they put themself in danger   5
To take bread at my hand; and now they range,
Busily seeking with a continual change.

Thanked be fortune it hath been otherwise
Twenty times better, but once in special,
In thin array after a pleasant guise   10
When her loose gown from her shoulders did fall,
And she me caught in her arms long and small,
Therewithal sweetly did me kiss,
And softly said, 'Dear heart, how like you this?'

It was no dream: I lay broad waking.   15
But all is turned thorough my gentleness
Into a strange fashion of forsaking,

There is little evidence that this is an allegory about fortune (cf., e.g., the shift
from *they* to *she*, and the eroticism of st. 2). As for the argument that st. 1
describes birds or deer, which would then be metaphorical for women, R. L.
Greene, *Bucknell Review*, XII, 3 (1964), 17–30, persuasively refutes those who
see st. 1 as referring to anything but women. But though he shows that, e.g., the
claim that the creatures are falcons is open to many objections, there may be
some suggestion of animal-like behaviour in the stanza, perhaps that of birds,
and WMT's quotation (note, 19) from Chaucer's *The Squire's Tale*, 610–1,
'Men loven of propre kynde newefangelnesse,/As briddes doon that men in
cages fede', is interesting.
1: Cf. Charles d'Orleans, 1347, 'They flee fro me'; also Greene about
flee='flee', not: 'fly'.
2 *stalking*: walking softly (e.g. in Chaucer, *LGW*, 1781—Nott), but cf. *OED*.
5 *danger*: risk; or: my power.
6 *To . . . hand*: the expression is elsewhere used of women (cf. Greene and
MT).
10 *guise*: manner, style.
12: Long and slender (*small*) arms were considered beautiful (WMT, note).

And I have leave to go of her goodness,
And she also to use newfangleness.
But since that I so kindly am served,   20
I would fain know what she hath deserved.

XXXVIII

There was never nothing more me pained,
Nor nothing more me moved,
As when my sweetheart her complained
That ever she me loved.
        Alas the while!   5

With piteous look she said and sighed:
'Alas, what aileth me
To love and set my wealth so light
On him that loveth not me?
        Alas the while!   10

'Was I not well void of all pain,
When that nothing me grieved?
And now with sorrows I must complain,
And cannot be relieved.
        Alas the while!   15

'My restful nights and joyful days
Since I began to love
Be take from me; all thing decays,
Yet can I not remove.
        Alas the while!'   20

18 *of*: by.   19 *newfangleness*: fickleness, or craze for novelty.
20 *kindly*: possibly 'according to her nature', but more likely ironic for
'unkindly, cruelly', as D's *gentillye* suggests.

8 *wealth*: well-being.
10: The refrain is here and in 15 and 20 spoken by the woman, or by W
looking back on the event (cf. 5, 25, and 30). It is perhaps taken from Chaucer,
'Complaynt d'Amours', 9 (F).

She wept, and wrung her hands withal,
The tears fell in my neck.
She turned her face, and let it fall,
Scarcely therewith could speak.
    Alas the while!   25

Her pains tormented me so sore
That comfort had I none,
But cursed my fortune more and more
To see her sob and groan.
    Alas the while!   30

XXXIX

Patience: though I have not
The thing that I require,
I must of force, God wot,
Forbear my most desire,
For no ways can I find   5
To sail against the wind.

Patience: do what they will
To work me woe or spite,
I shall content me still
To think both day and night: 10
To think, and hold my peace,
Since there is no redress.

Patience, withouten blame,
For I offended nought:
I know they know the same,   15
Though they have changed their thought.
Was ever thought so moved
To hate that it hath loved?

Patience of all my harm,
For fortune is my foe;   20
Patience must be the charm
To heal me of my woe.
Patience without offence
Is a painful patience.

1–2: These may form one sentence. Similarly 7–8.   4 *Forbear*: control.

XL

Patience for my device,
Impatience for your part!
Of contraries the guise
Is ever the overthwart:
Patience, for I am true,   5
The contrary for you.

Patience: a good cause why
You have no cause at all!
Therefore yours standeth awry,
Perchance sometime to fall.   10
Patience then, take him up,
And drink of patience' cup.

Patience, no force for that,
But brush your gown again.
Patience, spurn not thereat,   15
Let no man know your pain.
Patience, even at my pleasure
When yours is out of measure!

The other was for me,
This patience is for you.   20
Change when ye list let see,
For I have taken a new.
Patience with a good will
Is easy to fulfil.

A note in D connects this poem with XXXIX: 'patiens tho I had nott the &c/to her that saide this patiens was not for her but that the contrarye of myne was most metiste for her po^{r}posse/' However, in D, XXXIX is quite different from E's version, regularly with *she* for *they*, etc. W later seems to have made the application of XXXIX more general, with the result that its connection with XL has become more tenuous than in D.

1 *device*: motto (but cf. *OED*).   4 *overthwart*: opposite.

13 *no . . . that*: it is no matter.

19–22: 'In the previous poem I adopted patience for my device: now it is your turn. Show change whenever you like, for I have taken a new mistress.' (But *let see* may mean 'let us see', as in *CT*, A891.)

XLI

Ye know my heart, my lady dear,
That since the time I was your thrall
I have been yours both whole and clear,
Though my reward hath been but small:
So am I yet, and more than all.   5
And ye know well how I have served,
As if ye prove it shall appear
    How well, how long,
    How faithfully,
    And suffered wrong   10
    How patiently!
Then since that I have never swerved,
Let not my pains be undeserved.

Ye know also, though ye say nay,
That you alone are my desire,   15
And you alone it is that may
Assuage my fervent flaming fire.
Succour me then, I you require!
Ye know it were a just request,
Since ye do cause my heat, I say,   20
    If that I burn,
    That ye will warm,
    And not to turn
    All to my harm,
Sending such flame from frozen breast   25
Against all right for my unrest.

And I know well how frowardly
Ye have mistaken my true intent,
And hitherto how wrongfully
I have found cause for to repent.   30
But death shall rid me readily
If your hard heart do not relent;

18 *require*: implore.   22 *That*: depends on *request* (19).

And I know well all this ye know
    That I and mine
    And all I have   35
    Ye may assign
    To spill or save.
Why are ye then so cruel foe
Unto your own that loveth you so?

XLII

Who hath heard of such cruelty before?
That when my plaint remembered her my woe
That caused it, she cruel more and more
Wished each stitch as she did sit and sew
Had pricked mine heart, for to increase my sore.   5
And as I think, she thought it had been so:
For as she thought 'This is his heart indeed',
She pricked hard, and made herself to bleed.

XLIII

    If fancy would favour
    As my deserving shall,
    My love, my paramour,
    Should love me best of all.

    But if I cannot attain   5
    The grace that I desire,
    Then may I well complain
    My service and my hire.

34 *I and mine*: SCM (174) sees an appeal to Anne Boleyn here, whose motto was
'Me and Mine', and suggests (49) that 34–37 may speak literal truth.
37 *spill*: destroy.

2 *remembered*: caused to remember (Nott).

1 *fancy*: amorous inclination; caprice. For a discussion of this word and the
related *fantasy* (26), cf. D. M. Friedman, *JEGP*, 1968, 32–48.

Fancy doth know how
To further my true heart,   10
If fancy might avow
With faith to take part.

But fancy is so frail,
And flitting still so fast,
That faith may not prevail   15
To help me, first nor last.

For fancy at his lust
Doth rule all but by guess:
Whereto should I then trust
In truth or steadfastness?   20

Yet gladly would I please
The fancy of her heart
That may me only ease
And cure my careful smart.

Therefore, my lady dear,   25
Set once your fantasy
To make some hope appear
Of steadfast remedy.

For if he be my friend
And undertake my woe,   30
My grief is at an end
If he continue so.

Else fancy doth not right
As I deserve and shall,
To have you day and night,   35
To love me best of all.

11–12: The fancy is the lady's, the faith the lover's.
17 *lust*: (sexual) pleasure.
24 *careful*: full of grief.

XLIV

Alas, madame! for stealing of a kiss,
Have I so much your mind then offended?
Have I then done so grievously amiss
That by no means it may be amended?
Then revenge you, and the next way is this: 5
Another kiss shall have my life ended.
For to my mouth the first my heart did suck,
The next shall clean out of my breast it pluck.

XLV

What no, perdie, ye may be sure!
Think not to make me to your lure
With words and cheer so contrarying,
Sweet and sour counterweighing:
Too much it were still to endure.   5
Truth is tried where craft is in ure,
But though ye have had my heartes cure,
Trow ye I dote without ending?
     What no, perdie!

Though that with pain I do procure   10
For to forget that once was pure
Within my heart, shall still that thing
Unstable, unsure and wavering
Be in my mind without recure?
     What no, perdie!   15

---

5 *next*: nearest.

2: i.e. 'Don't think you can exercise the power of your lure over me'; cf.
Hawes, *Passetyme of Pleasure*, 4532, and LXXX, 5.
6: 'Honest loyalty is severely tested where deceit is practised.' *Ure*: cf. XXI, 17.
14 *recure*: remedy.

XLVI

The wandering gadling in the summer tide
That finds the adder with his reckless foot,
Starts not dismayed so suddenly aside
As jealous despite did, though there were no boot,
When he saw me, sitting by her side   5
That of my health is very crop and root.
It pleased me then to have so fair a grace
To sting that heart, that would have my place.

XLVII

The lively sparks that issue from those eyes
Against the which ne 'vaileth no defence
Have pressed mine heart, and done it none offence
With quaking pleasure more than once or twice.
Was never man could anything devise   5
The sunbeams to turn with so great vehemence
To daze man's sight as by their bright presence
Dazed am I, much like unto the guise
Of one ystricken with dint of lightning.
Blinded with the stroke, erring here and there,   10
So call I for help, I not when ne where,
The pain of my fall patiently bearing:
For after the blaze, as is no wonder,
Of deadly 'Nay!' hear I the fearful thunder.

The image of the wanderer stung by a snake is traditional, cf. Rollins and
MT.   1 *gadling*: wayfarer, cf. 'gadabout'.
4 *boot*: remedy.   6 *health*: welfare.
6 *crop and root*: 'head and root', i.e. the whole thing. Cf., e.g., *T & C*, II, 348.
7 *grace*: stroke of fortune.   8 *have*: should perhaps be *have had* (as in, e.g., P).

———
2 *ne*: not.
4 *quaking*: cf. 'A quaking heat' (CXIV, 16). Probably: 'causing me to quake'.
8 *guise*: manner.
9 *ystricken*: cf. IX, 6. But possibly='eye-stricken' (Buxton).
10 *erring*: wandering.
11 *not*:=*ne wot*, don't know.

XLVIII

What needeth these threatening words and wasted wind?
All this cannot make me restore my prey.
To rob your good iwis is not my mind,
Nor causeless your fair hand did I display.
Let love be judge or else whom next we meet   5
That may both hear what you and I can say.
She took from me an heart, and I a glove from her:
Let us see now, if the one be worth the other.

XLIX

Right true it is, and said full yore ago:
'Take heed of him that by thy back thee claweth',
For none is worse than is a friendly foe.
Though they seem good, all thing that thee delighteth,
Yet know it well, that in thy bosom creepeth: 5
For many a man such fire oft kindleth,
That with the blaze his beard singeth.

1 *threatening*: MS. *threning* (disyllabic).
1 *wind*: breath.
3 *good*: property.
3 *iwis*: certainly.
4 *display*: i.e. 'strip so as to reveal' (cf. It. *dispoglio*).
5 *meet*: may be intentional though it does not rhyme, since a scribe would hardly mistake a form like T's *finde* for *meit*.
6 *both hear*: i.e. hear both.

———

1 *full yore ago*: a very long time ago.
2: 'Beware of him that claps you on the back' (MT). Cf. *CT*, A4326 (proverbial, cf. Tilley, B17).
4 *thing*: uninflected plural.
5 *that . . . creepeth*: taken over from *CT*, D1993–5, which alludes to the treachery and ingratitude of the snake in Aesop's fable (I.X.), cf. *ODEP*, p. 747 (Tilley, V68), 'To nourish a snake in one's bosom', and to the 'Snake in the grass' (*ODEP*, p. 748; Tilley, S585).

L

What word is that, that changeth not
Though it be turned and made in twain?
It is mine answer, God it wot,
And eke the causer of my pain.
A love rewardeth with disdain,   5
Yet is it loved. What would ye more?
It is my health eke and my sore.

LI

At most mischief
I suffer grief,
For of relief
Since I have none,
My lute and I   5
Continually
Shall us apply
To sigh and moan.

Nought may prevail
To weep or wail: 10
Pity doth fail
In you alas.
Mourning or moan,
Complaint or none,
It is all one   15
As in this case.

A likely solution to this riddle is 'Anna', which T substituted for 'aunswer'
in his second edition; and 'aunswer' might be a pun, *Anne, Sir*, as R. C.
Harrier suggests (*N & Q*, 1959, 189). 'Anna' is presumably Anne Boleyn.
SCM (18) quotes a riddle from D, 'am el men', which he solves and believes
to be Anne's reply to L. But it is not in Anne's hand, and might equally well
be related to CXLII. Cf. also Baldi, 231–4.
7 *eke*: the MS. has a virgula before this.

1: 'At the highest pitch of suffering' (Tillyard).

For cruelty
Most that can be
Hath sovereignty
Within your heart,   20
Which maketh bare
All my welfare:
Nought do ye care
How sore I smart.

No tiger's heart   25
Is so pervert
Without desert
To wreak his ire:
And you me kill
For my good will,   30
Lo how I spill
For my desire!

There is no love
That can ye move,
And I can prove   35
None other way;
Therefore I must
Restrain my lust,
Banish my trust
And wealth away.   40

Thus in mischief
I suffer grief,
For of relief
Since I have none,
My lute and I   45
Continually
Shall us apply
To sigh and moan.

25 ff.: Cf. Tilley, L316, 'The lion spares the suppliant'.
31 *spill*: perish.   35 *prove*: cf. LV, 23.   40 *wealth*: well-being.

LII

Marvel no more although
The songs I sing do moan,
For other life than woe
I never proved none,
And in my heart also   5
Is graven with letters deep
A thousand sighs and mo,
A flood of tears to weep.

How may a man in smart
Find matter to rejoice?   10
How may a mourning heart
Set forth a pleasant voice?
Play who that can that part,
Needs must in me appear
How fortune overthwart   15
Doth cause my mourning cheer.

Perdie, there is no man,
If he never saw sight,
That perfectly tell can
The nature of the light.   20
Alas, how should I then,
That never tasted but sour,
But do as I began,
Continually to lour?

But yet perchance some chance   25
May chance to change my tune,
And when such chance doth chance
Then shall I thank fortune;

Nott suggested that this might refer to Mary Souche, one of Jane Seymour's
maids of honour (and cf. T's version), but added, 'in the original MS, nothing
justifies the supposition that any play on the word [such] was intended.' There
is, in fact, more play on the word *chance*.

4 *proved*: experienced.   15 *overthwart*: adverse, perverse.
17–20: Proverbial (*ODEP*, p. 63; Tilley, M80), cf., e.g., *T & C*, II, 21, 'A blynd
man kan nat juggen well in hewis'.

And if I have such chance,
Perchance ere it be long,   30
For such a pleasant chance
To sing some pleasant song.

LIII

Where shall I have at mine own will
Tears to complain? Where shall I fet
Such sighs that I may sigh my fill,
And then again my plaints repeat?

For though my plaint shall have none end,   5
My tears cannot suffice my woe.
To moan my harm have I no friend,
For fortune's friend is mishap's foe.

Comfort, God wot, else have I none
But in the wind to waste my words: 10
Nought moveth you my deadly moan,
But all you turn it into bourds.

I speak not now to move your heart
That you should rue upon my pain;
The sentence given may not revert: 15
I know such labour were but vain.

But since that I for you, my dear,
Have lost that thing that was my best,
A right small loss it must appear
To lose these words and all the rest.   20

The doubtfully authoritative tag (45) might suggest that this belongs to W's
Spanish years (1537–9).   2 *fet*: i.e. fetch.
8: Cf. *CT*, VII, 2244–5, 'For what man that hath freendes thurgh
Fortune,/Mishap wol maken hem enemys'; proverbial, cf. Tilley, T301.
10: Cf. Tilley, W831 and W833.   12 *bourds*: mockery; jests.
14 *rue*: pity.   15 *revert*: i.e. be recalled.

But though they sparkle in the wind,
Yet shall they show your falsed faith,
Which is returned unto his kind:
For like to like, the proverb sayeth.

Fortune and you did me advance: 25
Me thought I swam and could not drown,
Happiest of all; but my mischance
Did lift me up to throw me down.

And you with your own cruelness
Did set your foot upon my neck,   3°
Me and my welfare to oppress,
Without offence your heart to wreak.

Where are your pleasant words alas?
Where is your faith, your steadfastness?
There is no more, but all doth pass,   35
And I am left all comfortless.

But for because it doth you grieve
And also me, my wretched life,
Have here my truth: shall not relieve
But death alone my very strife.   40

Therefore farewell, my life, my death!
My gain, my loss! my salve, my sore!
Farewell also with you my breath!
For I am gone for evermore.

Podra esser che no es.   45

21 *sparkle*: disperse (cf. XII, 6).
24: Cf. XIX, 4.
37–40: 'But since my wretched life grieves both you and me, I promise you:
death, and nothing else, shall deliver me from my struggle.' (*Not* = nothing, cf.
OED 12).
45: Spanish-Italian (?), 'That which is not may some day be' (Maxwell).

LIV

She sat and sewed, that hath done me the wrong
Whereof I plain and have done many a day,
And whilst she heard my plaint in piteous song
Wished my heart the sampler as it lay.
The blind master, whom I have served so long,   5
Grudging to hear that he did hear her say,
Made her own weapon do her finger bleed,
To feel if pricking were so good in deed.

LV

'Ah, Robin,
Jolly Robin,
Tell me how thy leman doth,
And thou shall know of mine.'

'My lady is unkind, perdie!'   5
'Alack, why is she so?'
'She loveth another better than me,
And yet she will say no.'

Responce

'I find no such doubleness,
I find women true.
My lady loveth me doubtless,   10
And will change for no new.'

Cf. XLII, which follows this in D.
6 *Grudging*: discontented.

---

1 *Robin*: Padelford notes that the epithet 'jolly' was often applied to Robin
Hood. In January 1510, Henry VIII burst into the Queen's Chamber at
Westminster with ten men dressed as Robin Hood's men, as Edward Halle
relates (*Henry VIII*, ed. Charles Whibley, 1904, i, 15). Stevens (186) points out
that this incident belongs to a social 'game of love'; it included dances, and the
shorter version of this carol (cf. Appendix) would have fitted such an
occasion.   5 *unkind*: cf. XXV, 3.   8 *say no*: i.e. deny 7.

Le Plaintif

'Thou art happy while that doth last,
But I say as I find,
That women's love is but a blast,   15
And turneth like the wind.'

Responce

'If that be true yet as thou sayst,
That women turn their heart,
Then speak better of them thou mayst,
In hope to have thy part.'   20

Le Plaintif

'Such folks shall take no harm by love
That can abide their turn,
But I alas can no way prove
In love but lack and mourn.'

Responce

'But if thou wilt avoid thy harm,   25
Learn this lesson of me:
At other fires thyself to warm,
And let them warm with thee.'

LVI

Such vain thought as wonted to mislead me,
In desert hope, by well assured moan,
Maketh me from company to live alone
In following her whom reason bid me flee.
She fleeth as fast by gentle cruelty,   5
And after her mine heart would fain be gone,
But armed sighs my way do stop anon,
'Twixt hope and dread locking my liberty.

15–16: Proverbial, cf. Tilley, W698.   17 *If yet*: even if.
23 *prove*: try; experience.

---

2 : 'In lonely hope and undoubted moaning.' (But perhaps *by*= by means of.)

Yet as I guess under disdainful brow
One beam of pity is in her cloudy look   10
Which comforteth the mind that erst for fear shook,
And therewithal bolded I seek the way how
To utter the smart that I suffer within:
But such it is, I not how to begin.

LVII

Though I cannot your cruelty constrain
For my good will to favour me again,
Though my true and faithful love
Have no power your heart to move,
    Yet rue upon my pain.   5

Though I your thrall must evermore remain
And for your sake my liberty restrain,
The greatest grace that I do crave
Is that ye would vouchsafe
    To rue upon my pain.   10

Though I have not deserved to obtain
So high reward but thus to serve in vain,
Though I shall have no redress,
Yet of right ye can no less
    But rue upon my pain.   15

But I see well that your high disdain
Will nowise grant that I shall that attain;
Yet ye must grant at the least
This my poor and small request:
    Rejoice not at my pain.   20

---

14 *not*: = *ne wot*, don't know.

---

5 *rue*: pity.
17 *that* (2): i.e. 'that you will *rue upon my pain*'.

LVIII

To wish and want and not obtain,
To seek and sue ease of my pain,
Since all that ever I do is vain,
     What may it avail me?

Although I strive both day and hour   5
Against the stream with all my power,
If fortune list yet for to lour,
     What may it avail me?

If willingly I suffer woe,
If from the fire me list not go,   10
If then I burn to plain me so,
     What may it avail me?

And if the harm that I suffer
Be run too far out of measure,
To seek for help any further   15
     What may it avail me?

What though each heart that heareth me plain
Pitieth and plaineth for my pain,
If I no less in grief remain,
     What may it avail me?   20

Yea though the want of my relief
Displease the causer of my grief,
Since I remain still in mischief,
     What may it avail me?

Such cruel chance doth so me threat   25
Continually inward to fret,
Then of release for to entreat
     What may it avail me?

Fortune is deaf unto my call,
My torment moveth her not at all;   30
And though she turn as doth a ball,
     What may it avail me?

This appears to contain several proverbs, cf., e.g., Tilley, S927 (5–6; Rollins);
'Despair is a bad counsellor' (33; MT); 'Who speaks to the deaf, wastes his
words' (34; Rollins).   23 *mischief*: distress.

For in despair there is no rede;
To want of ear speech is no speed;
To linger still alive as dead   35
  What may it avail me?

LIX

Sometime I fled the fire that me brent
By sea, by land, by water and by wind;
And now I follow the coals that be quent
From Dover to Calais against my mind.
Lo how desire is both sprung and spent!   5
And he may see that whilom was so blind,
And all his labour now he laugh to scorn
Meshed in the briers that erst was all to-torn.

LX

He is not dead that sometime hath a fall:
The sun returneth, that was under the cloud,
And when fortune hath spit out all her gall
I trust good luck to me shall be allowed,
For I have seen a ship into haven fall   5
After the storm hath broke both mast and shroud,
And eke the willow that stoopeth with the wind
Doth rise again, and greater wood doth bind.

---

34 *speed*: profit, use.

W probably here compares his former feelings for Anne Boleyn with those he experiences while accompanying her (and Henry VIII) from Britain to Calais, France, in October 1532. Anne's marriage to the King took place soon after.
1 *brent*: burnt.   3 *coals*: MS. *coles*, perhaps disyllabic; *quent*: quenched.
7–8: 'And he who was at first torn to pieces while he was entangled in the briers can now laugh contemptuously about all the painful energy he has wasted.' *Briers*: proverbially used for 'difficulties' (cf. Tilley, B673). SCM (34) thinks of the briers through which the lover must force his way in *RR*. (Cf. *RR*, 1712.)

This may refer to W's imprisonment in the Fleet (1534)—or to any fall from fortune. The reflections are largely proverbial, cf. Tilley, F38 (1); C442 (2); S344 (5–6), W404 (7–8; which SCM, 28, compares with *T & C*, II, 1387–8).
4 *allowed*: allotted.

LXI

The furious gun in his raging ire,
When that the bowl is rammed in too sore
And that the flame cannot part from the fire,
Cracketh in sunder, and in the air doth roar
The shivered pieces. Right so doth my desire,   5
Whose flame increaseth from more to more,
Which to let out I dare not look nor speak:
So now hard force my heart doth all to-break.

LXII

My hope alas hath me abused,
And vain rejoicing hath me fed;
Lust and joy have me refused,
And careful plaint is in their stead.
Too much advancing slacked my speed,   5
Mirth hath caused my heaviness,
And I remain all comfortless.

Whereto did I assure my thought
Without displeasure steadfastly?
In fortune's forge my joy was wrought,   10
And is revolted readily.
I am mistaken wonderly,
For I thought nought but faithfulness,
Yet I remain all comfortless.

2 *bowl*: ball, bullet.
3 i.e. 'when no part of the fire can find an outlet'.
8 *to-break*: break into pieces.

---

3 *Lust*: pleasure.
4 *careful*: sorrowful.
5: Cf. 'The more haste the less speed' (Tilley, H198).
8–9: i.e. 'Why, when I was without sorrow, did I commit myself to constant service?'
11 *revolted*: '*turned*, as applied to the edge of a tool' (Padelford).

In gladsome cheer I did delight 15
Till that delight did cause my smart
And all was wrong where I thought right.
For right it was that my true heart
Should not from truth be set apart,
Since truth did cause my hardiness: 20
Yet I remain all comfortless.

Sometime delight did tune my song
And led my heart full pleasantly,
And to myself I said among:
My hap is coming hastily. 25
But it hath happed contrary:
Assurance causeth my distress,
And I remain all comfortless.

Then if my note now do vary
And leave his wonted pleasantness, 30
The heavy burden that I carry
Hath altered all my joyfulness.
No pleasure hath still steadfastness,
But haste hath hurt my happiness,
And I remain all comfortless. 35

LXIII

What death is worse than this,
When my delight,
My weal, my joy, my bliss,
Is from my sight?
Both day and night 5
My life alas I miss.

24 *among*: from time to time.
33: 'Constant allegiance procures no pleasure.'

For though I seem alive,
My heart is hence:
Thus bootless for to strive
Out of presence   10
Of my defence
Toward my death I drive.

Heartless alas what man
May long endure?
Alas, how live I then?   15
Since no recure
May me assure,
My life I may well ban.

Thus doth my torment grow
In deadly dread.   20
Alas, who might live so,
Alive as dead?
Alive to lead
A deadly life in woe?

LXIV

The enemy of life, decayer of all kind,
That with his cold withers away the green,
This other night me in my bed did find,
And offered me to rid my fever clean;
And I did grant, so did despair me blind.   5
He drew his bow with arrow sharp and keen,
And struck the place where love had hit before,
And drove the first dart deeper more and more.

9–12: 'My struggle is helpless since my heart is not here to protect me from death, so I drift fast towards my end.'
16 *recure*: remedy.

———
1–2: Death.
1 *all kind*: 'everything in nature' (Rollins).
7, 8 *struck*; *drove*: MS. *strake*; *drave*.

LXV

Once as me thought fortune me kissed,
And bade me ask what I thought best,
And I should have it as me list,
Therewith to set my heart in rest.

I asked nought but my dear heart   5
To have for evermore mine own:
Then at an end were all my smart,
Then should I need no more to moan.

Yet for all that a stormy blast
Had overturned this goodly day,   10
And fortune seemed at the last
That to her promise she said nay.

But like as one out of despair
To sudden hope revived I:
Now fortune showeth herself so fair   15
That I content me wonderly.

My most desire my hand may reach,
My will is alway at my hand;
Me need not long for to beseech
Her that hath power me to command.   20

What earthly thing more can I crave?
What would I wish more at my will?
No thing on earth more would I have,
Save that I have to have it still.

For fortune hath kept her promise   25
In granting me my most desire:
Of my sufferance I have redress,
And I content me with my hire.

18 *My will*: generally, 'what I desire'; or, specifically, 'what I sexually desire'—if the *dear heart* of 5 is a woman (the *Her* of 20, which may alternatively refer to fortune).   27 *sufferance*: suffering.

LXVI

My lute awake! Perform the last
Labour that thou and I shall waste,
And end that I have now begun;
For when this song is sung and past,
My lute be still, for I have done.   5

As to be heard where ear is none,
As lead to grave in marble stone,
My song may pierce her heart as soon.
Should we then sigh or sing or moan?
No, no, my lute, for I have done.   10

The rocks do not so cruelly
Repulse the waves continually
As she my suit and affection,
So that I am past remedy,
Whereby my lute and I have done.   15

Proud of the spoil that thou hast got
Of simple hearts thorough Love's shot,
By whom, unkind, thou hast them won,
Think not he hath his bow forgot,
Although my lute and I have done.   20

Vengeance shall fall on thy disdain
That makest but game on earnest pain!
Think not alone under the sun
Unquit to cause thy lovers plain,
Although my lute and I have done.   25

Moralized by John Hall in *The Court of Virtue*, who suggests that his version may
have been sung to the tune of 'My pen obey' which he provides. Cf. **CXX**.
6–9: 'It would be more easy for lead, which is the softest of metals, to engrave
characters on hard marble, than it is for me to make impression on her
obdurate heart' (Nott). Cf. *T & C*, II, 1241. The hardness of stone was
proverbial (Tilley, S878). Cf. also 'As deaf as a stone' (Tilley, S877).
13 *affection*: trisyllabic, with accents on the first and last syllable.
17 *Love's*: perhaps disyllabic.   18 *unkind*: cf. **XXV**, 3.
24 *Unquit*: unrequited.

Perchance thee lie withered and old
The winter night that are so cold,
Plaining in vain unto the moon:
Thy wishes then dare not be told.
Care then who list, for I have done.   30

And then may chance thee to repent
The time that thou hast lost and spent
To cause thy lovers sigh and swoon.
Then shalt thou know beauty but lent,
And wish and want as I have done.   35

Now cease, my lute: this is the last
Labour that thou and I shall waste,
And ended is that we begun.
Now is this song both sung and past:
My lute, be still, for I have done.   40

LXVII

If chance assigned
Were to my mind
By very kind
Of destiny,
Yet would I crave   5
Nought else to have
But only life and liberty.

Then were I sure
I might endure
The displeasure   10
Of cruelty,
Where now I plain
Alas in vain,
Lacking my life for liberty.

---

26 *Perchance*: i.e. 'it may chance that'.
27 *The winter night*: adverbial; *night* is an uninflected plural.
27: Cf. Gower, *Confessio Amantis*, V, 6668.

---

10 *displeasure*: injury.   14 *for liberty*: i.e. because of its absence, cf. 15–21.

For without the one   15
The other is gone,
And there can none
It remedy:
If the one be past,
The other doth waste,   20
And all for lack of liberty.

And so I drive,
As yet alive,
Although I strive
With misery;   25
Drawing my breath,
Looking for death
And loss of life for liberty.

But thou that still
Mayst at thy will   30
Turn all this ill
Adversity:
For the repair
Of my welfare
Grant me but life and liberty.   35

And if not so,
Then let all go
To wretched woe,
And let me die;
For the one or the other,   40
There is none other:
My death, or life with liberty.

15–21 *the one*: liberty; *the other*: life.
22 *drive*: cf. LXIII, 12.
27 *Looking for*: expecting.

LXVIII

Nature that gave the bee so feat a grace
To find honey of so wondrous fashion,
Hath taught the spider out of the same place
To fetch poison, by strange alteration.
Though this be strange, it is a stranger case   5
With one kiss by secret operation
Both these at once in those your lips to find,
In change whereof I leave my heart behind.

LXIX

I have sought long with steadfastness
To have had some ease of my great smart,
But nought availeth faithfulness
To grave within your stony heart.

But hap and hit or else hit not,   5
As uncertain as is the wind,
Right so it fareth by the shot
Of love alas, that is so blind.

Therefore I played the fool in vain,
With pity when I first began   10
Your cruel heart for to constrain,
Since love regardeth no doleful man.

But of your goodness all your mind
Is that I should complain in vain;
This is the favour that I find: 15
Ye list to hear how I can plain.

But though I plain to please your heart,
Trust me I trust to temper it so
Not for to care which do revert:
All shall be one, in wealth or woe.   20

1–4: The observations are traditional, cf. Rollins and F.

---

5 *hit . . . not*: cf. 'Hit or miss'.   6: Cf. Tilley, W412.
10 *pity*: i.e. an appeal to pity.   13 *of*: by.   20 *wealth*: well-being.

For fancy ruleth, though right say nay,
Even as the goodman kissed his cow;
None other reason can ye lay
But as who sayeth 'I reck not how'.

LXX

Like as the swan towards her death
Doth strain her voice with doleful note,
Right so sing I with waste of breath:
I die! I die! and you regard it not.

I shall enforce my fainting breath   5
That all that hears this deadly note
Shall know that you doth cause my death:
I die! I die! and you regard it not.

Your unkindness hath sworn my death,
And changed hath my pleasant note   10
To painful sighs that stops my breath:
I die! I die! and you regard it not.

Consumeth my life, faileth my breath:
Your fault is forger of this note.
Melting in tears, a cruel death   15
I die! I die! and you regard it not.

My faith with me after my death
Buried shall be, and to this note
I do bequeath my weary breath,
To cry: 'I died! and you regard it not!'   20

21–22: Proverbial (Flügel), a variant of 'Every man as he loves, quoth the good
man [goodman=head of household] when he kissed his cow' (Tilley, M103).
Fancy: cf. XLIII, 1.

The opening is traditional (cf. specific references in MT) and proverbial (Tilley,
S1028).   9 *unkindness*: cf. XXV, 3.
20 *regard it*: B *regardid*.

LXXI

In eternum I was once determed
For to have loved, and my mind affirmed
That with my heart it should be confirmed
    In eternum.

Forthwith I found the thing that I might like,   5
And sought with love to warm her heart alike,
For as me thought I should not see the like
    In eternum.

To trace this dance I put myself in press;
Vain hope did lead, and bade I should not cease   10
To serve, to suffer, and still to hold my peace
    In eternum.

With this first rule I furthered me apace,
That as me thought my truth had taken place
With full assurance to stand in her grace   15
    In eternum.

It was not long ere I by proof had found
That feeble building is on feeble ground,
For in her heart this word did never sound—
    In eternum.   20

In eternum then from my heart I kest
That I had first determed for the best:
Now in the place another thought doth rest
    In eternum.

1, 22 *determed*: determined.
3 *confirmed*: made strong.
9 *trace*: participate in (this dance of love); cf. VIII, 25.
9 *put . . . press*: exerted myself (*OED press* sb.¹, 5; Robbins, Glossary); but cf. also XV, 13.
15 *stand . . . grace*: 'enjoy her favour'; cf., e.g., *T & C*, III, 472.
18: 'That it is poor building on a shaky foundation'; cf. Tilley, F619.
21 *kest*: cast.

LXXII

Since ye delight to know
That my torment and woe
Should still increase
Without release,
I shall enforce me so   5
That life and all shall go,
For to content your cruelness.

And so this grievous train
That I too long sustain
Shall sometime cease   10
And have redress,
And you also remain
Full pleased with my pain,
For to content your cruelness.

Unless that be too light   15
And that ye would ye might
See the distress
And heaviness
Of one yslain outright,
Therewith to please your sight   20
And to content your cruelness.

Then in your cruel mood
Would God forthwith ye would
With force express
My heart oppress,   25
To do your heart such good
To see me bathe in blood,
For to content your cruelness.

Then could ye ask no more,
Then should ye ease my sore   30

8 *train*: delay; deceit.   19 *yslain*: cf. IX, 6.

And the excess
Of mine excess;
And you should evermore
Defamed be therefore,
For to repent your cruelness.   35

LXXIII

Heaven and earth, and all that hear me plain,
Do well perceive what care doth cause me cry,
Save you alone, to whom I cry in vain:
'Mercy, madame! Alas, I die, I die!'

If that you sleep, I humbly you require   5
Forbear a while, and let your rigour slake,
Since that by you I burn thus in this fire:
To hear my plaint, dear heart, awake, awake!

Since that so oft ye have made me to wake
In plaint and tears and in right piteous case,   10
Displease you not if force do now me make
To break your sleep, crying 'Alas! alas!'

It is the last trouble that ye shall have
Of me, madame, to hear my last complaint;
Pity at last your poor unhappy slave,   15
For in despair alas I faint, I faint!

It is not now, but long and long ago
I have you served as to my power and might
As faithfully as any man might do,
Claiming of you nothing of right, of right.   20

---

32 *excess*: immoderate grief.

There is a lute tablature for a song 'Heven and erth' in B. M. Roy. MSS., App.
58 (cf. Stevens, 135), but we do not know that LXXIII was written either for or
to a tune.   2, 27 *care*: grief.
5 *require*: implore.   6 *let slake*: relax.   7: May relate to 8 rather than 6.

Save of your grace only to stay my life,
That fleeth as fast as cloud afore the wind;
For since that first I entered in this strife
An inward death hath fret my mind, my mind.

If I had suffered this to you unware,   25
Mine were the fault, and you nothing to blame;
But since you know my woe and all my care,
Why do I die? Alas, for shame, for shame!

I know right well my face, my look, my tears,
Mine eyes, my words, and eke my dreary cheer   30
Have cried my death full oft unto your ears:
Hard of belief, it doth appear, appear!

A better proof I see that ye would have
How I am dead. Therefore when ye hear tell,
Believe it not, although ye see my grave.   35
Cruel! Unkind! I say farewell, farewell!

LXXIV

Comfort thyself, my woeful heart,
Or shortly on thyself thee wreak,
For length redoubleth deadly smart:
Why sighs thou, heart, and wilt not break?

To waste in sight were piteous death;   5
Alas, I find thee faint and weak.
Enforce thyself to lose thy breath:
Why sighs thou, heart, and wilt not break?

Thou knowest right well that no redress
Is thus to pine; and for to speak,   10
Perdie, it is remediless:
Why sighs thou then, and wilt not break?

21–22: Perhaps taken from Petrarch, cf. MT.   21 *of*: by.
30 *cheer*: aspect; mood.   36 *Unkind*: Cf. XXV, 3.
_____

5 *sight*: i.e. sighs (uninflected plural).   9 *redress*: aid, remedy.

It is too late for to refuse
The yoke when it is on thy neck;
To shake it off 'vaileth not to muse: 15
Why sighs thou then, and wilt not break?

To sob and sigh it were but vain,
Since there is none that doth it reck;
Alas, thou dost prolong thy pain:
Why sighs thou then, and wilt not break?   20

Then in her sight, to move her heart,
Seek on thyself thyself to wreak,
That she may know thou sufferedst smart:
Sigh there thy last, and therewith break!

LXXV

Desire, alas, my master and my foe:
So sore altered, thyself how mayst thou see?
Sometime I sought that drives me to and fro,
Sometime thou ledst that leadeth thee and me.
What reason is to rule thy subjects so   5
By forced law and mutability?
For where by thee I doubted to have blame,
Even now by hate again I doubt the same.

LXXVI

Venomous thorns that are so sharp and keen
Sometime bear flowers fair and fresh of hue;
Poison ofttime is put in medicine
And causeth health in man for to renew;
Fire that purgeth all thing that is unclean   5
May heal, and hurt: and if these been true,
I trust sometime my harm may be my health,
Since every woe is joined with some wealth.

15: 'It is of no avail to consider how the yoke may be shaken off, after it is once fastened on the neck' (Nott).

---

6 *forced*: enforced.   7 *doubted*: feared.

Largely proverbial, cf. Tilley, R179 (1–2); P457 (3–4); F258 (5–6); W188 (8).
2 *hue*: appearance.   8 *wealth*: well-being.

LXXVII

To cause accord or to agree
Two contraries in one degree
And in one point as seemeth me
To all man's wit it cannot be:
    It is impossible.   5

Of heat and cold when I complain
And say that heat doth cause my pain
When cold doth shake me every vein
And both at once, I say again
    It is impossible.   10

That man that hath his heart away,
If life liveth there as men do say,
That he heartless should last one day
Alive and not to turn to clay,
    It is impossible.   15

'Twixt life and death, say what who saith,
There liveth no life that draweth breath,
They join so near; and eke in faith
To seek for life by wish of death
    It is impossible.   20

Yet love that all thing doth subdue,
Whose power there may no life eschew,
Hath wrought in me that I may rue
These miracles to be so true
    That are impossible.   25

3 *point*: condition (*OED point* sb.¹, D.4), cf. ML, 75, 'in good point and accord'.
16 *say . . . saith*: no matter what anyone says.
22 *life*: living being.

LXXVIII

Though this thy port, and I thy servant true,
And thou thyself dost cast thy beams from high
From thy chief house, promising to renew
Both joy and eke delight, behold yet how that I,
Banished from my bliss, carefully do cry:　　　　5
'Help now, Cytherea, my lady dear,
My fearful trust, en vogant la galere!'

Alas the doubt that dreadful absence giveth!
Without thine aid, assurance is there none:
The firm faith, that in the water fleeteth,　　　　10
Succour thou therefore: in thee it is alone.
Stay that with faith that faithfully doth moan,
And thou also givest me both hope and fear:
Remember thou me, en vogant la galere.

By seas and hills elonged from thy sight,　　　　15
Thy wonted grace reducing to my mind,
Instead of sleep, thus I occupy the night:
A thousand thoughts and many doubts I find.
And still I trust thou canst not be unkind,
Or else despair my comfort and my cheer　　　　20
Would flee forthwith, en vogant la galere.

Cytherea (6) is Aphrodite (Venus in Roman mythology), here thought of as both goddess and planet (2–3), and called *Cytherea* because she was specially worshipped in Cythera, an island near the most southerly point of Laconia, Greece. (Cf. *Citherea*, *T & C*, III, 1255—F.) However, W actually seems to be thinking of his mistress in, e.g., 15; presumably he indirectly addresses her in st. 1 (otherwise his use of *thy* is inconsistent; and cf. LXV). Nott supposed that W wrote LXXVIII when crossing the Channel, en route to Spain in 1537, and that the mistress was Elizabeth Darrell (cf. ML, 83 ff.).

3 *chief house*: 'The first and seventh houses, of the twelve into which the celestial sphere was divided, were regarded as propitious. The reference here is almost certainly to the seventh' (MT). Cf. *T & C*, II, 681 (F).

5 *carefully*: sorrowfully.

7 *en . . . galere*: 'while rowing the galley'; MT also refers to *Et vogue la galere* = 'Come what may!'　　8 *doubt*: fear; suspicion.　　8 *dreadful*: full of fear.

15 *elonged*: separated.　　16 *reducing*: recalling.　　19 *unkind*: cf. XXV, 3.

21 *flee*: MS. *she*, which may, unexpectedly, refer to the mistress (if *thy sight*, 15, refers to Venus); *despair* (20) can mean 'cast into despair'.

Yet on my faith full little doth remain
Of any hope whereby I may myself uphold,
For since that only words do me retain
I may well think the affection is but cold.　　25
But since my will is nothing as I would,
But in thy hands it resteth whole and clear,
Forget me not, en vogant la galere.

LXXIX

Unstable dream, according to the place,
Be steadfast once, or else at least be true;
By tasted sweetness make me not to rue
The sudden loss of thy false feigned grace.
By good respect in such a dangerous case　　5
Thou broughts not her into this tossing mew,
But madest my sprite live my care to renew,
My body in tempest her succour to embrace.
The body dead, the sprite had his desire:
Painless was the one, the other in delight.　　10
Why then alas did it not keep it right,
Returning to leap into the fire,
And where it was at wish it could not remain?
Such mocks of dreams they turn to deadly pain.

LXXX

In doubtful breast, whilst motherly pity
With furious famine standeth at debate,
Saith the Hebrew mother: 'O child unhappy,
Return thy blood where thou hadst milk of late.

1 *according . . . place*: just like the place where I am.
5 *By . . . respect*: with proper consideration (MT).
6 *this . . . mew*: this hawk's cage in which I am tossing, i.e. my bed. Cf. also *OED toss* v., II.5, 'to be in mental agitation'.
7 *care*: sorrow.　　9 *dead*: i.e. asleep.
11: 'Why did not the spirit keep itself right by staying that way?' Cf. CXL, 9.

The discovery of the source in a Spanish MS., and perhaps LXXX's position in E, may suggest that W wrote the poem in Spain (1537–9).
2 *at debate*: at variance.
3 *the . . . mother*: Mary, the daughter of Eleazer, who acc. to Josephus in his *Jewish War*, killed her son and ate him, during the siege of Jerusalem, A.D. 70.

Yield me those limbs that I made unto thee,   5
And enter there where thou wert generate.
For of one body against all nature
To another must I make sepulture.'

LXXXI

Of Carthage he, that worthy warrior,
Could overcome, but could not use his chance,
And I likewise of all my long endeavour
The sharp conquest though fortune did advance
Could not it use: the hold that is given over   5
I unpossessed. So hangeth in balance
Of war my peace, reward of all my pain;
At Monçon thus I restless rest in Spain.

LXXXII

Process of time worketh such wonder
That water which is of kind so soft
Doth pierce the marble stone asunder
By little drops falling from aloft.

And yet an heart that seems so tender   5
Receiveth no drop of the stilling tears
That alway still cause me to render
The vain plaint that sounds not in her ears.

---

5 *made . . . thee*: made for you, or 'Brought into your possession or power (see *N.E.D.*, 9b)' (MT; cf. XLV, 2).

MT attempts to explain what this might allude to, but unfortunately none of the suggestions adequately accounts for W's sense of personal failure. The circumstances 'are so darkly hinted at, that they elude all conjecture' (Nott). W wrote a letter from Barbastra, near Monçon, Spain, on 16 October 1537 (cf. ML, 47).   1: Hannibal. (Cf. Livy's *History*, xii, 51—MT.)
3 *of*: in.
5–6 *the . . . unpossessed*: 'I did not possess the hold [over events] which is now abandoned altogether' (MT).

2–4: Cf. Tilley, D618.   7 *render*: emit.

So cruel alas is nought alive,
So fierce, so froward, so out of frame;   10
But some way, some time, may so contrive
By means the wild to temper and tame.

And I that always have sought and seek
Each place, each time for some lucky day,
This fierce tiger less I find her meek   15
And more denied the longer I pray.

The lion in his raging furor
Forbears that sueth meekness for his boot,
And thou alas in extreme dolour
The heart so low thou treads under thy foot!   20

Each fierce thing lo how thou dost exceed,
And hides it under so humble a face!
And yet the humble to help at need
Nought helpeth time, humbleness nor place.

LXXXIII

After great storms the calm returns,
And pleasanter it is thereby;
Fortune likewise that often turns
Hath made me now the most happy.

The heaven that pitied my distress,   5
My just desire and my cry,
Hath made my languor to cease,
And me also the most happy.

Whereto despaired ye, my friends?
My trust alway in Him did lie   10
That knoweth what my thought intends,
Whereby I live the most happy.

---

10 *out of frame*: perverse.
18: 'Spares one that sues for meekness to help him out of his plight', cf. LI,
25–28; or possibly *for his boot* = 'as a reward (for some service)' (MT).

---

10 *in Him did lie*: MS. *in hid ly*. Of all the emendations suggested in MT, this
seems to be the best. The line wants a syllable; *him did* could easily have been
copied as *hid*; and the reading fits the poem's meaning (cf., e.g., 17–20).

Lo, what can take hope from that heart
That is assured steadfastly?
Hope therefore, ye that live in smart,　　　　　　15
Whereby I am the most happy.

And I that have felt of your pain
Shall pray to God continually
To make your hope your health retain,
And me also the most happy.　　　　　　20

LXXXIV

All heavy minds
Do seek to ease their charge,
And that that most them binds
To let at large.

Then why should I　　　　　　5
Hold pain within my heart,
And may my tune apply
To ease my smart?

My faithful lute
Alone shall hear me plain,　　　　　　10
For else all other suit
Is clean in vain.

For where I sue
Redress of all my grief,
Lo, they do most eschew　　　　　　15
My heart's relief.

Alas my dear,
Have I deserved so
That no help may appear
Of all my woe?　　　　　　20

14 *assured*: pledged; or: made secure.
19: Perhaps with a comma after *hope* (Nott, etc.) the sense would be better, but
it may be: 'To make your hope preserve your well-being'.

14 *redress*: remedy.

Whom speak I to,
Unkind and deaf of ear?
Alas, lo, I go,
And wot not where.

Where is my thought?   25
Where wanders my desire?
Where may the thing be sought
That I require?

Light in the wind
Doth flee all my delight   30
Where truth and faithful mind
Are put to flight.

Who shall me give
Feathered wings for to flee,
The thing that doth me grieve   35
That I may see?

Who would go seek
The cause whereby to pain?
Who could his foe beseek
For ease of pain?   40

My chance doth so
My woeful case procure
To offer to my foe
My heart to cure.

What hope I then   45
To have any redress?
Of whom, or where, or when,
Who can express?

---

22 *Unkind*: cf. XXV, 3.   30, 34 *flee*: fly.
33 ff.: Cf. MT (Petrarch) and F (the Psalmist).
39 *beseek*: beseech.   42 *procure*: prevail upon.

No, since despair
Hath set me in this case,   50
In vain oft in the air
To say alas,

I seek nothing
But thus for to discharge
My heart of sore sighing,   55
To plain at large,

And with my lute
Sometime to ease my pain,
For else all other suit
Is clean in vain.   60

LXXXV

To seek each where where man doth live,
The sea, the land, the rock, the cliff,
France, Spain, and Ind, and everywhere,
Is none a greater gift to give,
Less set by oft, and is so lief and dear,   5
Dare I well say, than that I give to year.

I cannot give brooches nor rings,
These goldsmiths' work and goodly things,
Pierrie nor pearl orient and clear,
But for all that is no man brings   10
Liefer jewel unto his lady dear,
Dare I well say, than that I give to year.

Clearly a New Year's gift poem, punning on *year* and *ye* at the end of each stanza
(MS. *yere*; *to year* = for the year). Stevens suggests (210) that an emblem in the
shape of a heart would have accompanied the poem as a present. F's notion
that LXXXV was written in Spain (for the New Year of 1538 or 1539) may
derive support not only from its position in E, but also from the mention of
Spain (3).
3 *Ind*: India, seen as 'the farthest corner of the world' (F). Cf., e.g., *CT*,
C722.   5 *lief*: beloved; precious.
9 *Pierrie*: (cf. *OED perrie*) jewellery, (set) precious stones.

Nor I seek not to fetch it far,
Worse is it not though it be near,
And as it is it doth appear   15
Uncounterfeit mistrust to bar,
Left whole and pure withouten peer,
Dare I well say, the gift I give to year.

To thee therefore the same retain;
The like of thee to have again   20
France would I give, if mine it were!
Is none alive in whom doth reign
Lesser disdain: freely therefore lo here
Dare I well give, I say, my heart to year.

LXXXVI

O goodly hand
Wherein doth stand
My heart distressed in pain,
Fair hand alas
In little space   5
My life that doth restrain;

O fingers slight,
Departed right,
So long, so small, so round,
Goodly begone,   10
And yet alone
Most cruel in my wound;

With lilies white
And roses bright
Doth strive thy colour fair;   15
Nature did lend
Each finger's end
A pearl for to repair.

15–16: 'And it appears—as it is—the genuine thing, impossible to suspect.'

8 *Departed*: separated.   9 *small*: slender (cf. XXXVII, 12).
10: 'Exquisitely fashioned' (Tillyard).   18 *for to repair*: for adornment.

Consent at last,
Since that thou hast 20
My heart in thy demesne,
For service true
On me to rue,
And reach me love again.

And if not so, 25
Then with more woe
Enforce thyself to strain
This simple heart
That suffereth smart,
And rid it out of pain. 30

LXXXVII

1

Lo what it is to love!
Learn ye that list to prove
At me, I say,
No ways that may
The grounded grief remove, 5
My life alway
That doth decay:
Lo what it is to love!

Flee alway from the snare,
Learn by me to beware 10
Of such a train
Which doubles pain

---

21 *demesne*: possession, power.   23 *rue*: pity.

W's plan is indicated by the B version, where part 2 is preceded by the words 'the answer', and part 3 by 'the answer to thys'. In part 1, W argues against love. In part 2, we are to see a woman defending it. In part 3, W returns to the attack, criticizing the lady's behaviour rather than love, which she misuses. Thus *you* (85) is the haughty lady; *us* (91) refers to the abused lovers.

2, 27 *prove*: try; experience.   3 *At*: from.
4 *No ways*: not at all.   11ff. *train*: deceit.

And endless woe and care
That doth retain;
Which to refrain   15
Flee alway from the snare.

To love and to be wise,
To rage with good advice,
Now thus, now then,
Now off, now an,   20
Uncertain as the dice—
There is no man
At once that can
To love and to be wise.

Such are the divers throes,   25
Such that no man knows
That hath not proved
And once hath loved;
Such are the raging woes,
Sooner reproved   30
Than well removed:
Such are the divers throes.

Love is a fervent fire
Kindled by hot desire,
For a short pleasure   35
Long displeasure:
Repentance is the hire.
A poor treasure
Without measure,
Love is a fervent fire.   40

Lo what it is to love!

13ff. *care*: grief.   15 *refrain*: shun.
17: Cf. 'It is impossible to love and be wise' (Tilley, L558).
18 *advice*: wisdom, judgement.   20 *an*: on.
23 *can*: knows how to.
33ff.: MEW, 121, offers possible sources.   36 *displeasure*: sorrow.

2

Leave thus to slander love!
Though evil with such it prove
Which often use
Love to misuse   45
And loving to reprove,
Such cannot choose
For their refuse
But thus to slander love.

Flee not so much the snare: 50
Love seldom causeth care,
But by deserts
And crafty parts
Some lose their own welfare.
Be true of hearts   55
And for no smarts
Flee not so much the snare.

To love and not to be wise
Is but a mad device:
Such love doth last   60
As sure and fast
As chance on the dice—
A bitter taste
Comes at the last,
To love and not to be wise.   65

Such be the pleasant days,
Such be the honest ways;
There is no man
That fully can
Know it but he that says   70
Loving to ban
Were folly then:
Such be the pleasant days.

44–45 *use . . . misuse*: are in the habit of reviling love.
48: 'For their being refused' (Nott).   54, 80 *lose*: cf. CLIV, 28.
59, 99 *device*: motto; or: invention.   62: Cf. CXI, 18.

Love is a pleasant fire
Kindled by true desire,   75
And though the pain
Cause men to plain,
Sped well is oft the hire.
Then though some feign
And lose the gain,   80
Love is a pleasant fire.

3

Who most doth slander love
The deed must alway prove:
Truth shall excuse
That you accuse   85
For slander and reproof;
Not by refuse
But by abuse
You most do slander love.

Ye grant it is a snare   90
And would us not beware;
Lest that your train
Should be too plain
Ye colour all the care.
Lo how you feign   95
Pleasure for pain
And grant it is a snare!

To love and to be wise
It were a strange device,
But from that taste   100
Ye vow the fast;
On cinq though run your dice,
Ambs-ace may haste
Your pain to waste:
To love and to be wise!   105

78: i.e. 'the reward often is success'.
102–3 *cinq . . . Ambs-ace*: 'Five is a lucky throw, the double ace the unluckiest'
(MT); cf. *CT*, B124–5 (FS, 153).

Of all such pleasant days,
Of all such pleasant plays,
Without desert
You have your part,
And all the world so says.   110
Save that poor heart
That for more smart
Feeleth yet such pleasant days!

Such fire and such heat
Did never make ye sweat,   115
For without pain
You best obtain
Too good speed, and too great.
Whoso doth plain,
You best do feign   120
Such fire and such heat.

Who now doth slander love?

LXXXVIII

I lead a life unpleasant, nothing glad.
Cry and complaint offer, 'voids joyfulness:
So changeth me unrest, that nought shall fade.
Pain and despite hath altered pleasantness
Ago, long since, that she hath truly made   5
Disdain—for truth, set light in steadfastness.
I have cause good to sing this song:
Plain or rejoice who feeleth weal or wrong.

2: 'Crying and moaning offer themselves, while joyfulness avoids me.'
3 *that . . . fade*: which shall not grow weak at all (but cf. MT).
4–6: 'Pain and scorn have altered pleasantness, which my mistress has long
since turned into disdain—in exchange for my loyalty and honesty, slighted by
her for all my constancy.' *Truly* (5): 1 verily, 2 ironic.

LXXXIX

If in the world there be more woe
Than I have in my heart,
Whereso it is it doth come fro',
And in my breast there doth it grow,
For to increase my smart.   5
Alas, I am receipt of every care,
And of my life each sorrow claims his part.
Who list to live in quietness
By me let him beware,
For I by high disdain   10
Am made without redress,
And unkindness alas hath slain
My poor true heart all comfortless.

XC

The answer that ye made to me, my dear,
When I did sue for my poor heart's redress,
Hath so appalled my countenance and my cheer
That in this case I am all comfortless,
Since I of blame no cause can well express.   5

I have no wrong where I can claim no right,
Nought ta'en me fro' where I nothing have had,
Yet of my woe I cannot so be quite,
Namely since that another may be glad
With that that thus in sorrow maketh me sad.   10

Another? Why shall liberty be bond?
Free heart may not be bond but by desert.
        . . .

6 *receipt*: receptacle.   6 *care*: grief.
12 *unkindness*: cf. XXV, 3.

---

3 *appalled*: made pale.   3 *cheer*: face.
8 *quite*: i.e. quit; free.
9 *Namely*: especially.
9 *another*: Henry VIII? (Nott).   11ff.: incomplete stanza.

Nor none can claim, I say, by former grant
That knoweth not of any grant at all:
And by desert I dare well make avaunt   15
Of faithful will there is nowhere that shall
Bear you more truth, more ready at your call.

Now, good, then call again that friendly word,
That saith your friend, in saving of his pain,
And say, my dear, that it was said in bourd: 20
Late or too soon, let that not rule the gain
Wherewith free will doth true desert retain.

XCI

Most wretched heart, most miserable,
Since thy comfort is from thee fled,
Since all thy truth is turned to fable,
Most wretched heart, why art thou not dead?

'No, no, I live, and must do still,   5
Whereof I thank God, and no mo.
For I myself have all my will,
And he is wretched that weens him so.'

But yet thou hast both had and lost
The hope so long that hath thee fed,   10
And all thy travail and thy cost:
Most wretched heart, why art thou not dead?

18–20: 'So now, dear, repeal that "friendly" word—thus your friend (i.e.
lover) asks you to—so as to save him pain; and say that you spoke it in jest.' The
'friendly' word is the cruel answer of 1; cf. *it* (20) and *that* (21).

A dialogue between W and his heart in the traditional form of a debate, this
was perhaps written during W's imprisonment in 1541 (Nott). Thus 33–35
seems to refer to Bonner, W's principal accuser at his arrest after Cromwell's
fall in 1541, whose attempt to harm W in 1538 had then been foiled by C., W's
consistent protector. In his Defence (ML, 207), W (B.'s superior in Spain)
suggested that B. had been envious of him.   7: 'I fully control my will.'
8: 'And he is unhappy who considers himself such'; i.e. unhappiness is in the
mind, and subject to it. From Chaucer, 'Fortune', 25 (Padelford). Chaucer's
line is Boethian (cf. Robinson, note). See also QM, e.g., 459.

'Some other hope must feed me new:
If I have lost, I say: "What though?"
Despair shall not through it ensue,   15
For he is wretched that weens him so.'

The sun, the moon doth frown on thee,
Thou hast darkness in daylight's stead,
As good in grave as so to be:
Most wretched heart, why art thou not dead?   20

'Some pleasant star may show me light,
But though the heaven would work me woe,
Who hath himself shall stand up right,
And he is wretched that weens him so.'

Hath he himself that is not sure?   25
His trust is like as he hath sped,
Against the stream thou mayst not dure:
Most wretched heart, why art thou not dead?

'The last is worst: who fears not that,
He hath himself whereso he go.   30
And he that knoweth what is what
Saith he is wretched that weens him so.'

Seest thou not how they whet their teeth
Which to touch thee sometime did dread?
They find comfort for thy mischief: 35
Most wretched heart, why art thou not dead?

'What though that curse do fall by kind
On him that hath the overthrow?
All that cannot oppress my mind,
For he is wretched that weens him so.'   40

27: Cf. Tilley, S927.
31: Chaucer (F), or Boethius, or: 'he who is wise'.
35: 'It pleases them to hurt you.'

Yet can it not be then denied
It is as certain as thy creed
Thy great unhap thou canst not hide:
Unhappy then, why art thou not dead?

'Unhappy, but no wretch therefore!   45
For hap doth come again and go,
For which I keep myself in store,
Since unhap cannot kill me so.'

XCII

You that in love find luck and abundance
And live in lust and joyful jollity,
Arise for shame, do away your sluggardy!
Arise I say, do May some observance!
Let me in bed lie dreaming in mischance,   5
Let me remember the haps most unhappy
That me betide in May most commonly,
As one whom love list little to advance.
Sepham said true that my nativity
Mischanced was with the ruler of the May: 10
He guessed I prove of that the verity,
In May my wealth and eke my life I say
Have stood so oft in such perplexity.
Rejoice! Let me dream of your felicity.

42: 'It is as true as the gospel', cf. Tilley, C819.

W was imprisoned in May 1534 and May 1536; but (SCM, 28) Chaucer also
refers to May as a time of misfortune. Chaucer's influence shows in 3 (*CT*,
A1042), 4 (*CT*, A1045; but cf. also *T & C*, II, 112—Nott), and 8 (*T & C*, I,
518—Nott). Cf. W. H. Wiatt (*N & Q*, 1952, 244; and especially *ELN*, 1966,
89–92), who suggests that Sepham (Edward Sepham, a lecturer in logic at
Oxford, who also cast a horoscope for Edward VI—Flügel) guessed after 1536
what W already knew (cf. 11). Wiatt and F agree on May 1538 as a likely date for
the poem.   2 *lust*: (sexual) pleasure.
4: May morning was important in the Lover's calendar, celebrated with
romantic encounters, tournaments, etc.
10: The sign of Taurus was supposed to be governed by Venus.
11 *prove*: cf. CXLVIII, 29.   12 *wealth*: well-being.   13 *perplexity*: distress.

XCIII

And if an eye may save or slay
And strike more deep than weapon long,
And if an eye by subtle play
May move one more than any tongue,
How can ye say that I do wrong   5
Thus to suspect without desert?
For the eye is traitor of the heart.

To frame all well, I am content
That it were done unwittingly;
But yet I say, who will assent,   10
To do but well, do nothing why
That men should deem the contrary.
For it is said by men expert
That the eye is traitor of the heart.

But yet alas that look, all soul,   15
That I do claim of right to have,
Should not methinks go seek the school
To please all folk. For who can crave
Friendlier thing than heart? Vouchsafe
By look to give in friendly part: 20
For the eye is traitor of the heart.

And my suspect is without blame,
For as ye say, not only I
But other mo have deemed the same.
Then is it not of jealousy,   25
But subtle look of reckless eye
Did range too far, to make me smart,
For the eye is traitor of the heart.

1 *And if*: if.   7: Cf. Tilley, E231.
11 *To . . . well*: 'If you mean to do nothing but what is good' (Nott).
17 *seek the school*: 'seek to study (how to please all)' (MT).
20: i.e. to me (cf. 15–16), not to my rivals; *friendly*= 'as befits a lover'.
22 *suspect*: suspicion.   24 *mo*: besides.   25 *it*: my suspicion.

But I your friend shall take it thus,
Since you will so, as stroke of chance,   30
And leave further for to discuss
Whether the stroke did stick or glance.
But 'scuse who can, let him advance
Dissembled looks, but for my part
My eye must still betray my heart.   35

And of this grief ye shall be quit
In helping truth steadfast to go.
The time is long that that doth sit
Feeble and weak, and suff'reth woe.
Cherish him well, continue so,   40
Let him not fro' your heart astart:
Then fear not the eye to show the heart.

XCIV

Psalm 37. *Noli emulare in maligna*

Although thou see the outrageous climb aloft,
Envy not thou his blind prosperity;
The wealth of wretches, though it seemeth soft,
Move not thy heart by their felicity.
They shall be found like grass turned into hay,   5
And as the herbs that wither suddenly.
Stablish thy trust in God, seek right alway,
And on the earth thou shalt inhabit long.
Feed and increase such hope from day to day,
And if with God thou tune thy hearty song,   10
He shall thee give whatso thy heart can lust.
Cast upon God thy will that right thy wrong,

---

41 *astart*: escape.   42 *fear*: i.e. let fear (subjunctive).

Psalm 37 in the Authorized Version; No. 36 in the Vulgate.
1 *outrageous*: 'the excessively bold (one)' (Hughey).
11 *lust*: like (cf. 67).   12 *right*: subjunctive.

Give him the charge, for he upright and just
Hath cure of thee and of thy cares all,
And he shall make thy truth to be discussed   15
Bright as the sun, and thy righteousness shall
(The cursed's wealth though now do it deface)
Shine like the daylight, that we the noon call.
Patiently abide the Lord's assured grace,
Bear with even mind the trouble that he sends,   20
Dismay thee not though thou see the purchase
Increase of some, for such like luck God sends
To wicked folk . . .
Restrain thy mind from wrath that aye offends,
Do 'way all rage, and see thou do eschew   25
By their like deed such deeds for to commit,
For wicked folk their overthrow shall rue.
Who patiently abide and do not flit,
They shall possede the world from heir to heir:
The wicked shall of all his wealth be quit   30
So suddenly, and that without repair,
That all his pomp and his staring array
Shall from thine eye depart as blast of air.
The sober then the world shall wield I say,
And live in wealth and peace so plentiful.   35
Him to destroy the wicked shall essay,
And gnash his teeth eke with girning ireful.
The Lord shall scorn the threatenings of the wretch,
For he doth know the tide is nigh at full
When he shall sink and no hand shall him seech.   40
They have unsheathed eke their bloody bronds
And bent their bow to prove if they might reach

14 *cares*: disyllabic.   15 *discussed*: made known.
16 *righteousness*: MS. *rightwisnes*, with stress on *wis*.
17: 'Though now the prosperity of the wicked casts it in shade.'
20, 109 *trouble*: affliction.   21 *purchase*: prosperity.
29 *possede*: i.e. possess.   30 *quit*: deprived.
32 *staring*: ostentatious.
37 *with . . . ireful*: by showing his teeth in anger.
38 *scorn*: deride (cf. Camp., *ridebit*).
40 *seech*: i.e. seek.   41 *bronds*: swords.

To overthrow the . . .
Bare of relief the harmless to devour.
The sword shall pierce the heart of such that fonds, 45
Their bow shall break in their most endeavour.
A little living gotten rightfully
Passeth the riches and eke the high power
Of that that wretches have gathered wickedly;
Perish shall the wicked's posterity, 50
And God shall stablish the just assuredly.
The just men's days the Lord doth know and see:
Their heritage shall last for evermore,
And of their hope beguiled they shall not be.
When dismal days shall wrap the t'other sore, 55
They shall be full when other faint for food;
Therewhilst shall fail these wicked men therefore.
To God's enemies such end shall be allowed
As hath lambs' grease wasting in the fire
That is consumed into a smoky cloud. 60
Borrowth the unjust without will or desire
To yield again, the just freely doth give
Where he seeth need as mercy doth require.
Who willth Him well for right therefore shall live,
Who banneth Him shall be rooted away. 65
His steps shall God direct still and relieve
And please him shall what life him lust essay,
And though he fall under foot lie shall not he,
Catching his hand for God shall straight him stay.
. . . 70
Nor yet his seed foodless seen for to be.
The just to all men merciful hath been,
Busy to do well: therefore his seed I say
Shall have abundance alway fresh and green. 75

43: Incomplete. F conj. *just; stretched forth their honds.*   45 *fonds*: plays the fool.
48 *riches*: cf. CVIII, 164.   50, 96, 107 *wicked's*: plural.
51 *stablish*: make firm, strengthen.   58 *allowed*: allotted.
62 *yield again*: pay back.
65 *banneth*: speak ill of, curse. MS. *bannyshe*, but cf. Camp. *maledicunt.*
70–71: Omitted from the MS. M conj. *The righteous yet, though age has stolen on me,/Forsaken by the Lord I ne'er have seen.*

Flee ill, do good, that thou mayst last alway,
For God doth love for evermore the upright:
Never his chosen doth he cast away,
For ever he them mindeth day and night;
And wicked seed alway shall waste to nought.   80
The just shall wield the world as their own right,
And long thereon shall dwell as they have wrought.
With wisdom shall the wise man's mouth him able,
His tongue shall speak alway even as it ought,
With God's learning he hath his heart stable,   85
His foot therefore from sliding shall be sure.
The wicked watcheth the just for to disable
And for to slay him doth his busy cure,
But God will not suffer him for to quail
By tyranny, nor yet by fault unpure   90
To be condemned in judgement without fail.
Await therefore the coming of the Lord;
Live with his laws in patience to prevail,
And he shall raise thee of thine own accord
Above the earth, in surety to behold   95
The wicked's death, that thou may it record.
I have well seen the wicked sheen like gold,
Lusty and green as laurel lasting aye,
But even anon and scant his seat was cold:
When I have passed again the selfsame way   100
Where he did reign, he was not to be found—
Vanished he was for all his fresh array.

80 *wicked*: Camp. *impiorum*; but in W perhaps an adjective.
83 *able*: strengthen.
85 *learning*: teaching (Camp. *Doctrina*).
86 *sure*: secure (Camp. *securus*).
88 *slay*: MS. *se*. Flügel conj. *sle*. Cf., e.g., Camp. *occidat*.
88 *doth . . . cure*: applies himself diligently.
89–90 *him . . . tyranny*: 'that the just man be destroyed by the cruel power of the wicked man'; 1535 is clearer in what follows than W: 'ner let him be condemned of ungodlynesse when hys cause shalbe handled in iudgment'.
96 *record*: witness, see.

Let uprightness be still thy steadfast ground,
Follow the right: such one shall alway find
Himself in peace and plenty to abound.   105
All wicked folk reversed shall untwind,
And wretchedness shall be the wicked's end;
Health to the just from God shall be assigned.
He shall them strength whom trouble should offend;
The Lord shall help I say, and them deliver   110
From cursed's hands, and health unto them send,
For that in him they set their trust for ever.

XCV

From these high hills as when a spring doth fall,
It trilleth down with still and subtle course,
Of this and that it gathers aye and shall
Till it have just off-flowed the stream and force,
Then at the foot it rageth over all: 5
So fareth love when he hath ta'en a source;
His rein is rage, resistance 'vaileth none:
The first eschew is remedy alone.

XCVI

(fragment)

Prove whether I do change, my dear,
Or if that I do still remain
Like as I went or far or near;
And if ye find . . .

---

106 *untwind*: 'untwine', be destroyed.   108, 111 *Health*: welfare.

---

2 *trilleth*: trickles.
4: 'Until it is just strong enough to burst away at the sides of the central current.' The stream is shaping into a less disciplined waterfall. But cf. MT also.
7 *rein*: MS. *rayne*, probably for *rein*, cf. Petrarch's *frena* and IV, 7. Love's rage is unbridled.
8: 'The only remedy is to avoid love in the beginning' (Rollins), cf. *PF*, 140 (Flügel).

XCVII

If waker care, if sudden pale colour,
If many sighs with little speech to plain,
Now joy, now woe, if they my cheer distain,
For hope of small, if much to fear therefore,
To haste, to slack my pace less or more,   5
Be sign of love, then do I love again.
If thou ask whom, sure since I did refrain
Brunet that set my wealth in such a roar
The unfeigned cheer of Phyllis hath the place
That Brunet had: she hath and ever shall.   10
She from myself now hath me in her grace:
She hath in hand my wit, my will, and all.
My heart alone well worthy she doth stay
Without whose help scant do I live a day.

XCVIII

In Spain

So feeble is the thread that doth the burden stay
Of my poor life, in heavy plight that falleth in decay,
That but it have elsewhere some aid or some succours,
The running spindle of my fate anon shall end his course.

1 *waker care*: sleepless grief.   2 *many sighs*: object of *plain*.
3 *cheer*: face.   3 *distain*: stain.
4–5: 'If—in hope of little, therefore fearing much—I vary my pace according
to these feelings . . .'   7 *refrain*: give up; avoid.
W revised 8 (originally 'her that did set our country in a rore'), no doubt
because it was too clear a reference to Anne Boleyn (fittingly described as
Brunet). Phyllis is quite possibly Elizabeth Darrell (cf. LXXVIII).
8 *wealth*: well-being.
8 *roar*: confusion (*OED roar* sb.²). Cf. *T & C*, V, 45 (Nott).
12 *wit*: mind.   13 *alone*: i.e. *she*.

W's revision *At other will* (88) probably refers to the King's will that W was to
stay in Spain. If so, it is likely (MT) that he was revising the poem early in 1539,
'at which point his frustration and anxiety to be recalled reached their peak'
(cf. ML, 86–87). The mistress alluded to may well be Elizabeth Darrell (cf.
XCVII).   2 *that*: i.e. my life.
4: 'W brings in the common classical metaphor of the spinning Fates' (MT).

For since the unhappy hour that did me to depart   5
From my sweet weal, one only hope hath stayed my life apart,
Which doth persuade such words unto my sorry mind:
'Maintain thyself, O woeful sprite, some better luck to find:
For though thou be deprived from thy desired sight,
Who can thee tell if thy return be for thy most delight?   10
Or who can tell thy loss if thou once mayst recover?
Some pleasant hour thy woe may rape and thee defend and
                                        cover.'
This is the trust that yet hath my life sustained,
And now alas I see it faint, and I by trust am trained.
The time doth fleet, and I perceive the hours how they bend   15
So fast that I have scant the space to mark my coming end.
Westward the sun from out the east scant doth show his light,
When in the west he hides him straight within the dark of
                                        night,
And comes as fast where he began his path awry:
From east to west, from west to the east, so doth his journey
                                        lie.   20
The life so short, so frail, that mortal men live here,
So great a weight, so heavy charge the body that we bear,
That when I think upon the distance and the space
That doth so far divide me from my dear desired face,
I know not how to attain the wings that I require   25
To lift my weight that it might flee to follow my desire.
Thus of that hope that doth my life something sustain
Alas I fear—and partly feel—full little doth remain.
Each place doth bring me grief where I do not behold
Those lively eyes which of my thoughts were wont the keys to
                                        hold.   30
Those thoughts were pleasant sweet whilst I enjoyed that grace,
My pleasure past, my present pain, where I might well
                                        embrace.

6 *apart*: i.e. alone.   7 *persuade*: urge, counsel.
9 *desired*: MS. *desyerd* shows the pronunciation.
14 *trained*: drawn out, protracted (It. *attempo*).
15 *the hours . . . bend*: i.e. how the sun inclines through the zodiac (MT).
16 *space*: time.   21 *The . . . short*: cf. *PF*, 1.   26, 100 *flee*: fly.

But for because my want should more my woe increase,
In watch, in sleep, both day and night, my will doth never cease
That thing to wish whereof since I did lose the sight   35
I never saw the thing that might my faithful heart delight.
The uneasy life I lead doth teach me for to mete
The floods, the seas, the land and hills that doth them
                                        entermete
'Tween me and those shining lights that wonted to clear
My dark pangs of cloudy thoughts, as bright as Phoebus'
                                        spear;   40
It teacheth me also what was my pleasant state,
The more to feel by such record how that my wealth doth
                                        bate.
If such record alas provoke the enflamed mind
Which sprang that day that I did leave the best of me behind,
If love forget himself, by length of absence let,   45
Who doth me guide, O woeful wretch, unto this baited net
Where doth increase my care? Much better were for me
As dumb as stone, all thing forgot, still absent for to be.
Alas, the clear crystal, the bright transparent glass,
Doth not bewray the colour hid which underneath it has,   50
As doth the accumbered sprite thoughtful throes discover
Of fierce delight, of fervent love, that in our hearts we cover.
Out by these eyes it showth, that ever more delight
In plaint and tears to seek redress, and that both day and night.
These new kinds of pleasures, wherein most men rejoice,   55
To me they do redouble still of stormy sighs the voice:

34 *In watch*: when I am awake.
38 *entermete*: put (themselves) between.
39 *lights*: i.e. eyes.
40 *Phoebus*: Phoebus Apollo, the sun.
42 *record*: memory.
42 *wealth*: well-being.
44 *sprang*: i.e. to life (MT).
47 *care*: sorrow.
48 *As . . . stone*: cf. Chaucer, *House of Fame*, 656.
51 *accumbered*: (cf. *encumbered*) crushed.
53 *by*: through (It. *Per*).
54 ff. *redress*: remedy, aid.

For I am one of them whom plaint doth well content,
It sits me well, mine absent wealth me seems me to lament,
And with my tears for to essay to charge mine eyes twain,
Like as mine heart above the brink is fraughted full of pain.   60
And for because thereto of those fair eyes to treat
Do me provoke: I shall return, my plaint thus to repeat,
For there is nothing else that touches me so within,
Where they rule all, and I alone nought but the case or skin.
Wherefore I do return to them as well or spring   65
From whom descends my mortal woe above all other thing.
So shall mine eyes in pain accompany mine heart,
That were the guides that did it lead of love to feel the smart.
The crisped gold that doth surmount Apollo's pride,
The lively streams of pleasant stars that under it doth glide,   70
Wherein the beams of love doth still increase their heat,
Which yet so far touch me so near in cold to make me sweat,
The wise and pleasant talk, so rare or else alone,
That did me give the courteous gift that such had never none,
Be far from me alas, and every other thing   75
I might forbear with better will than that that did me bring
With pleasant word and cheer redress of lingered pain,
And wonted oft in kindled will to virtue me to train.
Thus am I driven to hear and hearken after news;
My comfort scant, my large desire in doubtful trust renews.   80
And yet with more delight to moan my woeful case
I must complain: those hands, those arms that firmly do
                                             embrace
Me from myself and rule the stern of my poor life,
The sweet disdains, the pleasant wraths, and eke the lovely
                                             strife

60 *brink*: brim, i.e. of a vessel.   60 *fraughted*: (cf. *freighted*) loaded.
64 *case*: skin.   70 *streams*: cf. CLXVI, 13.
73 *else alone*: 'even unique' (MT).
76 *forbear*: go without.
78 *train*: draw.
80 *doubtful*: apprehensive.
82–83 *that . . . myself*: cf. Horace, IV, Ode 13, 20, 'Quae me surpuerat mihi'.
83 *stern*: rudder and helm (of a ship). Cf. ML, 39.
84 *lovely*: loving.

That wonted well to tune in temper just and meet,   85
The rage that oft did make me err, by furor undiscreet—
All this is hid me fro' with sharp and cragged hills.
At other will my long abode my deep despair fulfils.
But if my hope sometime rise up by some redress,
It stumbleth straight for feeble faint, my fear hath such

                                                        excess.   90
Such is the sort of hope, the less for more desire,
Whereby I fear and yet I trust to see that I require:
The resting place of love, where virtue lives and grows,
Where I desire my weary life also may take repose.
My song, thou shalt attain to find that pleasant place   95
Where she doth live by whom I live, may chance thee have this

                                                        grace—
When she hath read and seen the dread wherein I starve,
Between her breasts she shall thee put: there shall she thee

                                                        reserve.
Then tell her that I come, she shall me shortly see:
If that for weight the body fail, this soul shall to her flee.   100

XCIX

In Spain

        Tagus farewell, that westward with thy streams
        Turns up the grains of gold already tried:
        With spur and sail for I go seek the Thames
        Gainward the sun that showth her wealthy pride

87: Cf. LXXVIII, 15; *with*: by.   88 *fulfils*: makes full.
91 *the less . . . desire*: made worse by my growing desire.
97 *starve*: die (i.e. from deprivation).

---

1 *Tagus*: one of the main rivers in Spain and Portugal.
2 *already tried*: 'already sifted from the dross' (WMT). Cf. Chaucer, *Boece*, III,
Metrum 10, 11 ff., and Robinson's note.
3–6: 'For I with spur and sail am going to seek the Thames that shows her
abundant splendour towards the sun and that like a crescent moon lends her
beautiful side to the town which B. sought by dreams.'

And to the town which Brutus sought by dreams   5
Like bended moon doth lend her lusty side.
My king, my country, alone for whom I live,
Of mighty love the wings for this me give.

I flee

C

Of purpose Love chose first for to be blind,
For he with sight of that that I behold
Vanquished had been against all godly kind:
His bow your hand and truss should have unfold,
And he with me to serve had been assigned.   5
But for he blind and reckless would him hold,
And still by chance his deadly strokes bestow,
With such as see I serve and suffer woe.

C I

What rage is this? What furor of what kind?
What power, what plague doth weary thus my mind?
Within my bones to rankle is assigned
        What poison pleasant sweet?

Lo, see, mine eyes swell with continual tears,   5
The body still away sleepless it wears,
My food nothing my fainting strength repairs,
        Nor doth my limbs sustain.

---

5 *the town*: London. Brutus, descendant of Aeneas, was told by Diana, who
appeared to him in a dream, to found a kingdom in Albion (to which he lent
his name). Cf. Geoffrey of Monmouth (Nott).
7–8: W was allowed to return to Britain in 1539, having stayed in Spain longer
than he liked. He left—and probably wrote XCIX—early in June.
9 *flee*: fly.

4: 'Your hand would have unwrapped his bow and bundle of arrows.'

In deep wide wound the deadly stroke doth turn
To cured scar that never shall return.   10
Go to, triumph, rejoice thy goodly turn,
    Thy friend thou dost oppress.

Oppress thou dost, and hast of him no cure,
Nor yet my plaint no pity can procure.
Fierce tiger fell! Hard rock without recure!   15
    Cruel rebel to love!

Once may thou love, never beloved again,
So love thou still, and not thy love obtain,
So wrathful love with spites of just disdain
    May threat thy cruel heart!   20

CII

(fragment?)

From thought to thought, from hill to hill love doth me lead;
Clean contrary from restful life these common paths I tread.

CIII

Vulcan begot me, Minerva me taught,
Nature my mother, craft nourished me year by year,
Three bodies are my food, my strength is in nought,
Slaughter, wrath, waste and noise are my children dear.
Guess, friend, what I am, or how I am wrought: 5
Monster of land, sea, or elsewhere?
Have me and use me, and I may thee defend,
And if I be thine enemy, I may thy life end.

---

10 *that*: i.e. the wound (9), which will never be restored to a cured scar. Cf.
CLXII, 14.   12 *friend*: lover.   13 *cure*: care.
15: Cf. CXLVIII, 9–12.   15 *recure*: remedy.

Cf. Appendix, CIII.
1 *Vulcan*: the Roman god of fire, and the divine smith.
1 *Minerva*: Roman goddess of wisdom; also protector of handicrafts and
goddess of war.
3 *in nought*: cf. Lat. *de nihilo*. 'In the O of the gun's mouth' (S).
4 *waste*: destruction, ruin (Lat. *ruina*).

CIV

Iopas' Song (unfinished)

When Dido feasted first the wandering Trojan knight
Whom Juno's wrath with storms did force in Libyc sands to light,
That mighty Atlas did teach, the supper lasting long,
With crisped locks, on golden harp, Iopas sang in his song.
'That same,' quod he, 'that we the world do call and name,   5
Of heaven and earth, with all contents, it is the very frame,
Or thus: of heavenly powers, by more power kept in one,
Repugnant kinds, in mids of whom the earth hath place alone,
Firm, round, of living things the mother place and nurse;
Without the which, in equal weight, this heaven doth hold his
course,   10
And it is called by name the first moving heaven.
The firmament is next, containing other seven:
Of heavenly powers that same is planted full and thick,
As shining lights, which we call stars, that therein cleave and
stick.

This expounds essentially the Ptolemaic system. The earth is seen as central, not the sun, which with the moon is considered to be one of the planets revolving round the earth. Copernicus' theories were getting known in the 1530s; perhaps W was responding to them, either in writing his poem or in abandoning it. He may, of course, not have lived to complete his poem; or possibly the task became too much for him. Scott (cf. Appendix) suggests that W wrote the poem in October 1539, when a clock was constructed to celebrate the arrival of Anne of Cleves, but interrupted his labour when sent out once again, in November, to Charles V.

1–4: Cf. Virgil's *Aeneid*, I, 723–47; particularly 740–2. Aeneas, Trojan hero, on his wanderings was driven by a storm to Libya and Dido, Queen of Carthage. When she first feasted him, Iopas, 'That (i.e. whom) mighty Atlas did teach', sang about the structure of the universe.

2 *Juno's wrath*: cf. *Aeneid* I, 4 (MT).

3 *Atlas*: legendary king of Mauretania, changed by Perseus into Mt. Atlas, and so forced to bear the heavens.   6, 7 *Of*: depends on *frame*.

7 *heavenly powers*: the heavens were thought of as spheres or shells (cf. 41), concentric, transparent and hollow globes, revolving round the earth, and carrying the heavenly bodies with them. The outermost sphere is the *primum mobile* ('the first moving heaven', 11), which contains the others, and which W describes first.

12 *The firmament*: the sphere of the fixed stars. It contains the spheres of the seven planets.

With great swift sway the first, and with his restless source,   15
Carrieth itself and all those eight in even continual course.
And of this world so round, within that rolling case,
There be two points, that never move, but firmly keep their
                                                            place.
The t'one we see alway: the t'other stands object
Against the same, dividing just the round by line direct   20
Which by imagination drawn from the one to the other
Toucheth the centre of the earth—way there is none other.
And these been called the poles, described by stars not bright:
Arctic the t'one northward we see, Antarctic the other hight.
The line that we devise from the one to the other so   25
As axle is, upon the which the heavens about doth go,
Which of water nor earth, of air nor fire have kind:
Therefore the substance of those same were hard for man to
                                                            find.
But they been uncorrupt, simple and pure unmixed,
And so we say been all those stars that in those same been
                                                            fixed,   30
And eke those erring seven, in circles as they stray,
So called because against that first they have repugnant way,
And smaller byways too, scant sensible to man—
Too busy work for my poor harp: let sing them he that can.
The widest save the first of all these nine above   35
One hundred year doth ask of space for one degree to move,
Of which degrees we make, in the first moving heaven,
Three hundred and three score in parts justly divided even.
And yet there is another between those heavens two
Whose moving is so sly, so slack, I name it not for now.   40
The seventh heaven or the shell next to the starry sky
All those degrees that gatherth up, with aged pace so sly,

15 *source*: flight.   19 *object*: opposite.   24 *hight*: is called.
27: W refers to the four elements of which all material bodies were thought to
be composed.   31 *those . . . seven*: the planets; *erring*: wandering.
36, 57 *space*: duration.
39 *another*: W has so far talked of nine spheres. Now he thinks of
another—scholarship was uncertain about the exact number.
41, 70 *the starry sky*: the firmament.

And doth perform the same, as elders' count hath been,
In nine and twenty years complete, and days almost sixteen,
Doth carry in his bout the star of Saturn old,   45
A threatener of all living things, with drought and with his
                                                              cold.
The sixth whom this contains doth stalk with younger pace
And in twelve year doth somewhat more than the other's
                                                        voyage was.
And this in it doth bear the star of Jove benign,
'Tween Saturn's malice and us men friendly defending sign.   50
The fifth bearth bloody Mars that in three hundred days
And twice eleven, with one full year, hath finished all those
                                                             ways.
A year doth ask the fourth, and hours thereto six,
And in the same the day his eye, the sun, therein he sticks.
The third that governed is by that that governth me   55
And love for love—and for no love—provokes as oft we see,
In like space doth perform that course that did the t'other.
So doth the next to the same, that second is in order,
But it doth bear the star that called is Mercury,
That many a crafty secret step doth tread as calkers try.   60
That sky is last and first, next us those ways hath gone
In seven and twenty common days, and eke the third of one,
And beareth with his sway the diverse moon about,
Now bright now brown, now bent now full, and now her·light
                                                            is out.
Thus have they of their own two movings all those seven: 65
One wherein they be carried still each in his several heaven,

45 *bout*: circuit.
45 *star*: was common for 'planet' and 'fixed star'.
47 *this*: Saturn's sphere, which contains the sixth sphere, that of Jupiter.
47 *stalk*: move quietly.
47 *with . . . pace*: 'with quicker movement' (Rollins).
55 *The third*: Venus.   60 *calkers*: astronomers.   60 *try*: find.
61 *last*: i.e. in my description; *first* because closest to the earth.
61 *next us*: 'which nearest to us'.   64 *bent*: crescent.
65 *of their own*: i.e. not counting their being carried by the *primum mobile*.

Another of himselves where their bodies been laid
In byways and in lesser rounds, as I afore have said,
Save of them all the sun doth stray least from the straight.
The starry sky hath but one course, that we have called the
                                                    eight. 70
And all these movings eight are meant from west to the east,
Although they seem to climb aloft I say from east to west;
But that is but by force of the first moving sky,
In twice twelve hours from east to the east that carrieth them by
                                                    and by.
But mark we well also these movings of these seven   75
Be not about that axle tree of the first moving heaven,
For they have their two poles directly the one to the other . . .'

C V
Satire I

Mine own John Poyntz, since ye delight to know
The cause why that homeward I me draw,
And flee the press of courts whereso they go
Rather than to live thrall under the awe
Of lordly looks, wrapped within my cloak   5
To will and lust learning to set a law:
It is not for because I scorn or mock
The power of them to whom fortune hath lent
Charge over us, of right to strike the stroke;

---

74 *by and by*: on and on.

Written after either W's first imprisonment in the Tower (1536), or his second
(1541). Nott favoured 1541. Certainly 89–99 seems to refer to past experience
rather than the future. The *clog* of 86 may refer to some unpleasant experience
W had to accept when released (cf. ML, 209) or to whatever he saw as a
restriction; or, if the poem was written in 1536, W may hint that he is on parole
to his father, enjoying relative freedom only. His imprisonment in 1536 had in
his opinion been due to the machinations of the Duke of Suffolk and he had
witnessed the execution of Anne Boleyn, so he had reason not to look
favourably on life at court. However, this was even more true in 1541.
1 *John Poyntz*: a courtier contemporary with W, of whom little is known.
3 *press*: crowd. But cf. also XV, 13, and CLXXXI, 4.
5 *wrapped . . . cloak*: Nott mentions Horace's 'mea/virtute me involvo' (Odes,
III, No. 29, 54–55) as the source, and perhaps as an explanation.

But true it is that I have always meant 10
Less to esteem them than the common sort
Of outward things that judge in their intent
Without regard what doth inward resort.
I grant sometime that of glory the fire
Doth touch my heart: me list not to report 15
Blame by honour and honour to desire,
But how may I this honour now attain
That cannot dye the colour black a liar?
My Poyntz, I cannot frame my tune to feign,
To cloak the truth for praise without desert 20
Of them that list all vice for to retain.
I cannot honour them that sets their part
With Venus and Bacchus all their life long,
Nor hold my peace of them although I smart.
I cannot crouch nor kneel, to do so great a wrong 25
To worship them like God on earth alone
That are as wolves these seely lambs among.
I cannot with my word complain and moan
And suffer nought, nor smart without complaint,
Nor turn the word that from my mouth is gone. 30
I cannot speak and look like a saint,
Use wiles for wit, and make deceit a pleasure,
And call craft counsel, for profit still to paint.
I cannot wrest the law to fill the coffer,
With innocent blood to feed myself fat, 35
And do most hurt where most help I offer.
I am not he that can allow the state

10–13: 'I esteem the great less than the common sort of people do, who in their intent, i.e. view of things, judge of persons by their outward appearance, without regard to what is their internal merit' (Nott; cf. the It.). *The common sort*: cf. QM, 450.
15–16: *me . . . desire*: 'I do not like to talk censoriously about honour while yet I desire it.'
18: 'Who cannot add to a liar's blackness'; cf. Tilley, B436. **22** *part*: interest.
27 *seely*: (cf. *silly*) innocent. See Matthew 10:16, and Whiting, W455.
30: Cf. Tilley, W777. *Turn*: i.e. call back.
32 *Use . . . wit*: substitute deceitful subtleties for reason.
33 *paint*: flatter, deceive.   37 *allow*: praise.

Of him Caesar, and damn Cato to die,
That with his death did 'scape out of the gate
From Caesar's hands, if Livy do not lie,   40
And would not live where liberty was lost,
So did his heart the common weal apply.
I am not he such eloquence to boast
To make the crow singing as the swan,
Nor call the lion of coward beasts the most,   45
That cannot take a mouse as the cat can,
And he that dieth for hunger of the gold
Call him Alexander, and say that Pan
Passeth Apollo in music manifold,
Praise Sir Thopas for a noble tale   50
And scorn the story that the knight told,
Praise him for counsel that is drunk of ale,
Grin when he laugheth that beareth all the sway,
Frown when he frowneth and groan when he is pale,
On others' lust to hang both night and day: 55
None of these points would ever frame in me—
My wit is nought, I cannot learn the way.
And much the less of things that greater be,
That asken help of colours of device
To join the mean with each extremity: 60

38 *him*: D, C, CC. But possibly this should be *high* (A, P, T).
38 *damn*: sentence.
38 *Cato*: 'Brutus' uncle, Cato of Utica, who . . . fought for freedom against Caesar, and who committed suicide after the battle of Thapsus in 46 B.C.' (MT). Cf. the Epitome of Book cxiv of Livy's *History* (Nott).
42 *the common weal*: 'the old republic, and the general good' (Nott).
45 *lion*: cf. the heraldic 'Lion Coward' (*OED coward*, adj., 2).
48–49: W contrasts Pan and his pipe with Apollo, the higher god who—amongst many civilized functions—was the patron of music. Both are Greek deities.
50–51: W contrasts Chaucer's *Sir Thopas*, a deliberately clumsy parody of a chivalric tale, with the genuine thing—*The Knight's Tale*, also by C.
55 *On . . . hang*: to depend on the wishes of others. Cf. 78.
56 *frame*: fit; prosper.
59 *colours of device*: ingenious disguises; distortions.

With the nearest virtue to cloak alway the vice,
And as to purpose likewise it shall fall
To press the virtue that it may not rise,
As drunkenness good fellowship to call,
The friendly foe with his double face   65
Say he is gentle, and courteous therewithal,
And say that favel hath a goodly grace
In eloquence, and cruelty to name
Zeal of justice and change in time and place,
And he that sufferth offence without blame   70
Call him pitiful, and him true and plain
That raileth reckless to every man's shame,
Say he is rude that cannot lie and feign,
The lecher a lover, and tyranny
To be the right of a prince's reign: 75
I cannot, I—no, no, it will not be!
This is the cause that I could never yet
Hang on their sleeves that weigh as thou mayst see
A chip of chance more than a pound of wit.
This maketh me at home to hunt and to hawk,   80
And in foul weather at my book to sit,
In frost and snow then with my bow to stalk:
No man doth mark whereso I ride or go,
In lusty lease at liberty I walk,
And of these news I feel nor weal nor woe,   85
Save that a clog doth hang yet at my heel—
No force for that, for it is ordered so

61 ff.: For possible sources, cf. Nott.
62: 'And likewise as it shall be opportune' (MT).
67 *favel*: probably 'flattery' rather than 'deceit'; cf. the context and Nott's
examples. Not necessarily a personification, and without a capital in E.
70–71 *And . . . pitiful*: 'and call him compassionate who tolerates offences
against people who do not deserve them'.
78: *Hang on sleeves*: fawn on, be obsequious to. But cf. 55.
79: Proverbial (Rollins), cf. Tilley, O85.
83 *go*: walk.   84 *lusty*: delightful.
84 *lease*: pasture; cf. Kenneth A. Bleeth (*N & Q*, 1971, 214), who compares
T & C, II, 750–2.
86: Proverbial (cf. Rollins).
87 *No . . . that*: never mind about that.

That I may leap both hedge and dike full well.
I am not now in France to judge the wine,
With savoury sauce the delicates to feel;   90
Nor yet in Spain, where one must him incline,
Rather than to be, outwardly to seem—
I meddle not with wits that be so fine;
Nor Flanders' cheer letteth not my sight to deem
Of black and white, nor taketh my wit away   95
With beastliness, they beasts do so esteem;
Nor I am not where Christ is given in prey
For money, poison and treason, at Rome
A common practice used night and day:
But here I am in Kent and Christendom   100
Among the Muses where I read and rhyme,
Where if thou list, my Poyntz, for to come,
Thou shalt be judge how I do spend my time.

CVI

Satire 2

My mother's maids, when they did sew and spin,
They sang sometime a song of the fieldmouse,
That for because her lyvelood was but thin

89: F notes that W was granted a licence to import wine when serving in Calais, September 1529.
90 *feel*: taste and smell.
94–96: 'Nor does the merry-making of the Flemish prevent me from seeing the difference between black and white, or replace my brains with beastliness—the way one would expect from their high opinion of beasts as models.'
100 *Kent and Christendom*: the history of Kent, with Canterbury, as the centre of English Christendom (to which it was first converted) had become proverbial (cf. *ODEP*, p. 420; Tilley, K16). But W expresses his own feeling, and Allington Castle, the home of the Wyatt family, is in Kent.
101 *Muses*: cf. QM, 446, 'the best remedy is with the muses . . .'

---

3 *lyvelood*: i.e. livelihood.

Would needs go seek her townish sister's house.
She thought herself endured too much pain: 5
The stormy blasts her cave so sore did souse
That when the furrows swimmed with the rain
She must lie cold and wet in sorry plight;
And worse than that, bare meat there did remain
To comfort her when she her house had dight—   10
Sometime a barley corn, sometime a bean,
For which she laboured hard both day and night
In harvest time whilst she might go and glean.
And when her store was 'stroyed with the flood,
Then wellaway, for she undone was clean.   15
Then was she fain to take instead of food
Sleep if she might, her hunger to beguile.
'My sister,' quod she, 'hath a living good,
And hence from me she dwelleth not a mile.
In cold and storm she lieth warm and dry   20
In bed of down. The dirt doth not defile
Her tender foot, she laboureth not as I:
Richly she feedeth, and at the rich man's cost,
And for her meat she needs not crave nor cry.
By sea, by land, of delicates the most   25
Her cater seeks, and spareth for no peril.
She feedeth on boiled bacon meat and roast,
And hath thereof neither charge nor travail,
And when she list, the liquor of the grape
Doth glad her heart, till that her belly swell.'   30
And at this journey she maketh but a jape,
So forth she goeth, trusting of all this wealth
With her sister her part so for to shape
That if she might keep herself in health
To live a lady while her life doth last.   35
And to the door now is she come by stealth,

9, 24 *meat*: food.
10 *dight*: put in order.
26 *cater*: i.e. caterer.
26 *and . . . peril*: 'and no danger restrains him'.
28 *charge*: burden; or: cost (cf. 23).
29 *liquor*: i.e. juice, cf. *CT*, C452.

And with her foot anon she scrapeth full fast.
The other for fear durst not well scarce appear,
Of every noise so was the wretch aghast.
At last she asked softly who was there,   40
And in her language as well as she could,
'Peep,' quod the other, 'sister, I am here.'
'Peace,' quod the towny mouse, 'why speakest thou so loud?'
And by the hand she took her fair and well.
'Welcome,' quod she, 'my sister, by the rood!'   45
She feasted her that joy it was to tell
The fare they had—they drank the wine so clear,
And as to purpose now and then it fell
She cheered her with 'How, sister, what cheer?'
Amids this joy befell a sorry chance,   50
That wellaway the stranger bought full dear
The fare she had. For as she looked askance
Under a stool she spied two steaming eyes
In a round head with sharp ears: in France
Was never mouse so feared, for though the unwise   55
Had not yseen such a beast before,
Yet had nature taught her after her guise
To know her foe and dread him evermore.
The towny mouse fled: she knew whither to go.
The other had no shift, but wonders sore   60
Feared of her life; at home she wished her tho.
And to the door alas as she did skip,
The heaven it would, lo, and eke her chance was so,

41 *could*: knew how to.
46: Cf. *T & C*, III, 1228 (MEW, 167).
48: 'As it fell into conversation' (Nott, who compares *T & C*, III, 1131).
50: Cf. *T & C*, II, 464.
53 *steaming*: flaming. (Cf. *CT*, Gen. Prol., 201–2.)
56 *yseen*: cf. IX, 6.
57 *guise*: fashion.
60 *shift*: solution, expedient.
60 *wonders*: prob. a verb; otherwise: wondrously.
61 *tho*: then.

At the threshold her seely foot did trip,
And ere she might recover it again   65
The traitor Cat had caught her by the hip,
And made her there against her will remain
That had forgotten her poor surety and rest
For seeming wealth wherein she thought to reign.
Alas my Poyntz, how men do seek the best,   70
And find the worst, by error as they stray!
And no marvel: when sight is so oppressed
And blind the guide, anon out of the way
Goeth guide and all in seeking quiet life.
O wretched minds! There is no gold that may   75
Grant that ye seek, no war, no peace, no strife—
No, no: although thy head were hooped with gold,
Sergeant with mace, halbert, sword, nor knife
Cannot repulse the care that follow should!
Each kind of life hath with him his disease: 80
Live in delight even as thy lust would,
And thou shalt find when lust doth most thee please
It irketh straight and by itself doth fade.
A small thing it is that may thy mind appease.
None of ye all there is that is so mad   85
To seek grapes upon brambles or briers,
Nor none (I trow) that hath his wit so bad

64 *seely*: innocent, pitiful. Cf. CV, 27.
66 *hip*: cf. 'To have one on the hip' = to have one at a disadvantage (Tilley,
H474).
68 *poor surety*: 'the security which she derived from her poverty' (Nott).
70: Nott rightly compares *CT*, A1266–7, and Arcite's speech generally.
70: *Poyntz*: cf. CV, 1.
75 *gold*: cf. QM, 462, 'So nouther gorgiousnesse . . .'
78 *Sergeant*: i.e. a bodyguard.   78 *knife*: dagger.
79: 'Cannot repel the anxiety that is bound to follow'. Nott compares Horace,
Odes, II, 16.   80 *his disease*: its distress.
84: 'The thing which can set your mind at rest is only small.'
86: Proverbial (Rollins), cf. Tilley, G411.

To set his hay for conies over rivers,
Ne ye set not a drag-net for an hare:
And yet the thing that most is your desire   90
Ye do misseek with more travail and care.
Make plain thine heart, that it be not knotted
With hope or dread, and see thy will be bare
From all affects whom vice hath ever spotted;
Thyself content with that is thee assigned,   95
And use it well that is to thee allotted:
Then seek no more out of thyself to find
The thing that thou hast sought so long before,
For thou shalt feel it sitting in thy mind—
Mad if ye list to continue your sore,   100
Let present pass, and gape on time to come,
And deep yourself in travail more and more.
Henceforth, my Poyntz, this shall be all and some:
These wretched fools shall have nought else of me,
But to the great God and to his high doom   105
None other pain pray I for them to be
But when the rage doth lead them from the right
That looking backward virtue they may see
Even as she is, so goodly fair and bright;
And whilst they clasp their lusts in arms across   110
Grant them, good Lord, as thou mayst of thy might,
To fret inward for losing such a loss.

---

88 *hay for conies*: hunting-net for rabbits.
89: Cf. QM, 452, 'them that . . . hunt an hart with a dragge net'. *Ne*: nor.
93–94 *bare . . . affects*: 'free from the dominion of all passion' (Nott).
97: Cf. Persius, I, 7, 'Nec te quaesiveris extra'.
97 *out of*: outside.
99 *it*: i.e. 98—satisfaction, mental peace.
100 *Mad*: in apposition to *thou* (99). Cf. QM, 455, 'for foles let good thynges passe tho they be present . . . so moche doth their thoughtes gape gredily after thynges to come'.
101 *gape on*: long for.
102 *travail*: agony.
103 *all and some*: the sum total.
105 ff.: Cf. Persius, III, 35–38 (e.g. in Rollins, II, 214).

CVII

Satire 3

A spending hand that alway poureth out
Had need to have a bringer in as fast,
And on the stone that still doth turn about
There groweth no moss: these proverbs yet do last.
Reason hath set them in so sure a place   5
That length of years their force can never waste.
When I remember this, and eke the case
Wherein thou stands, I thought forthwith to write,
Brian, to thee, who knows how great a grace
In writing is to counsel man the right.   10
To thee therefore, that trots still up and down
And never rests: but running day and night
From realm to realm, from city, street, and town,
Why dost thou wear thy body to the bones
And mightst at home sleep in thy bed of down   15

W addressed CXLV also to Sir Francis Brian. CXLV was written in prison, and its language is like that of W's Declaration and Defence. Therefore, it is possible that CVII, too, was written in 1541 (and cf. CV), at the time of W's second imprisonment in the Tower, as is suggested by Nott and Mason (204), who points to the resemblance between 11–13 and a passage in W's Defence (cf. ML, 181). Others believe that all three verse epistles were written in 1536–7.

Hughey (II, 185) refers to the friendship for Brian evident in CXLV. W knew B. well (cf. ML). Like W, B. was a courtier 'constantly employed by Henry in business of a confidential nature' (Nott, lxxxiv). Both men were esteemed as poets (cf. Rollins, II, 82). W's poetry shows that like B. he was fond of proverbs. W's irony, therefore, is no doubt aimed at other courtiers, not B., who within the poem plainly dissociates himself from the kind of life which W denounces (cf. 80 ff.). However, cf. MT, which continues an argument begun by J. P. Collier in *Archaeologica*, 1836, 446–53.

1–2: i.e. 'A spendthrift needs a constant supply.' Cf. Tilley, S738. W once lent B. £200 (ML, 20), and may be poking gentle fun at him.

3–4: Cf. Tilley, S885.

10: The line ends with a question mark in E, perhaps correctly. *Who* (9) is preceded by a virgula.

And drink good ale so nappy for the nonce,
Feed thyself fat and heap up pound by pound?
Likest thou not this? 'No.' Why? 'For swine so groins
In sty and chaw the turds moulded on the ground,
And drivel on pearls, the head still in the manger,   20
Than of the harp the ass to hear the sound.
So sacks of dirt be filled up in the cloister,
That serves for less than do these fatted swine.
Though I seem lean and dry, without moisture,
Yet will I serve my prince, my lord and thine,   25
And let them live to feed the paunch that list,
So I may feed to live both me and mine.'
By God, well said! But what and if thou wist
How to bring in as fast as thou dost spend?
'That would I learn.' And it shall not be missed   30
To tell thee how. Now hark what I intend.
Thou knowst well, first, whoso can seek to please
Shall purchase friends where truth shall but offend.
Flee therefore truth: it is both wealth and ease.
For though that truth of every man hath praise,   35
Full near that wind goeth truth in great misease.
Use virtue as it goeth nowadays:
In word alone to make thy language sweet,
And of the deed yet do not as thou says,
Else be thou sure thou shalt be far unmeet   40
To get thy bread, each thing is now so scant.
Seek still thy profit upon thy bare feet;

18 *groins*: grunt.
21 *Than*: MS. *then*, for *than*=as (*OED* 5). Swine value pearls (cf. Matthew 7:6—Rollins) as little as an ass cares for music (cf., e.g., *T & C*, I, 731–5).
22 *dirt*: excrement. W refers to 'sensual and voluptuous monks' (Nott).
28 *and . . . wist*: if you knew.
33: Cf. *ODEP*, p. 843 (Tilley, T570), particularly the reference to Terence's *Andria* (Nott; cf. 78).
34 *it*: i.e. to flee the truth.
36: 'Yet in proximity to that talk truth is considered too close.' In practice, people do not value truth as much as they say.

Lend in no wise, for fear that thou do want,
Unless it be as to a dog a cheese,
By which return be sure to win a cant 45
Of half at least: it is not good to lese.
Learn at Kytson, that in a long white coat
From under the stall, without lands or fees
Hath leapt into the shop, who knoweth by rote
This rule that I have told thee here before. 50
Sometime also rich age beginneth to dote:
See thou when there thy gain may be the more,
Stay him by the arm whereso he walk or go,
Be near alway, and if he cough too sore,
When he hath spit, tread out and please him so. 55
A diligent knave that picks his master's purse
May please him so that he withouten mo
Executor is, and what is he the worse?
But if so chance you get nought of the man,
The widow may for all thy charge deburse: 60
A rivelled skin, a stinking breath, what then?
A toothless mouth shall do thy lips no harm,
The gold is good, and though she curse or ban,
Yet where thee list thou mayst lie good and warm:
Let the old mule bite upon the bridle 65
Whilst there do lie a sweeter in thine arm.

44 *a dog*: i.e. do not give a dog a bone (which he will keep), but a cheese, which
he will return—with at least half an additional portion (*cant*). (So: make sure
that the interest on your loans is excessive.)
46 *lese*: lose.
47 *Kytson*: prob. Sir Thomas Kytson, a prosperous merchant (cf. S, in
N & Q, 1974, 403–4).
48 *fees*: goods.
56 *knave*: servant; rogue.
60: Cf. QM, 454, 'or to lye with a riche old woman'.
60 *charge*: cf. CVI, 28.
60 *deburse*: disburse.
61 *what then*: so what.
65: Proverbial (Rollins); cf. Tilley, B670. 'Let the old woman (cf. also XXXV)
vex herself.'

In this also see you be not idle:
Thy niece, thy cousin, thy sister or thy daughter,
If she be fair, if handsome by her middle,
If thy better hath her love besought her,   70
Advance his cause, and he shall help thy need:
It is but love, turn it to a laughter.
But 'ware, I say, so gold thee help and speed,
That in this case thou be not so unwise
As Pandar was in such a like deed: 75
For he, the fool, of conscience was so nice
That he no gain would have for all his pain.
Be next thyself, for friendship bears no price.
Laughst thou at me? Why, do I speak in vain?
'No, not at thee, but at thy thrifty gest!   80
Wouldest thou I should for any loss or gain
Change that for gold that I have ta'en for best
Next godly things: to have an honest name?
Should I leave that? Then take me for a beast!'
Nay then farewell, and if you care for shame   85
Content thee then with honest poverty,
With free tongue what thee mislikes to blame,
And for thy truth sometime adversity,
And therewithal this thing I shall thee give:
In this world now little prosperity,   90
And coin to keep as water in a sieve.

69 *by her middle*: in her waist, cf., e.g., Chaucer, *RR*, 1032.
75 *Pandar*: cf. *T & C*, particularly III, 260 ff. and 400 ff. (Nott). Pandarus
helped Troilus without accepting any gift from him.
78 *Be next thyself*: 'Look after Number One' (WMT). From Terence's *Andria*,
IV, 1, 12, 'Proximus sum egomet mihi' (Nott).
80 *thrifty*: (also) proper.
80 *gest*: tale.
83 *honest*: cf. ML, 38 ff.
91: Proverbial (Rollins); cf. Tilley, W111.

CVIII

Penitential Psalms

Prologue

Love to give law unto his subject hearts
Stood in the eyes of Barsabe the bright,
And in a look anon himself converts
Cruelly pleasant before King David's sight;
First dazed his eyes, and further forth he starts   5
With venomed breath, as softly as he might
Touched his senses, and overruns his bones
With creeping fire, sparpled for the nonce.

And when he saw that kindled was the flame,
The moist poison in his heart he lanced,   10
So that the soul did tremble with the same.
And in this brawl as he stood and tranced,
Yielding unto the figure and the frame
That those fair eyes had in his presence glanced,
The form that Love had printed in his breast   15
He honourth it as thing of thinges best.

Cf. Appendix. Preceded by Surrey's 'The great Macedon' (cf. ed. Emrys Jones,
p. 29), which must have been added later. W's references to enemies and
imminent death have suggested to scholars that he wrote CVIII at the time of
either his imprisonment in 1536, or that in 1541. (A date earlier than 1534,
when Aretino was published, is impossible.) Mason prefers 1536; for counter
arguments cf., e.g., ML, 256, and SCM, 168. The sources do not settle the
question one way or the other, nor does the poem's position in E. We may
remember W's repentant tone in his letters to his son (ML, 38 ff.), written in
1537; on the other hand, 364 ff. would quite well fit the circumstances of W's
imprisonment in 1541 (cf., e.g., XCI).

In the first prologue, W treats 'the story of David's love for Uriah's wife
Bathsheba, the warnings of the prophet Nathan, and his repentance, as told in
2 Samuel, 11–12' (MT). As Hughey notes, W is indebted to Aretino 'for the
romantic concept of the Psalms as repentant laments . . . with the dramatic
and psychological progression secured through the prologues.'

Prologue

2 *Barsabe*: (Aretino: *Bersabe*) Bathsheba.   8 *sparpled*: scattered.
12 *brawl*: 'a kind of French dance resembling a cotillon' (*OED*'s gloss, *brawl*
sb.³).

So that forgot the wisdom and forecast
(Which woe to realms when that these kings doth lack),
Forgetting eke God's majesty as fast,
Yea and his own, forthwith he doth to make   20
Uriah to go into the field in haste,
Uriah I say, that was his idol's make,
Under pretence of certain victory
For enemies' swords a ready prey to die.

Whereby he may enjoy her out of doubt   25
Whom more than God or himself he mindeth.
And after he had brought this thing about
And of that lust possessed himself, he findeth
That hath and doth reverse and clean turn out
Kings from kingdoms and cities undermindeth: 30
He blinded thinks this train so blind and close
To blind all thing that nought may it disclose.

But Nathan hath spied out this treachery,
With rueful cheer and sets afore his face
The great offence, outrage and injury   35
That he hath done to God as in this case,
By murder for to cloak adultery.
He showeth him eke from heaven the threats alas
So sternly sore, this prophet, this Nathan,
That all amazed this aged woeful man.   40

Like him that meets with horror and with fear
The heat doth straight forsake the limbs cold;
The colour eke droopeth down from his cheer,
So doth he feel his fire manifold;

17 *forecast*: foresight, prudence.   22 *make*: mate.
29 *reverse*: overturn.   30 *undermindeth*: i.e. undermines.
31–32: 'Blinded himself, he thinks this deceitful deed sufficiently out of sight
and hidden to blind everything, so that nothing can reveal it.'
34: 'And with a mournful countenance sets forth the great offence before
David's face' (Nott; cf. Aretino).
40: 'That David became utterly panic-stricken.'
43, 69 *cheer*: face.   44 *fire*: MS. *fyer*, disyllabic.

His heat, his lust and pleasure all in fear   45
Consume and waste, and straight his crown of gold,
His purple pall, his sceptre he lets fall,
And to the ground he throwth himself withal.

The pompous pride of state and dignity
Forthwith rebates repentant humbleness;   50
Thinner vile cloth than clotheth poverty
Doth scantly hide and clad his nakedness;
His fair hoar beard of reverent gravity
With ruffled hair, knowing his wickedness,
More like was he the selfsame repentance   55
Than stately prince of worldly governance.

His harp he taketh in hand to be his guide,
Wherewith he offerth his plaints his soul to save
That from his heart distils on every side,
Withdrawing him into a dark cave   60
Within the ground, wherein he might him hide,
Fleeing the light, as in prison or grave:
In which as soon as David entered had
The dark horror did make his fault adrad.

But he without prolonging or delay   65
Of that that might his Lord his God appease
Fallth on his knees, and with his harp I say
Afore his breast, fraughted with disease

49 *The . . . dignity*: direct object.
55 *the . . . repentance*: repentance itself.
64 *adrad*: feared, i.e. by him.
66 *Of*: controversial reading. Some modern scholars read *rof* (i.e. *rove*). But in
65 *or* replaces earlier *of*, and in 66 *rof that that* would take the place of W's earlier
the thing that. Rove, pace R. C. Harrier (*N & Q*, 1953, 234) does not simply mean
'took'; and it cannot be parallel to It. *prendendo, pace* MT. *Of* gives easier sense,
and was adopted by A, R, and Q.
68 *fraughted*: cf. XCVIII, 60.
68 *disease*: discomfort, suffering.

Of stormy sighs, his cheer coloured like clay,
Dressed upright, seeking to counterpese   70
His song with sighs and touching of the strings
With tender heart, lo thus to God he sings:

Psalm 6. *Domine ne in furore*

[1] 'O Lord, since in my mouth thy mighty name
     Sufferth itself my Lord to name and call,
     Here hath my heart hope taken by the same,   75
     That the repentance which I have and shall
     May at thy hand seek mercy as the thing
     Only comfort of wretched sinners all.
     Whereby I dare with humble bemoaning
     By thy goodness of thee this thing require: 80
     Chastise me not for my deserving
     According to thy just conceived ire!
     O Lord, I dread, and that I did not dread
     I me repent, and evermore desire
     Thee, thee to dread! I open here and spread   85
     My fault to thee, but thou for thy goodness
     Measure it not in largeness nor in bread,
     Punish it not as asketh the greatness
     Of thy furor, provoked by my offence.
[2] Temper, O Lord, the harm of my excess   90
     With mending will that I for recompense
     Prepare again, and rather pity me,
     For I am weak, and clean without defence:
     More is the need I have of remedy,
     For of the whole the leech taketh no cure.   95
     The sheep that strayth the shepherd seeks to see:

70 *Dressed upright*: directed upwards.
70 *counterpese*: i.e. counterpoise.

Psalm 6
80 *require*: implore.
87 *bread*: i.e. breadth.
95: 'For the physician does not take care of those who are healthy.'

I, Lord, am strayed; I, sick without recure,
Feel all my limbs, that have rebelled, for fear
Shake in despair unless thou me assure.
My flesh is troubled, my heart doth fear the spear   100
That dread of death, of death that ever lasts,
Threateth of right and draweth near and near.

[3] Much more my soul is troubled by the blasts
Of these assaults, that come as thick as hail,
Of worldly vanity, that temptation casts   105
Against the weak bulwark of the flesh frail,
Wherein the soul in great perplexity
Feeleth the senses with them that assail
Conspire, corrupt by use and vanity,
Whereby the wretch doth to the shade resort   110
Of hope in thee, in this extremity.
But thou, O Lord, how long after this sort
Forbearest thou to see my misery?
Suffer me yet, in hope of some comfort,
Fear and not feel that thou forgettest me.   115

[4] Return, O Lord, O Lord, I thee beseech,
Unto thy old, wonted benignity!
Reduce, revive my soul: be thou the leech,
And reconcile the great hatred and strife
That it hath ta'en against the flesh, the wretch   120
That stirred hath thy wrath by filthy life.
See how my soul doth fret it to the bones:
Inward remorse so sharpth it like a knife
That but thou help the caitiff that bemoans
His great offence, it turns anon to dust.   125
Here hath thy mercy matter for the nonce,

97 *recure*: remedy.   98 *rebelled*: followed by W's virgula in E.
100 *troubled*: perturbed, afflicted. So 155.
102 *near and near*: nearer and nearer (Nott).
104 *that . . . hail*: cf. *LGW*, 655 (Mason).
107 *perplexity*: distress.   109 *corrupt*: i.e. corrupted.
109 *use*: i.e. 'by my excessive use of them'.
113 *Forbearest*: dost tolerate.
115 *feel*: perception, experience.
118 *Reduce*: restore.   124 *caitiff*: wretch.

For if thy righteous hand that is so just
Suffer no sin or strike with damnation,
Thy infinite mercy want needs it must
Subject matter for his operation: 130
[5]   For that in death there is no memory
Among the damned, nor yet no mention
Of thy great name, ground of all glory.
Then if I die and go whereas I fear
To think thereon, how shall thy great mercy   135
Sound in my mouth unto the world's ear?
For there is none that can thee laud and love,
For that thou nilt no love among them there.
Suffer my cries thy mercy for to move,
That wonted is a hundred years' offence   140
In moment of repentance to remove.
[6]   How oft have I called up with diligence
This slothful flesh long afore the day
For to confess his fault and negligence,
That to the down for ought that I could say   145
Hath still returned to shroud itself from cold,
Whereby it sufferth now for such delay.
By nightly plaints, instead of pleasures old,
I wash my bed with tears continual,
[7]   To dull my sight that it be never bold   150
To stir my heart again to such a fall.
Thus dry I up among my foes in woe,
That with my fall do rise and grow withal
And me beset even now where I am, so
With secret traps to trouble my penance.   155
Some do present to my weeping eyes, lo,

138: It is God's will that love be excluded from the region of the damned.
Nilt = ne wilt, wilt not.
145 *down*: R's *doune* (MEW).
146 *shroud*: shelter.
152 *my foes*: i.e. the senses.

The cheer, the manner, beauty and countenance
Of her whose look alas did make me blind;
Some other offer to my remembrance
Those pleasant words, now bitter to my mind;   160
And some show me the power of my armour,
Triumph and conquest, and to my head assigned
Double diadem; some show the favour
Of people frail, palais, pomp, and riches.
To these mermaids and their baits of error   165
I stop mine ears with help of thy goodness,
And for I feel it cometh alone of thee
That to my heart these foes have none access
[8]   I dare them bid: "Avoid, wretches, and flee!
The Lord hath heard the voice of my complaint;   170
Your engines take no more effect in me.
[9]   The Lord hath heard I say, and seen me faint
Under your hand, and pitieth my distress.
He shall do make my senses by constraint
Obey the rule that reason shall express,   175
Where the deceit of your glozing bait
Made them usurp a power in all excess."
[10] Shamed be they all that so lie in wait
To compass me, by missing of their prey!
Shame and rebuke redound to such deceit!   180
Sudden confusion's stroke without delay
Shall so deface their crafty suggestion
That they to hurt my health no more essay,
Since I, O Lord, remain in thy protection.'

157 *cheer*: cf. 43.
164 *palais* (French form): palaces (Aretino: *palazzi*). *Pomp*: triumphal
processions. *Riches*: cf. OF *richesse*; stressed on the last syllable (Nott), as is
palais.
171 *engines*: machinations, snares.
180 *rebuke*: disgrace.
182 *suggestion*: incitement to evil.
183 *health*: welfare, salvation.

Prologue

Whoso hath seen the sick in his fever   185
After truce taken with the hot or cold
And that the fit is past of his fervour
Draw fainting sighs, let him I say behold
Sorrowful David after his languor,
That with the tears that from his eyes down rolled   190
Paused his plaint, and laid adown his harp,
Faithful record of all his sorrows sharp.

It seemed now that of his fault the horror
Did make afeared no more his hope of grace,
The threats whereof in horrible error   195
Did hold his heart as in despair a space
Till he had willed to seek for his succour,
Himself accusing, beknowing his case,
Thinking so best his Lord for to appease:
Eased—not yet healed—he feeleth his disease.   200

Seemeth horrible no more the dark cave
That erst did make his fault for to tremble;
A place devout, or refuge for to save
The succourless it rather doth resemble.
For who had seen so kneel within the grave   205
The chief pastor of the Hebrews' assemble,
Would judge it made by tears of penitence
A sacred place worthy of reverence.

With vapoured eyes he looketh here and there,
And when he hath a while himself bethought,   210
Gathering his sprites that were dismayed for fear,
His harp again into his hand he raught.

Prologue
186 *hot*: heat (*OED hot* sb.²).   192 *record*: witness.
198 *beknowing*: confessing.
200 *disease*: cf. 68.
212 *raught*: (mod. *reached*) seized.

Tuning accord by judgement of his ear,
His heartes bottom for a sigh he sought,
And therewithal upon the hollow tree   215
With strained voice again thus crieth he:

Psalm 32. *Beati quorum remisse sunt*

[1]   'O happy are they that have forgiveness got
      Of their offence—not by their penitence
      As by merit which recompenseth not,
      Although that yet pardon hath none offence   220
      Without the same—but by the goodness
      Of Him that hath perfect intelligence
      Of heart contrite, and coverth the greatness
      Of sin within a merciful discharge.
      And happy are they that have the wilfulness   225
      Of lust restrained afore it went at large,
      Provoked by the dread of God's furor,
      Whereby they have not on their backs the charge
      Of other's fault to suffer the dolour,
      For that their fault was never execute   230
      In open sight, example of error.
[2]   And happy is he to whom God doth impute
      No more his fault, by knowledging his sin,
      But cleansed now the Lord doth him repute,

215 *the . . . tree*: i.e. the harp.
216 *strained*: Aretino's *accordato* may support MT's 'with the pitch of his voice matched to his harp', but this is less straightforward than *OED*'s 'exerted by an abnormal effort to an abnormal degree' (the sense in, e.g., 412), and W first wrote *lowd*.

Psalm 32 (Vulgate 31)

218–21 *not by . . . but by*: 'not by their penitence, for recompense is not due to that, as though it deserves it (although no sin is forgiven without penitence), but by . . .' Cf. Mason, 215.
227 *Provoked*: i.e. 'motivated, by fear of God's anger, to control their lust before it could come out into the open'.
228–31: 'They have not burdened themselves with the grief of someone else's sin, for, because their sinful intention was never carried out in public, they have not made it an example.'
233 *knowledging*: confessing (cf. *acknowledge*).

As adder fresh, new, stripped from his skin,   235
Nor in his sprite is ought undiscovered.
[3] I for because I hid it still within,
Thinking by state in fault to be preferred,
Do find by hiding of my fault my harm,
As he that feels his health to be hindered   240
By secret wound concealed from the charm
Of leech's cure, that else had had redress,
And feel my bones consume and wax unfirm
By daily rage, roaring in excess.
[4] Thy heavy hand on me was so increased   245
Both day and night, and held my heart in press
With pricking thoughts bereaving me my rest,
That withered is my lustiness away
As summer heats that hath the green oppressed;
[5] Wherefore I did another way essay,   250
And sought forthwith to open in thy sight
My fault, my fear, my filthiness I say,
And not to hide from thee my great unright.
"I shall," quod I, "against myself confess
Unto the Lord all my sinful plight."   255
And thou forthwith didst wash the wickedness
Of mine offence, of truth right thus it is,
[6] Wherefore they that have tasted thy goodness
At me shall take example as of this,
And pray and seek in time for time of grace: 260
Then shall the storms and floods of harm him miss,
And him to reach shall never have the space.
[7] Thou art my refuge and only safeguard
From the troubles that compass me the place.

238: 'Thinking to be advanced by remaining in sin.'
240 *hindered*: harmed.
242 *leech*: cf. 65. *Redress*: remedy.
249 *green*: MS. *grene*, possibly=grain, cf. Camp. *aristae* (MT).
262: 'And shall never get near him.'
264: 'From the afflictions that besiege me here.' Or perhaps *place*=field of combat.

Such joy as he that 'scapes his enemies' ward   265
With loosed bonds hath in his liberty,
Such joy, my joy, thou hast to me prepared;
That as the seaman in his jeopardy
By sudden light perceived hath the port,
So by thy great merciful property   270

[8]   Within thy look thus read I my comfort:
"I shall thee teach and give understanding,
And point to thee what way thou shalt resort
For thy address, to keep thee from wandering;
Mine eye shall take the charge to be thy guide.   275

[9]   I ask thereto of thee alone this thing:
Be not like horse or mule that man doth ride,
That not alone doth not his master know,
But for the good thou dost him must be tied
And bridled lest his guide he bite or throw."   280

[10]   O divers are the chastisings of sin,
In meat, in drink, in breath that man doth blow,
In sleep, in watch, in fretting still within,
That never suffer rest unto the mind
Filled with offence, that new and new begin   285
With thousand fears the heart to strain and bind!
But for all this he that in God doth trust
With mercy shall himself defended find.

[11]   Joy and rejoice I say, ye that be just,
In Him that maketh and holdeth you so still;   290
In Him your glory alway set you must,
All ye that be of upright heart and will.'

267 *my joy*: possibly object complement.
270 *property*: quality.
274 *address*: direction.
282 *meat*: food.
283 *watch*: waking.

Prologue

This song ended, David did stint his voice,
And in that while about he with his eye
Did seek the cave, with which withouten noise   295
His silence seemed to argue and reply
Upon this peace, this peace that did rejoice
The soul with mercy that mercy so did cry
And found mercy at mercy's plentiful hand,
Never denied but where it was withstand.   300

As the servant that in his master's face
Finding pardon of his passed offence
Considering his great goodness and his grace
Glad tears distils, as gladsome recompense,
Right so David, that seemed in that place   305
Marble image of singular reverence
Carved in the rock with eyes and hands on high,
Made as by craft to plain, to sob, to sigh.

This while a beam that bright sun forth sends,
That sun the which was never cloud could hide,   310
Pierceth the cave, and on the harp descends,
Whose glancing light the cords did overglide,
And such lustre upon the harp extends
As light of lamp upon the gold clean tried,
The turn whereof into his eyes did start,   315
Surprised with joy by penance of the heart.

Prologue

296–7 *His . . . peace*: 'David's silence seemed to converse or reason with the cave about the peace he had made with God' (MT).

299 *mercy's plentiful*: F. W first wrote *mercy full*, then *plentifull* above it. Nott: *plentiful Mercy's*.

314 *tried*: refined. (As in VIII, 4.)

315 *turn*: reflection (MT).

He then inflamed with far more hot affect
Of God than he was erst of Bersabe
His left foot did on the earth erect,
And just thereby remainth the t'other knee;   320
To his left side his weight he doth direct.
Sure hope of health, and harp again taketh he;
His hand his tune, his mind sought his lay,
Which to the Lord with sober voice did say:

Psalm 38. *Domine ne in furore tuo arguas me*

[1] 'O Lord, as I thee have both prayed and pray   325
      (Although in thee be no alteration
      But that we men like as ourselves we say,
      Measuring thy justice by our mutation),
      Chastise me not, O Lord, in thy furor,
      Nor me correct in wrathful castigation,   330
[2] For that thy arrows of fear, of terror,
      Of sword, of sickness, of famine and fire
      Sticks deep in me. I, lo, from mine error
      Am plunged up as horse out of the mire
      With stroke of spur. Such is thy hand on me   335
[3] That in my flesh for terror of thy ire
      Is not one point of firm stability,
      Nor in my bones there is no steadfastness,
      Such is my dread of mutability,

317 *affect*: passionate love.   318 *Bersabe*: cf. 2.

319–20: David rests the sole of his left foot on the ground, so that the lower part of his leg is straightened up. His right knee remains level (*just*) with the earth.

322 *health*: cf. 183.

323 'With his hand he sought the music, with his mind the words of his song.'

Psalm 38 (Vulgate 37)

326–8: W means that 'there is no alteration in God, except what we men, being men, think we see, judging His justice by human standards of changeability' (MT).

334 *plunged up*: heaved up.

For that I know my frailful wickedness: 340

[4]   For why my sins above my head are bound
       Like heavy weight that doth my force oppress,
       Under the which I stoop and bow to ground
       As willow plant haled by violence;

[5]   And of my flesh each not well cured wound,   345
       That festered is by folly and negligence,
       By secret lust hath rankled under skin,
       Not duly cured by my penitence.

[6]   Perceiving thus the tyranny of sin
       That with his weight hath humbled and depressed   350
       My pride by grudging of the worm within
       That never dieth, I live withouten rest.

[7]   So are mine entrails infect with fervent sore,
       Feeding the harm that hath my wealth oppressed,
       That in my flesh is left no health therefore.   355

[8]   So wondrous great hath been my vexation
       That it hath forced my heart to cry and roar.

[9]   O Lord, thou knowst the inward contemplation
       Of my desire, thou knowst my sighs and plaints,
       Thou knowst the tears of my lamentation   360
       Cannot express my heart's inward restraints.

[10]   My heart panteth, my force I feel it quail,
       My sight, mine eyes, my look decays and faints.

[11]   And when mine enemies did me most assail,
       My friends most sure, wherein I set most trust,   365
       Mine own virtues, soonest then did fail,
       And stood apart: reason and wit unjust
       As kin unkind were farthest gone at need.

[12]   So had they place their venom out to thrust

---

341 *For why*: for; because (as W wrote first, and cf. the sources).
344 *plant*: young tree.   351 *grudging*: inward vexation.
351 *the worm*: W refers to the pricking of conscience (F), which is eternal. Cf.
also *OED*, I.6.b.   354 *wealth*: well-being.
356 *my vexation*: the attack on me, my affliction.
361 *restraints*: lit., what is restrained in the heart, and which ought to be
expressed (MT).   368 *unkind*: disloyal.

That sought my death by naughty word and deed: 370
Their tongues reproach, their wits did fraud apply,
[13] And I like deaf and dumb forth my way yede,
[14] Like one that hears not, nor hath to reply
One word again, knowing that from thy hand
[15] These things proceed and thou, O Lord, shalt supply   375
My trust in thee, wherein I stick and stand.
[16] Yet have I had great cause to dread and fear
That thou wouldst give my foes the over hand,
For in my fall they showed such pleasant cheer;
[17] And therewithal I alway in the lash   380
Abide the stroke, and with me everywhere
I bear my fault, that greatly doth abash
[18] My doleful cheer, for I my fault confess,
And my desert doth all my comfort dash.
[19] In the meanwhile mine enemies safe increase   385
And my provokers hereby do augment,
That without cause to hurt me do not cease.
[20] In evil for good against me they be bent,
And hinder shall my good pursuit of grace.
[21] Lo now, my God, that seest my whole intent,   390
My Lord, I am thou knowst well in what case:
Forsake me not, be not far from me gone,
[22] Haste to my help, haste, Lord, and haste apace,
O Lord, the Lord of all my health alone!'

Prologue

Like as the pilgrim that in a long way   395
Fainting for heat, provoked by some wind,
In some fresh shade lieth down at mids of day,
So doth of David the wearied voice and mind

370 *naughty*: wicked.   372 *yede*: went.
378 *over hand*: upper hand, victory.   379: Cf. XCI, 35.
385 *safe*: in good health, strong.   385 *increase*: thrive.
390 *intent*: endeavour.
394 *health*: cf. 183.

Take breath of sighs when he had sung this lay
Under such shade as sorrow hath assigned;   400
And as the t'one still minds his voyage end,
So doth the t'other to mercy still pretend.

On sonore cords his fingers he extends,
Without hearing or judgement of the sound;
Down from his eyes a storm of tears descends   405
Without feeling that trickle on the ground,
As he that bleeds in bain right so intends
The altered senses to that that they are bound.
But sigh and weep he can none other thing,
And look up still unto the heaven's king.   410

But who had been without the cave's mouth
And heard the tears and sighs that he did strain,
He would have sworn there had out of the south
A lukewarm wind brought forth a smoky rain.
But that so close the cave was and uncouth   415
That none but God was record of his pain,
Else had the wind blown in all Israel's ears
The woeful plaint and of their king the tears.

Of which some part when he up supped had,
Like as he whom his own thought affrays   420
He turns his look: him seemeth that the shade
Of his offence again his force essays
By violence despair on him to lade:
Starting like him whom sudden fear dismays
His voice he strains, and from his heart out brings   425
This song that I not whether he cries or sings.

Prologue

401 *The t'one*: the pilgrim.   403 *sonore*: i.e. sonorous.
406: With his senses transformed by God, David can only direct them towards
Him, and hence does not notice the loss of his tears. He is just like someone
who in his bath feels only the water, and not the loss of his blood.
411 *cave's*: disyllabic.   414 *smoky rain*: cf. *T & C*, III, 628 (Nott).
415 *uncouth*: unknown.   416 *record*: cf. 192.
420 *affrays*: frightens.   426 *not* = *ne wot*, don't know.

Psalm 51. *Miserere mei domine*

[1]   'Rue on me, Lord, for thy goodness and grace,
That of thy nature art so bountiful,
For that goodness that in the world doth brace
Repugnant natures in quiet wonderful.   430
And for thy mercies number without end,
In heaven and earth perceived so plentiful
That over all they do themselves extend:
For those mercies much more than man can sin
Do 'way my sins that so thy grace offend.   435

[2]   Again wash me, but wash me well within,
And from my sin that thus maketh me afraid
Make thou me clean, as aye thy wont hath been:
For unto thee no number can be laid
For to prescribe remissions of offence   440
In hearts returned, as thou thyself hast said.

[3]   And I beknow my fault, my negligence,
And in my sight my sin is fixed fast,
Thereof to have more perfect penitence.

[4]   To thee alone, to thee have I trespassed,   445
For none can measure my fault but thou alone:
For in thy sight I have not been aghast
For to offend, judging thy sight as none
So that my fault were hid from sight of man,
Thy majesty so from my mind was gone.   450
This know I and repent. Pardon thou then,
Whereby thou shalt keep still thy word stable,
Thy justice pure and clean: because that when
I pardoned am, then forthwith justly able,
Just I am judged by justice of thy grace.   455

[5]   For I myself, lo thing most unstable,

Psalm 51 (Vulgate 50)

427 *rue*: pity.   429 *brace*: i.e. embrace.
439 *laid*: imposed (MT).
442 *beknow*: cf. 198.   454 *able*: fit.
455 *just*: see 488.

Formed in offence, conceived in like case,
Am nought but sin from my nativity.
Be not this said for my excuse alas,
[6]   But of thy help to show necessity,   460
For lo thou loves the truth of inward heart,
Which yet doth live in my fidelity
Though I have fallen by frailty overthwart,
For wilful malice led me not the way
So much as hath the flesh drawn me apart.   465
Wherefore, O Lord, as thou hast done alway,
Teach me the hidden wisdom of thy lore,
Since that my faith doth not yet decay;
[7]   And as the Jews do heal the leper sore,
With hyssop cleanse, cleanse me, and I am clean.   470
Thou shalt me wash, and more than snow therefore
I shall be white, how foul my fault hath been.
[8]   Thou of my health shalt gladsome tidings bring:
When from above remission shall be seen
Descend on earth, then shall for joy up spring   475
The bones that were afore consumed to dust.
[9]   Look not, O Lord, upon mine offending,
But do away my deeds that are unjust.
[10] Make a clean heart in the mids of my breast
With sprite upright, voided from filthy lust.   480
[11] From thine eyes' cure cast me not in unrest,
Nor take from me thy sprite of holiness.
[12] Render to me joy of thy help and rest,
My will confirm with sprite of steadfastness.
[13] And by this shall these goodly things ensue: 485
Sinners I shall into thy ways address,

463 *overthwart*: 'opposed, thwarted' (MT), cf. Camp. *uictus*.
469: 'Brief reference to the law followed by the Jews in the cleansing of lepers
(Leviticus 14)' (Hughey). *The leper sore*: the plague of leprosy.
472 *how*: however.   473 *health*: cf. 183.
474 ff.: W appears to refer to the doctrine of remission of sins through the
coming of Jesus Christ (Hughey).
480 *voided*: emptied.   484 *confirm*: make strong.
485 *by this*: refers to what goes before; *these things* to what follows.
486 *address*: direct, teach.

They shall return to thee and thy grace sue;
[14] My tongue shall praise thy justification;
[15] My mouth shall spread thy glorious praises true.
But of thyself, O God, this operation 490
It must proceed, by purging me from blood,
Among the just that I may have relation;
And of thy lauds for to let out the flood
Thou must, O Lord, my lips first unloose.
[16] For if thou hadst esteemed pleasant good 495
The outward deeds that outward men disclose,
I would have offered unto thee sacrifice.
But thou delightes not in no such gloze
Of outward deed as men dream and devise.
[17] The sacrifice that the Lord liketh most 500
Is sprite contrite: low heart in humble wise
Thou dost accept, O God, for pleasant host.
[18] Make Sion, Lord, according to thy will
Inward Sion, the Sion of the ghost:
Of heart's Jerusalem strength the walls still. 505
[19] Then shalt thou take for good these outward deeds
As sacrifice thy pleasure to fulfil.
Of thee alone thus all our good proceeds.'

Prologue

Of deep secrets that David here did sing,
Of mercy, of faith, of frailty, of grace, 510
Of God's goodness and of justifying,
The greatness did so astun himself a space

488 *justification*: 'the action whereby man is justified, or freed from the penalty of sin, and accounted or made righteous by God' (*OED* 4). Perhaps influenced by Luther, cf. Mason, 217, and MEW, 189.
497 *sacrifice*: i.e. instead of *lauds* (493) and *sprite contrite* (501), David would have offered a holocaust (or other 'outward' sacrifice).
498 *gloze*: false show, pretence.   502 *host*: sacrifice.
504: 'Spiritual Sion, the Sion of the heart, formed to the will of God' (Nott).
506 *deeds*: now signs of internal 'justice'.

Prologue
509 *Of*: depends on *greatness* (512).   512 *astun*: astound, overwhelm.

As who might say: 'Who hath expressed this thing?
I, sinner I, what have I said, alas,
That God's goodness would within my song entreat?   515
Let me again consider and repeat.'

And so he doth, but not expressed by word,
But in his heart he turneth and peiseth
Each word that erst his lips might forth afford.
He points, he pauseth, he wonders, he praiseth   520
The mercy that hides of justice the sword,
The justice that so his promise 'complisheth,
For his word's sake, to worthiless desert,
That gratis his graces to men doth depart.

Here hath he comfort when he doth measure   525
Measureless mercies to measureless fault,
To prodigal sinners infinite treasure,
Treasure termless that never shall default.
Yea when that sin shall fail and may not dure,
Mercy shall reign, 'gain whom shall no assault   530
Of hell prevail, by whom lo at this day
Of heaven gates remission is the key.

And when David hath pondered well and tried,
And seeth himself not utterly deprived
From light of grace, that dark of sin did hide,   535
He finds his hope so much therewith revived,
He dare importune the Lord on every side
(For he knowth well to mercy is ascribed
Respectless labour), importune, cry, and call,
And thus beginth his song therewithal: 540

515 *entreat*: discuss.
518 *turneth and peiseth*: turns and reflects upon (cf. *poiseth*).
520 *points*: hints, suggests (Hughey).
524 *depart*: bestow.
531 *by whom*: 'By means of mercy remission of sins is the key to the gates of heaven' (MT). Cf. MEW, 185–7.
538–9 *For . . . labour*: 'for he knows well that his reckless effort will be considered due to mercy'.

Psalm 102. *Domine exaudi orationem meam*

[1] 'Lord hear my prayer, and let my cry pass
     Unto the Lord without impediment.
     Do not from me turn thy merciful face,

[2] Unto myself leaving my government.
     In time of trouble and adversity   545
     Incline to me thine ear and thine intent,
     And when I call help my necessity;
     Readily grant the effect of my desire.
     These bold demands do please thy majesty,
     And eke my case such haste doth well require: 550

[3] For like as smoke my days been passed away,
     My bones dried up as furnace with the fire,

[4] My heart, my mind is withered up like hay,
     Because I have forgot to take my bread,
     My bread of life, the word of truth, I say;   555
     And for my plaintful sighes and my dread
     My bones, my strength, my very force of mind
     Cleaved to the flesh, and from thy sprite were fled,
     As desperate thy mercy for to find.

[5] So made I me the solein pelican,   560
     And like the owl that fleeth by proper kind
     Light of the day, and hath herself beta'en
     To ruin life out of all company;

[6] With waker care, that with this woe began,
     Like the sparrow was I solitary,   565
     That sits alone under the houses' eaves.

[7] This while my foes conspired continually,

Psalm 102 (Vulgate 101)

544 *government*: management (of myself).
545 *trouble*: cf. 100.
546 *intent*: attention.
560 *solein*: solitary, lonely.
561 *by . . . kind*: by its very nature.
564 *waker care*: cf. XCVII, 1.

And did provoke the harm of my disease.

[8]   Wherefore like ashes my bread did me savour,
        Of thy just word the taste might not me please;   570
        Wherefore my drink I tempered with liquor
        Of weeping tears, that from mine eyes do rain.

[9]   Because I know the wrath of thy furor,
        Provoked by right, had of my pride disdain,
        For thou didst lift me up to throw me down,   575
        To teach me how to know myself again,

[10]   Whereby I knew that helpless I should drown.
        My days like shadow decline, and I do dry:

[11]   And thee forever eternity doth crown,
        World without end doth last thy memory.   580

[12]   For this frailty, that yoketh all mankind,
        Thou shalt awake, and rue this misery,
        Rue on Sion, Sion that as I find
        Is the people that live under thy law:
        For now is time, the time at hand assigned,   585

[13]   The time so long that doth thy servants draw
        In great desire to see that pleasant day,
        Day of redeeming Sion from sin's awe.
        For they have ruth to see in such decay,
        In dust and stones, this wretched Sion lour.   590

[14]   Then the Gentiles shall dread thy name alway,
        All earthly kings thy glory shall honour,

[15]   Then, when thy grace thy Sion thus redeemeth,
        When thus thou hast declared thy mighty power

[16]   The Lord his servants' wishes so esteemeth   595
        That he him turnth unto the poor's request.

[17]   To our descent this to be written seemeth,
        Of all comforts as consolation best,
        And they that then shall be regenerate
        Shall praise the Lord therefore, both most and least.   600

568 *disease*: cf. 68.   581 *this frailty*: i.e. original sin (MT).
582 *rue*: cf. 427.   590 *lour*: be depressed
591 *Gentiles*: in the sense of 'Heathen' (MT).
594 *declared*: shown.   594 *mighty*: W myght.   597 *descent*: i.e. descendants.
600 *both . . . least*: the greatest and the meanest; 'attached to *thei* (l. 599)'
(MT).

[18]   For he hath looked from the height of his estate,
        The Lord from heaven in earth hath looked on us,

[19]   To hear the moan of them that are algate
        In foul bondage, to loose and to discuss
        The sons of death out from their deadly bond,   605

[20]   To give thereby occasion gracious
        In this Sion his holy name to stond
        And in Jerusalem his lauds lasting aye;

[21]   When in one church the people of the lond
        And realms been gathered to serve, to laud, to pray   610
        The Lord alone, so just and merciful.

[22]   But to this 'semble running in the way
        My strength faileth to reach it at the full.
        He hath abridged my days, they may not dure
        To see that term, that term so wonderful,   615

[23]   Although I have with hearty will and cure
        Prayed to the Lord: Take me not, Lord, away,
        In mids of my years, though thine ever sure
        Remain eterne, whom time cannot decay.

[24]   Thou wroughtst the earth, thy hands the heavens did
                                make; 620

[25]   They shall perish, and thou shalt last alway,
        And all things age shall wear and overtake
        Like cloth, and thou shalt change them like apparel,
        Turn and translate, and they in worth it take.

[26]   But thou thyself the self remainest well   625
        That thou wast erst, and shalt thy years extend.

[27]   Then since to this there may nothing rebel,

---

601 *estate*: status, standing (Hughey).
603 *algate*: always.
604 *discuss*: set free.
605 *bond*: imprisonment.
612–13: 'But as I run in the journey to this assembly (*samble*), my strength fails so that I do not quite reach it' (MT).
615 *term*: time.
616 *cure*: care, concern.
617 *Take*: the remainder of this Psalm is David's prayer.
624 *Turn and translate*: change and transform.
624 *and they . . . take*: Cf. CXXVII, 8.

The greatest comfort that I can pretend
Is that the children of thy servants dear,
That in thy word are got, shall without end   630
Before thy face be stablished all in fere.'

Prologue

When David had perceived in his breast
The sprite of God returned that was exiled,
Because he knew he hath alone expressed
These great thinges that greater sprite compiled   635
As shawm or pipe lets out the sound impressed
By music's art forged tofore and filed,
I say when David had perceived this,
The sprite of comfort in him revived is.

For thereupon he maketh argument   640
Of reconciling unto the Lord's grace,
Although sometime to prophecy have lent
Both brute beasts and wicked hearts a place—
But our David judgeth in his intent
Himself by penance clean out of this case,   645
Whereby he hath remission of offence,
And 'ginneth to allow his pain and penitence.

But when he weighth the fault and recompense,
He damnth his deed, and findeth plain
Atween them two no whit equivalence,   650
Whereby he takes all outward deed in vain

631 *in fere*: together.

Prologue
635 *compiled*: composed.   637 *tofore*: before.
640–1: i.e. 'he calls in question the process of reconciliation to God',
mistakenly assuming that it is completed, and due to his own merit.
644 *intent*: opinion.   647 *allow*: praise.
649–52: *findeth . . . penitence*: 'clearly finds that the two, i.e. his fault and God's
recompense, are not at all equivalent, an assumption according to which he
had vainly thought that every outward action on our part deserves the name of
rightful penitence'.

To bear the name of rightful penitence,
Which is alone the heart returned again
And sore contrite that doth his fault bemoan,
And outward deed the sign or fruit alone.   655

With this he doth defend the sly assault
Of vain allowance of his void desert,
And all the glory of his forgiven fault
To good alone he doth it whole convert:
His own merit he findeth in default.   660
And whilst he pondered these things in his heart,
His knee his arm, his hand sustained his chin,
When he his song again thus did begin:

Psalm 130. *De profundis clamavi*

[1] 'From depth of sin, and from a deep despair,
     From depth of death, from depth of heartes sorrow, 665
     From this deep cave, of darkness deep repair,
     Thee have I called, O Lord, to be my borrow;
     Thou in my voice, O Lord, perceive and hear
[2] My heart, my hope, my plaint, my overthrow,
     My will to rise, and let by grant appear   670
     That to my voice thine ears do well intend.
     No place so far that to thee is not near,
     No depth so deep that thou ne mayst extend
     Thine ear thereto: hear then my woeful plaint.
[3] For, Lord, if thou do observe what men offend   675

655: Luther-Tyndale, cf. Mason, 218–19 (or MEW, 189–90).
656–60: 'Realizing this, he wards off the sly temptation vainly to praise his own
non-existing merit. He transfers the glory of forgiveness to God's goodness, as
exclusively due to Him. He discovers that his own merit is deficient.'

Psalm 130 (Vulgate 129)
666 *of . . . repair*: 'the deep haunt or resort of darkness' (MT).
667 *borrow*: deliverer from prison.
671 *intend*: attend.

And put thy native mercy in restraint,
If just exaction demand recompense,
Who may endure, O Lord? Who shall not faint
At such account? Dread, and not reverence,
Should so reign large. But thou seeks rather love,   680
[4]   For in thy hand is mercy's residence,
By hope whereof thou dost our heartes move.
[5]   I in thee, Lord, have set my confidence,
My soul such trust doth evermore approve.
Thy holy word of eterne excellence,   685
Thy mercy's promise, that is alway just,
Have been my stay, my pillar, and pretence.
[6]   My soul in God hath more desirous trust
Than hath the watchman looking for the day
By the relief to quench of sleep the thrust.   690
[7]   Let Israel trust unto the Lord alway,
For grace and favour arn his property:
Plenteous ransom shall come with him I say,
[8]   And shall redeem all our iniquity.'

Prologue

This word redeem that in his mouth did sound   695
Did put David, it seemeth unto me,
As in a trance to stare upon the ground
And with his thought the height of heaven to see,
Where he beholds the Word that should confound
The sword of death, by humble ear to be   700
In mortal maid, in mortal habit made,
Eternal life in mortal veil to shade.

---

684 *approve*: find good through experience.   687 *pretence*: perhaps
'defence' (Nott); but cf. 726. Tillyard suggests: 'the cause I have for
claiming merit'.   690 *thrust*: i.e. thirst (Nott), with metathesis of *r*.
692 *arn*: early form of *are*.   692 *property*: cf. 270.   693 *ransom*: i.e. Christ.

Prologue

700 *humble ear*: 'W probably means that the Virgin Mary by listening to the
Word, became the mother of Christ' (MT).
702 *in . . . shade*: '"in mortal veil to shroud" (cf. the use of "veil" to describe
that which divides mortal from eternal life in *Hebrews* 6:19)' (MT).

He seeth that Word, when full ripe time should come,
Do 'way that veil, by fervent affection
Torn off with death, for death should have her doom;   705
And leapeth lighter from such corruption
The glint of light that in the air doth loom.
Man redeemed, death hath her destruction,
That mortal veil hath immortality,
David assurance of his iniquity.   710

Whereby he frames this reason in his heart:
'That goodness which doth not forbear his son
From death for me and can thereby convert
My death to life, my sin to salvation,
Both can and will a smaller grace depart   715
To him that sueth by humble supplication,
And since I have his larger grace assayed,
To ask this thing why am I then afraid?

'He granteth most to them that most do crave,
And he delights in suit without respect.   720
Alas, my son pursues me to the grave,
Suffered by God my sin for to correct;
But of my sin since I my pardon have,
My son's pursuit shall shortly be reject:
Then will I crave with 'sured confidence.'   725
And thus begins the suit of his pretence:

706–7: 'And the gleam of light which appears in the air rises the more brightly away from that destroyer, death.'

710 *assurance*: the certainty that Christ has saved his soul by delivering him from sin; cf. *OED* 8.b. See 714.

712 *forbear*: spare.

715 *depart*: cf. 524.

717 *assayed*: tasted.

720 *respect*: partiality (MT).

721–4: 'W sets the dramatic time as the interval just preceding the final battle with the hostile forces led by David's son Absalom (II Samuel 18)' (Hughey, who also compares II Samuel 15:30 and 16:8).

726 *pretence*: professed aim.

Psalm 143. *Domine exaudi orationem meam*

[1] 'Hear my prayer, O Lord, hear my request,
'Complish my boon, answer to my desire,
Not by desert, but for thine own behest,
In whose firm truth thou promist mine empire   730
To stand stable. And after thy justice
Perform, O Lord, the thing that I require,

[2] But not of law after the form and guise
To enter judgement with thy thrall bondslave
To plead his right, for in such manner wise   735
Before thy sight no man his right shall save.
For of myself lo this my righteousness
By scourge and whip and pricking spurs I have
Scant risen up, such is my beastliness;

[3] For that my enemy hath pursued my life   740
And in the dust hath foiled my lustiness;
For that in hains, to flee his rage so rife,
He hath me forced as dead to hide my head;

[4] And for because within myself at strife
My heart and sprite with all my force were fled.   745

[5] I had recourse to times that have been past,
And did remember thy deeds in all my dread,
And did peruse thy works that ever last,
Whereby I knew above those wonders all

[6] Thy mercies were. Then lift I up in haste   750
My hands to thee, my soul to thee did call
Like barren soil for moisture of thy grace.

[7] Haste to my help, O Lord, afore I fall,

Psalm 143 (Vulgate 142)
729: 'Not because I deserve it, but because of thine own promise.'
732 *require*: cf. 80.
733 *guise*: manner.
741 *foiled*: trodden under foot.
742 *hains*: enclosed places (cf. Camp. *locis obscurissimis*).
748 *did peruse*: considered one by one.
750 *lift*: i.e. lifted.

      For sure I feel my sprite doth faint apace.

      Turn not thy face from me, that I be laid   755

      In count of them that headling down do pase

[8]   Into the pit. Show me betimes thine aid,

      For on thy grace I wholly do depend.

      And in thy hand since all my health is stayed,

      Do me to know what way thou wilt I bend,   760

      For unto thee I have raised up my mind.

[9]   Rid me, O Lord, from that that do intend

      My foes to me, for I have me assigned

      Alway within thy secret protection.

[10]   Teach me thy will, that I by thee may find   765

      The way to work the same in affection.

      For thou, my God, thy blessed upright sprite,

      In land of truth shall be my direction.

[11]   Thou for thy name, Lord, shalt revive my sprite

      Within the right that I receive by thee,   770

      Whereby my life of danger shall be quite.

[12]   Thou hast fordone their great iniquity

      That vexed my soul, thou shalt also confound

      My foes, O Lord, for thy benignity:

      For thine am I, thy servant aye most bound.'   775

755–6 *laid/In count of*: 'reckoned among' (MT).

756 *pase*: i.e. *pass*, not *pace*.

759 *health*: cf. 183.

766 *way*: Camp. *viam*.

771 *quite*: i.e. quit; free.

773 *vexed*: afflicted (Camp. *affligunt*).

II

POEMS FROM
THE DEVONSHIRE
MANUSCRIPT

A. Ascribed Poems
B. Unascribed Poems

A. ASCRIBED POEMS

CIX

Take heed betime, lest ye be spied!
Your loving eye ye cannot hide,
At last the truth will sure be tried.
　　Therefore take heed!

For some there be of crafty kind;　　　　5
Though you show no part of your mind,
Surely their eyes ye cannot blind.
　　Therefore take heed!

For in like case theirselves hath been,
And thought right sure none had them seen;　　10
But it was not as they did ween.
　　Therefore take heed!

Although they be of divers schools
And well can use all crafty tools,
At length they prove themself but fools.　　15
　　Therefore take heed!

If they might take you in that trap,
They would soon leave it in your lap.
To love unspied is but a hap:
　　Therefore take heed!　　　　20

CX

What meaneth this? When I lie alone
I toss, I turn, I sigh, I groan,
My bed me seems as hard as stone:
　　What meaneth this?

1 *lest . . . spied*: cf. ML, 199.　　3 *tried*: cf. CXXXVI, 24.
5 ff.: Cf. Robbins, 177, 45–46.　　9 *like*: i.e. 'the same as you'.
18: 'They would forcefully confront you with it.'
19 *but a hap*: a matter of mere luck.

———

3 *as hard as stone*: cf. LXVI, 7.
4: Cf. Lydgate, 'Floure of Curtesy', 68.

I sigh, I plain continually,   5
The clothes that on my bed do lie
Always methink they lie awry:
    What meaneth this?

In slumbers oft for fear I quake,
For heat and cold I burn and shake,   10
For lack of sleep my head doth ache:
    What meaneth this?

Amornings then when I do rise,
I turn unto my wonted guise,
All day after muse and devise: 15
    What meaneth this?

And if perchance by me there pass
She unto whom I sue for grace,
The cold blood forsaketh my face:
    What meaneth this?   20

But if I sit near her by,
With loud voice my heart doth cry,
And yet my mouth is dumb and dry:
    What meaneth this?

To ask for help no heart I have,   25
My tongue doth fail what I should crave,
Yet inwardly I rage and rave:
    What meaneth this?

Thus have I passed many a year
And many a day, though nought appear   30
But most of that that most I fear:
    What meaneth this?

---

13 *Amornings*: in the morning.   14 *guise*: manner.
15 *muse and devise*: wonder and guess.   26 *doth fail*: lacks.
30–31 *though . . . fear*: 'though nothing appears other than most of what I fear
most (i.e. refusals, etc.)'.

CXI

Is it possible
That so high debate,
So sharp, so sore, and of such rate,
Should end so soon, and was begun so late?
Is it possible?   5

Is it possible:
So cruel intent,
So hasty heat, and so soon spent,
From love to hate, and thence for to relent?
Is it possible?   10

Is it possible
That any may find
Within one heart so diverse mind
To change or turn as weather and wind?
Is it possible?   15

Is it possible
To spy it in an eye
That turns as oft as chance on die,
The truth whereof can any try?
Is it possible?   20

It is possible
For to turn so oft,
To bring that lowest that was most aloft,
And to fall highest yet to light soft:
It is possible.   25

All is possible,
Whoso list believe.
Trust therefore first, and after prove
As men wed ladies by licence and leave
All is possible.   30

2 *debate*: strife.   14 *as . . . wind*: cf., e.g., Tilley, W439.
19 *try*: cf. CXXXVI, 24.   28 *prove*: cf. CXLVIII, 29.
29 *by . . . leave*: a reference to the wedding ceremony, but also to the woman's lawlessness and her dismissal of her husband (cf. XV, 5). W may hint that his wife, Elizabeth Brooke, was unfaithful to him.

CXII

And wilt thou leave me thus?
Say nay, say nay, for shame,
To save thee from the blame
Of all my grief and grame!
And wilt thou leave me thus?   5
    Say nay, say nay!

And wilt thou leave me thus,
That hath loved thee so long
In wealth and woe among?
And is thy heart so strong   10
As for to leave me thus?
    Say nay, say nay!

And wilt thou leave me thus,
That hath given thee my heart
Never for to depart,   15
Neither for pain nor smart?
And wilt thou leave me thus?
    Say nay, say nay!

And wilt thou leave me thus,
And have no more pity   20
Of him that loveth thee?
Alas thy cruelty!
And wilt thou leave me thus?
    Say nay, say nay!

Baldi (231) compares 'And will ye serve me so', in Wynkyn de Worde's *Part-Song Book* (1530).

4 *grame*: sorrow.
9 *wealth*: well-being.
9 *among*: all the time.
10 *strong*: oppressive; flagrantly guilty.

CXIII

The restful place, reviver of my smart,
The labour's salve, increasing my sorrow,
The body's ease, and troubler of my heart,
Quieter of mind, and my unquiet foe,
Forgetter of pain, remembering my woe,   5
The place of sleep, wherein I do but wake,
Besprent with tears, my bed, I thee forsake!

The frost, the snow, may not redress my heat,
Nor yet no heat abate my fervent cold.
I know nothing to ease my paines meet: 10
Each cure causeth increase by twentyfold,
Reviving cares upon my sorrows old.
Such overthwart affects they do me make
Besprent with tears my bed for to forsake.

Yet helpeth it not: I find no better ease   15
In bed or out. This most causeth my pain:
Where most I seek how best that I may please,
My lost labour alas is all in vain,
Yet that I gave I cannot call again.
No place fro' me my grief away can take,   20
Wherefore with tears, my bed, I thee forsake.

CXIV

So unwarely was never no man caught
With steadfast look upon a goodly face
As I of late: for suddenly me thought
My heart was torn out of his place.

5 *Forgetter, remembering*: used causatively.
7 *Besprent with tears*: perhaps suggested by Chaucer, 'Complaint unto Pity', 10.
9 *fervent*: severe.
12 *cares*: griefs.
13 *overthwart affects*: contrarious passions.
19 *again*: back.

Thorough mine eye the stroke from hers did slide,   5
Directly down unto my heart it ran,
In help whereof the blood thereto did slide,
And left my face both pale and wan.

Then was I like a man for woe amazed,
Or like the bird that flieth into the fire,   10
For while that I upon her beauty gazed
The more I burnt in my desire.

Anon the blood start in my face again,
Enflamed with heat that it had at my heart,
And brought therewith thereout in every vein   15
A quaking heat with pleasant smart.

Then was I like the straw when that the flame
Is driven therein by force and rage of wind.
I cannot tell alas what I shall blame,
Nor what to seek, nor what to find.   20

But well I wot the grief holds me so sore,
In heat and cold, betwixt hope and dread,
That but her help to health doth me restore
This restless life I may not lead.

CXV

Blame not my lute, for he must sound
Of this or that as liketh me:
For lack of wit the lute is bound
To give such tunes as pleaseth me.

5–6: Cf. *CT*, A1096–7 (Nott).   9 *amazed*: stupefied.
10: Cf. XXIV. T reads *fowle* for D's *byrde*.
15 *thereout*: i.e. the heart.   16 *quaking*: causative.

On the difficult question of the relation of this poem to music, cf. Stevens, 135 ff. W may have written the poem to be sung to a fashionable tune (e.g. that in Folger MS. 448.16, which, however, has no words except the title). Hall's *Court of Virtue* (cf. CXX) contains a moralized version of the poem with a different tune, for one voice.

Then though my songs be somewhat strange   5
And speaks such words as touch thy change,
    Blame not my lute.

My lute alas doth not offend,
Though that perforce he must agree
To sound such tunes as I intend   10
To sing to them that heareth me.
Then though my songs be somewhat plain
And toucheth some that use to feign,
    Blame not my lute.

My lute and strings may not deny,   15
But as I strike they must obey:
Break not them then so wrongfully,
But wreak thyself some wiser way.
And though the songs which I indite
Do quit thy change with rightful spite,   20
    Blame not my lute.

Spite asketh spite, and changing change,
And falsed faith must needs be known;
The fault so great, the case so strange,
Of right it must abroad be blown.   25
Then since that by thine own desert
My songs do tell how true thou art,
    Blame not my lute.

Blame but thyself, that hast misdone
And well deserved to have blame,   30
Change thou thy way so evil begone,
And then my lute shall sound that same.
But if till then my fingers play
By thy desert their wonted way,
    Blame not my lute.   35

5 *Then though*: MS. *tho*; but cf., e.g., 12.
6 *speaks*: the subject is *my songs* (5).   13 *use to*: are in the habit of.
31 *evil begone*: 'surrounded by (i.e. steeped in) evil'.

Farewell, unknown, for though thou break
My strings in spite with great disdain,
Yet have I found out for thy sake
Strings for to string my lute again.
And if perchance this foolish rhyme   40
Do make thee blush at any time,
　　　Blame not my lute.

CXVI

All in thy sight my life doth whole depend:
Thou hidest thyself, and I must die therefore.
But since thou mayst so easily save thy friend,
Why dost thou stick to heal that thou madest sore?
Why do I die, since thou mayst me defend?   5
For if I die, then mayst thou live no more:
Since the one by the other doth live and feed the heart,
I with thy sight, thou also with my smart.

CXVII

My love took scorn my service to retain,
Wherein me thought she used cruelty,
Since with good will I lost my liberty
To follow her which causeth all my pain.
Might never care cause me for to refrain,   5
But only this, which is extremity,

---

36 *unknown*: i.e. sexually, cf. *OED know*, II.7; or W plays on the phrase 'unknown, unkissed' (cf. *OED unkissed*).

---

3 *friend*: lover.
4 *stick*: perhaps 'hesitate' (Rollins), but cf. *OED* 15; 'stab' is possible, if *heal* is ironic.
7–8: 'For each of us lives and feeds his heart by means of the other person—I by looking at you, and you by feeding on my grief.' 7 *the* (3): D *thy*, no doubt in error for *the* (cf. It. *il*).   8 *thou*: D may have *then* or *thin*, i.e. *thine*.

5: 'Grief could never lead me to cease serving her.'

Giving me nought, alas, not to agree
That as I was her man I might remain.
But since that thus ye list to order me
That would have been your servant true and fast,   10
Displease thee not my doting days be past,
And with my loss to live I must agree.
For as there is a certain time to rage,
So is there time such madness to assuage.

CXVIII

Perdie, I said it not,
Nor never thought to do:
As well as I ye wot
I have no power thereto.
And if I did, the lot   5
That first did me enchain
Do never slake the knot
But straiter to my pain.

And if I did, each thing
That may do harm or woe   10
Continually may wring
My heart whereso I go.
Report may always ring
Of shame of me for aye,
If in my heart did spring   15
The word that ye do say.

If I said so, each star
That is in heaven above
May frown on me to mar
The hope I have in love;   20

7–8: 'Giving me nothing at all, alas, in that she did not grant me to remain her lover, as I was before.'   12 *live*: MS. *leve*; Nott reads *leave*, with T.

7–8: 'May never loosen the knot other than so as to become more tight.'
9 ff. *And if*: if.

And if I did, such war
As they brought into Troy
Bring all my life afar
Fro' all this lust and joy.

And if I did so say,   25
The beauty that me bound
Increase from day to day
More cruel to my wound;
With all the moan that may
To plaint may turn my song;   30
My life may soon decay
Without redress by wrong.

If I be clear for thought,
Why do ye then complain?
Then is this thing but sought   35
To turn me to more pain.
Then that that ye have wrought
Ye must it now redress,
Of right therefore ye ought
Such rigour to repress.   40

And as I have deserved,
So grant me now my hire;
Ye know I never swerved,
Ye never found me liar.
For Rachel have I served   45
(For Leah cared I never),
And her I have reserved
Within my heart for ever.

22 *into*: B (T: *unto*); but D's *owt of* may be correct.
24 *lust*: pleasure.
32 *by*: i.e. in the presence of.
33 *for*: as regards.
45–46 *Rachel*; *Leah*: it is not known which ladies might parade under these
biblical names (cf. Gen. 29), which perhaps pun (MT) on *rake-hell* (debauchee)
and *liar*; cf. B's *Rakhell* and *Lya*.

CXIX

Driven by desire I did this deed,
To danger myself without cause why:
To trust the untrue, not like to speed,
To speak and promise faithfully.
But now the proof doth verify   5
That whoso trusteth or he know
Doth hurt himself and please his foe.

B. UNASCRIBED POEMS

CXX

My pen, take pain a little space
To follow that which doth me chase
And hath in hold my heart so sore;
But when thou hast this brought to pass,
My pen I prithee write no more.   5

Remember oft thou hast me eased
And all my pains full well appeased,
But now I know unknown before,
For where I trust I am deceived,
And yet, my pen, thou canst no more.   10

---

1 *this deed*: prob. W's decision to become a woman's 'servant'. Cf., e.g.,
LXII, 8–9.
6–7: Cf., e.g., 'Try your friend before you trust' (*ODEP*, p. 845; Tilley, T595).

Moralized by John Hall in his *The Court of Virtue* (ed. Russell A. Fraser, London,
1961), who presents his version with music for one voice. As with LXVI and
CXV, we need not assume that there is any connection between Hall's music
and W's poem; cf. Stevens, 136 ff.
3, 28 *in hold*: in captivity (cf. I, 10).
9: Proverbial, cf. SCM, 64.

A time thou haddest as other have
To write which way my hope to crave.
That time is past, withdraw therefore;
Since we do lose that other save,
As good leave off and write no more.   15

In worth to use another way
(Not as we would, but as we may—
For once my loss is past restore,
And my desire is my decay),
My pen yet write a little more.   20

To love in vain whoever shall,
Of wordly pain it passeth all,
As in like case I find. Wherefore
To hold so fast and yet to fall?
Alas, my pen, now write no more!   25

Since thou hast taken pain this space
To follow that which doth me chase
And hath in hold my heart so sore,
Now hast thou brought my mind to pass:
My pen, I prithee write no more.   30

CXXI

I love loved, and so doth she,
And yet in love we suffer still;
The cause is strange as seemeth me,
To love so will and want our will.

14: Cf. Tilley, M337.
16 *In worth*: perhaps 'patiently' (cf. Nott and CXXVII, 8), but 'with dignity'
would also fit.
18 *once*: once for all (?).
18 *restore*: i.e. restoration; repair.

---

1 *I . . . loved*: I love while being loved; cf. Stevens, 424, 'I love unloved'
(WMT).
4 ff. *will*: sexual desire (or satisfaction); with a pun on *well*.

O deadly yea! O grievous smart!   5
Worse than refuse, unhappy gain!
I love: whoever played this part,
To love so will and live in pain?

Was ever heart so will agreed,
Since love was love as I do trow,   10
That in their love so evil did speed,
To love so will and live in woe?

This mourn we both and hath done long,
With woeful plaint and careful voice.
Alas, alas! It is a grievous wrong   15
To love so will and not rejoice.

And here an end of all our moan!
With sighing oft my breath is scant,
Since of mishap ours is alone—
To love so will and it to want.   20

But they that causer is of this,
Of all our cares God send them part,
That they may trow what grief it is
To love so will and live in smart.

CXXII

Farewell, all my welfare!
My shoe is trod awry.
Now may I cark and care
To sing lullay-by-by.
Alas, what shall I do thereto?   5
There is no shift to help me now.

10, 23 *trow*: experience (*OED* 7).   14 *careful*: sorrowful. Cf. 22.
19 *alone*: unique (cf. XCVIII, 73).

2: 'I have been seduced.' Proverbial (Nott), cf. Tilley, S373.
3 *cark and care*: mourn and grieve.   6 *shift*: expedient.

Who made it such offence
To love for love again?
God wot that my pretence
Was but to ease his pain   10
For I had ruth to see his woe:
Alas, more fool, why did I so?

For he from me is gone,
And makes thereat a game,
And hath left me alone   15
To suffer sorrow and shame.
Alas, he is unkind doubtless
To leave me thus all comfortless.

It is a grievous smart
To suffer pains and sorrow,   20
But most grieved my heart
He laid his faith to borrow;
And falsehood hath his faith and truth,
And he forsworn by many an oath.

All ye lovers, perdie,   25
Hath cause to blame his deed,
Which shall example be
To let you of your speed;
Let never woman again
Trust to such words as men can feign.   30

For I unto my cost
Am warning to you all
That they whom you trust most
Soonest deceive you shall.
But complaint cannot redress   35
Of my great grief the great excess.

9 *pretence*: intention.   17 *unkind*: cf. XXV, 3.
17 *doubtless*: most certainly.   21 *grieved*: l. 22 is the subject.
22: 'That he pledged loyalty' (*borrow*=pledge). Cf. *CT*, A1622.
23 *falsehood*: Nott conj. *falsed*; cf. CXV, 23.   24: Cf. *LGW*, 666.
28: 'To prevent you from succeeding in your design.'
33-34: Cf. CXX, 9.

CXXIII

Alas, poor man, what hap have I,
That must forbear that I love best?
I trow it be my destiny
Never to live in quiet rest.

No wonder is though I complain— 5
Not without cause, ye may be sure:
I seek for that I cannot attain,
Which is my mortal displeasure.

Alas, poor heart, as in this case
With pensive plaints thou art oppressed, 10
Unwise thou were to desire place
Whereas another is possessed.

Do what I can to ease thy smart,
Thou wilt not let to love her still.
Hers and not mine I see thou art: 15
Let her do by thee as she will.

A careful carcass full of pain
Now hast thou left to mourn for thee.
The heart once gone, the body is slain;
That ever I saw her woe is me! 20

Mine eye alas was cause of this,
Which her to see had never his fill;
To me that sight full bitter is,
In recompense of my good will.

She that I serve all other above 25
Hath paid my hire, as ye may see:
I was unhappy, and that I prove,
To love above my poor degree.

Nott suggests that W expresses in this how he was obliged to relinquish all
claim to Anne Boleyn's affection. As for loving above one's 'degree' and its
consequences, cf. SCM, 24.

8 *displeasure*: grief.   12 *another*: cf., e.g., XC, 9 ff.
17 *careful*: sorrowful.   27 *prove*: cf. CXLVIII, 29.
28 *degree*: rank (particularly social).

CXXIV

It was my choice, it was no chance,
That brought my heart in other's hold,
Whereby it hath had sufferance
Longer, perdie, than reason would.
Since I it bound where it was free,   5
Me thinks iwis of right it should
    Accepted be.

Accepted be without refuse,
Unless that fortune have the power
All right of love for to abuse,   10
For as they say, one happy hour
May more prevail than right or might.
If fortune then list for to lour,
    What 'vaileth right?

What 'vaileth right if this be true?   15
Then trust to chance and go by guess:
Then whoso loveth may well go sue
Uncertain hope for his redress.
Yet some would say assuredly
Thou mayst appeal for thy release   20
    To fantasy.

To fantasy pertains to choose.
All this I know, for fantasy
First unto love did me induce,
But yet I know as steadfastly   25
That if love have no faster knot,
So nice a choice slips suddenly:
    It lasteth not.

Cf. XLIII.   2 *hold*: captivity (cf. I, 10).
3 *sufferance*: suffering.   6 *iwis*: for sure.
11–12: No exact parallel comes to hand, but cf. Tilley, H741, and Whiting,
H600.   21 *fantasy* (29 *Fancy*): amorous inclination; caprice.

It lasteth not that stands by change:
Fancy doth change, fortune is frail,   30
Both these to please the ways is strange.
Therefore me thinks best to prevail:
There is no way that is so just
As truth to lead, though t'other fail,
      And thereto trust.   35

CXXV

Full well it may be seen
To such as understand,
How some there be that ween
They have their wealth at hand:
Through love's abused band   5
But little do they see
The abuse wherein they be.

Of love there is a kind
Which kindleth by abuse,
As in a feeble mind   10
Whom fancy may induce
By love's deceitful use
To follow the fond lust
And proof of a vain trust.

---

28 *stands by*: depends upon.
29 *Fortune is frail*: cf., e.g., Tilley, F606.
31 *prevail*: i.e., apparently, 'to try and become stronger, in my loyalty, than
fancy and fortune together'.

---

4 *wealth*: well-being.
4 *at hand*: at their disposal. F and MT, in contrast to Nott, connect 4–5,
not 5–6.
5–7: 'Victims of a lovers' agreement violated by the deceit of their mistresses,
they hardly see their plight.'
11 *fancy*: cf. CXXIV, 21.

As I myself may say   15
By trial of the same,
No wight can well bewray
The falsehood love can frame.
I say 'twixt grief and game
There is no living man   20
That knows the craft love can.

For love so well can feign
To favour for the while
That such as seeks the gain
Are served with the guile;   25
And some can this concile,
To give the simple leave
Themselves for to deceive.

What thing may more declare
Of love the crafty kind   30
Than see the wise, so ware,
In love to be so blind?
If so it be assigned,
Let them enjoy the gain
That thinks it worth the pain.   35

CXXVI

Since love is such that as ye wot
Cannot always be wisely used,
I say therefore then blame me not
Though I therein have been abused;
For as with cause I am accused—   5
Guilty, I grant, such was my lot—
And though it cannot be excused,
Yet let such folly be forgot.

21 *can*: is skilled in.
26–28: 'And this can lull some, so as to allow the innocent to deceive themselves.'
31 *so ware*: i.e. 'normally so vigilant'.

For in my years of reckless youth
Me thought the power of love so great   10
That to her laws I bound my truth
And to my will there was no let.
Me list no more so far to fet
Such fruit lo as of love ensueth:
The gain was small that was to get,   15
And of the loss the less the ruth.

And few there is but first or last
A time in love once shall they have,
And glad I am my time is past,
Henceforth my freedom to withsave.   20
Now in my heart there shall I grave
The grounded grace that now I taste:
Thanked be fortune, that me gave
So fair a gift, so sure and fast.

Now such as have me seen or this,   25
When youth in me set forth his kind
And folly framed my thought amiss,
The fault whereof now well I find,
Lo since that so it is assigned
That unto each a time there is,   30
Then blame the lot that led my mind
Sometime to live in love's bliss.

But from henceforth I do protest
By proof of that that I have passed
Shall never cease within my breast   35
The power of love so late outcast:
The knot thereof is knit full fast,
And I thereto so sure professed,
For evermore with me to last
The power wherein I am possessed.   40

---

12 *will*: sexual desire. Immature love is contrasted with a ripe, stable
relationship, the 'grounded (i.e. firmly based) grace' of 22.
13 *fet*: i.e. fetch.   20 *withsave*: preserve.   32 *love's*: disyllabic.

CXXVII

Lo how I seek and sue to have
That no man hath, and may be had!
There is no more but sink or save,
And bring this doubt to good or bad.
To live in sorrows always sad,   5
I like not so to linger forth:
Hap evil or good, I shall be glad
To take that comes as well in worth.

Should I sustain this great distress,
Still wandering forth thus to and fro,   10
In dreadful hope to hold my peace,
And feed myself with secret woe?
Nay, nay, certain I will not so!
But sure I shall myself apply
To put in proof this doubt to know   15
And rid this danger readily.

I shall essay by secret suit
To show the mind of mine intent,
And my deserts shall give such fruit
As with my heart my words be meant.   20
So by the proof of this consent
Soon out of doubt I shall be sure,
For to rejoice or to repent,
In joy or pain for to endure.

CXXVIII

Now must I learn to live at rest
And wean me of my will,
For I repent where I was pressed
My fancy to fulfil.

---

4 ff. *doubt*: suspicion; fear.   8 *take in worth*: bear patiently (Nott).
11 *dreadful*: full of fear.   21 *by . . . consent*: by putting this feeling to the test.

---

2 *will*: cf. CXXVI, 12.   4 *fancy*: cf. CXXIV, 21.

I may no longer more endure 5
My wonted life to lead,
But I must learn to put in ure
The change of womanhed.

I may not see my service long
Rewarded in such wise, 10
Nor I may not sustain such wrong
That ye my love despise.

I may not sigh in sorrows deep,
Nor wail the want of love,
Nor I may neither crouch nor creep 15
Where it doth not behove.

But I of force must needs forsake
My faith so fondly set,
And from henceforth must undertake
Such folly to forget. 20

Now must I seek some other ways
Myself for to withsave,
And as I trust by mine essays
Some remedy to have.

I ask none other remedy 25
To recompense my wrong
But once to have the liberty
That I have lacked so long.

CXXIX

Forget not yet the tried intent
Of such a truth as I have meant,
My great travail so gladly spent
    Forget not yet.

7 *put in ure*: i.e. 'get used to'.　　22 *withsave*: cf. CXXVI, 20.
23 *essays*: cf. CXXIX, 9.　　27 *once*: one day.

Padelford notes: 'Music composed for this song is to be found in *Royal Ms. App.*
58, p. 50, 53 *b*.'　　1 *intent*: endeavour.

Forget not yet when first began 5
The weary life ye know since when,
The suit, the service none tell can,
    Forget not yet.

Forget not yet the great essays,
The cruel wrong, the scornful ways, 10
The painful patience in denays,
    Forget not yet.

Forget not yet, forget not this,
How long ago hath been and is
The mind that never meant amiss, 15
    Forget not yet.

Forget not then thine own approved,
The which so long hath thee so loved,
Whose steadfast faith yet never moved,
    Forget not this. 20

CXXX

Me list no more to sing
Of love nor of such thing
How sore that it me wring,
For what I sung or spake,
Men did my songs mistake. 5

My songs were too diffuse,
They made folk to muse.
Therefore, me to excuse,
They shall be sung more plain,
Neither of joy nor pain. 10

9 *essays*: perhaps 'tribulations' rather than 'attempts'.
11 *denays*: i.e. denials; refusals.
17 *thine own approved*: 'him whom you yourself approved of (or: have found good through experience)'.

6 *diffuse*: obscure, vague.   7 *muse*: wonder, guess at the meaning.

What 'vaileth then to skip
At fruit over the lip?
For fruit withouten taste
Doth nought but rot and waste.

What 'vaileth under key   15
To keep treasure alway
That never shall see day?
If it be not used,
It is but abused.

What 'vaileth the flower   20
To stand still and wither?
If no man it savour,
It serves only for sight,
And fadeth towards night.

Therefore fear not to essay   25
To gather, ye that may,
The flower that this day
Is fresher than the next:
Mark well, I say, this text.

Let not the fruit be lost   30
That is desired most:
Delight shall quite the cost.
If it be ta'en in time,
Small labour is to climb.

And as for such treasure   35
That maketh thee the richer
And no deal the poorer,
When it is given or lent
Me thinks it were well spent.

11 ff.: A line is missing from this stanza, probably the first.
13 *withouten taste*: i.e. untasted.
22 *savour*: smell.   29 *text*: adage.   30–34: Cf. *ODEP*, p. 215.
32 *quite*: i.e. quit; repay.   37 *no deal*: not at all.

If this be under mist   40
And not well plainly wist,
Understand me who list:
For I reck not a bean,
I wot what I do mean.

CXXXI

To rail or jest ye know I use it not
Though that such cause sometime in folks I find;
And though to change ye list to set your mind,
Love it who list, in faith I like it not.
And if ye were to me as ye are not,   5
I would be loth to see you so unkind;
But since your faith must needs be so by kind,
Though I hate it, I pray you leave it not.
Things of great weight I never thought to crave—
This is but small, of right deny it not: 10
Your feigning ways as yet forget them not,
But like reward let others have;
That is to say, for service true and fast
Too long delays, and changing at the last.

CXXXII

Pain of all pain, the most grievous pain
Is to love heartily and cannot be loved again.

Love with unkindness is causer of heaviness,
Of inward sorrow and sighs painful.
Whereas I love is no redress   5

---

40 *under mist*: i.e. not clear.   41 *wist*: known, grasped (by you).
43: 'I don't care at all' (cf. Tilley, B118).

1: 'You know I am not in the habit of rallying or jesting.'
5–8: 'If you were loyal to me (which you are not), I should hate you to be cruel
to me. But since, detestably enough, it is not in your nature to be loyal to me, I
hope you *will* be cruel—to others, as a small favour to me (cf. 9 ff.).'

---

3 ff. *unkindness*: cf. XXV, 3.   5–6 *Whereas . . . pastime*: i.e. 'where I love
there is no remedy, no matter how I spend my time'.

To no manner of pastime: the sprites so dull
With privy mournings and looks rueful;
The body all wearish, the colour pale and wan,
More like a ghost than like a living man,

When Cupido hath enflamed the heart's desires   10
To love thereas is disdain;
Of good or ill the mind oblivious,
Nothing regarding but love to attain,
Always imagining by what mean or train
It may be at rest, thus in a moment   15
Now here, now there, being never content,

Tossing and turning when the body would rest,
With dreams oppressed and visions fantastical.
Sleeping or waking, love is ever pressed,
Sometime to weep, sometime to cry and call,   20
Bewailing his fortune and life bestial,
Now in hope of recure, and now in despair.
This is a sorry life, to live alway in care!

Record of Terence in his comedies poetical:
In love is jealousy, and injuries many one,   25
Anger and debate, with mind sensual,
Now war, now peace, musing all alone,
Sometime all mort and cold as any stone.
This causeth unkindness of such as cannot skill
Of true love, assured with heart and good will.   30

8 *wearish*: sickly, feeble.   14 *train*: trick.
17 *Tossing*: cf. LXXIX, 6.
18 *fantastical*: of what exists in the imagination only (cf. LXXIX).
22 *recure*: remedy.   23 *care*: grief.
24 *Record of*: witness.
24 *Terence*: Roman writer of comedies, 195–159 B.C.
26 *debate*: quarrelling.
28 *mort*: dead.
28 *cold . . . stone*: cf. Tilley, S876.
29 *cannot skill*: do not know.
30 *assured*: pledged.

Lucrece the Roman, for love of her lord
And because perforce she had commit adultery
With Tarquinus, as the story doth record,
Herself did slay with a knife most piteously
Among her nigh friends because that she   35
So falsely was betrayed. Lo, this was the guerdon
Whereas true love hath no dominion!

To make rehearsal of old antiquity
What needeth it? We see by experience
Among lovers it chanceth daily: 40
Displeasure and variance for none offence.
But if true love might give sentence
That unkindness and disdain should have no place,
But true heart for true love, it were a great grace.

O Venus, lady, of love the goddess,   45
Help all true lovers to have love again!
Banish from thy presence disdain and unkindness,
Kindness and pity to thy service retain.
For true love once fixed in the cordial vein
Can never be revulsed by no manner of art,   50
Unto the soul from the body depart.

CXXXIII

Lament my loss, my labour, and my pain,
All ye that hear my woeful plaint and cry;
If ever man might once your heart constrain

31 *Lucrece*: Lucretia. Cf. Livy and Ovid, but particularly Chaucer's version in
LGW (F), acc. to which L's husband, L. Tarquinius Collatinus, invited Sextus
Tarquinius (33) to his home to exhibit his virtuous wife. When S. T. raped her,
L. felt morally compelled to commit suicide.
31 *her*: MS.: *or* (i.e. *our*) may be correct, cf. MT and *LGW*, 1870–1 and 1879–82.
34 *knife*: dagger.   39–40: Cf. Robbins, poem 181, 42.
49 *cordial*: of the heart.
50: 'Can never be torn away by any kind of trick.'   51 *Unto*: until.

Chambers, p. 110, suggests that CXXXIII confirms his impression derived
from E that W meant to publish his poems. But W's revisions in E are not
necessarily intended for a printer, and the anonymous poem may be an *Envoi*
to a manuscript collection. Cf. CXLII, 5.

To pity words of right, it should be I,
That since the time that youth in me did reign   5
My pleasant years to bondage did apply,
Which as it was I purpose to declare,
Whereby my friends hereafter may beware.

And if perchance some readers list to muse
What meaneth me so plainly for to write,   10
My good intent the fault of it shall 'scuse,
Which mean nothing but truly to indite
The craft and care, the grief and long abuse
Of lovers' law, and eke her puissant might,
Which though that men ofttimes by pains doth know,   15
Little they wot which ways the guiles doth grow.

Yet well ye know it will renew my smart
Thus to rehearse the pains that I have passed:
My hand doth shake, my pen scant doth his part,
My body quakes, my wits begin to waste,   20
'Twixt heat and cold in fear I feel my heart
Panting for pain. And thus as all aghast
I do remain, scant wotting what I write,
Pardon me then, rudely though I indite.

And patiently, O reader, I thee pray   25
Take in good part this work as it is meant,
And grieve thee not with ought that I shall say,
Since with good will this book abroad is sent
To tell men how in youth I did assay
What love did mean, and now I it repent: 30
That moaning me my friends might well beware,
And keep them free from all such pain and care.

9 *muse*: wonder. Cf. CX, 15–16.
13, 32 *care*: grief.
27 *grieve thee not*: take no offence.
29 *assay*: examine; learn by experience.
31 *moaning*: MS. *moving*. Chambers suggests *musing*; MEW (80) *noting*. But in
XXII, 14, D's *moving* parallels E's *complayning*.

CXXXIV

Divers doth use, as I have heard and know,
When that to change their ladies do begin,
To mourn and wail and never for to lin,
Hoping thereby to 'pease their painful woe.
And some there be that when it chanceth so   5
That women change and hate where love hath been,
They call them false, and think with words to win
The hearts of them which otherwhere doth grow.
But as for me, though that by chance indeed
Change hath outworn the favour that I had,   10
I will not wail, lament, nor yet be sad,
Nor call her false that falsely did me feed,
But let it pass, and think it is of kind
That often change doth please a woman's mind.

CXXXV

Spite hath no power to make me sad,
Nor scornfulness to make me plain:
It doth suffice that once I had,
And so to leave it is no pain.

Let them frown on that least doth gain: 5
Who did rejoice must needs be glad,
And though with words thou weenest to reign,
It doth suffice that once I had.

Since that in checks thus overthwart
And coyly looks thou dost delight,   10
It doth suffice that mine thou wert,
Though change hath put thy faith to flight.

---

1 *Divers doth use*: 'various men are accustomed' (WMT).
3 *lin*: cease.   8 *which*: refers to *hearts*.
13: Cf. Stevens, 359, 'To lett itt over pass, and thynk . . .'
14: Proverbial, cf. Tilley, W673 (WMT); also W674 and W698.

---

7 *reign*: MS. *rayne*, perhaps=*rein* (cf. XI, 1; and *checks*, 9).
9 *overthwart*: cf. LII, 15.   10 *coyly*: disdainful.

Alas, it is a peevish spite
To yield thyself and then to part,
But since thou setst thy faith so light, 15
It doth suffice that mine thou wert.

And since thy love doth thus decline
And in thy heart such hate doth grow,
It doth suffice that thou wert mine,
And with good will I quite it so. 20

Sometime my friend, farewell my foe,
Since that thou change I am not thine:
But for relief of all my woe
It doth suffice that thou wert mine.

Praying you all that hears this song 25
To judge no wight, nor none to blame:
It doth suffice she doth me wrong
And that herself doth know the same.

And though she change, it is no shame:
Their kind it is, and hath been long. 30
Yet I protest she hath no name:
It doth suffice she doth me wrong.

CXXXVI

Greeting to you both in hearty wise,
As unknown I send and this my intent
As I do here, you to advertise,
Lest that perchance your deeds you do repent.
The unknown man dreads not to be shent, 5
But says as he thinks: so fares it by me,
That neither fear nor hope in no degree.

13 *peevish*: malicious; capricious.
20 *quite*: i.e. quit; abandon.   29–30: Cf. CXXXIV, 13–14.
31: A typical note in poetry of the period, cf., e.g., Stevens, 395, H28.

For the proverbs cf. Tilley, S725 (6); F724 (13); SCM, 64 (14); Tilley, W794 (22);
H94 (23); T338 (24); W781 (29).   5 *shent*: blamed (cf. 12).

The body and the soul to hold together,
It is but right, and reason will the same,
And friendly for the one to love the other,   10
It increaseth your bruit and also your fame.
But mark well my words, for I fear no blame:
Trust well yourselves, but 'ware ye trust no mo,
For such as ye think your friend may fortune be your foe.

Beware hardily ere ye have any need,   15
And to friends reconciled trust not greatly:
For they that once with hasty speed
Exiled themselves out of your company,
Though they turn again and speak sweetly,
Feigning themselves to be your friends fast,   20
Beware of them, for they will deceive you at last.

Fair words makes fools fain,
And bearing in hand causeth much woe,
For time trieth truth: therefore refrain.
And from such as be ready to do—   25
None do I name, but this I know,
That by this fault cause causeth much,
Therefore beware, if you do know any such.

'To wise folks few words' is an old saying,
Therefore at this time I will write no more,   30
But this short lesson take for a warning:
By such light friends set little store,
If ye do otherwise ye will repent it sore.
And thus of this letter making an end,
To the body and the soul I me commend.   35

8: i.e. in harmony.
9 *will*: cf. XV, 8.
14 *fortune*: perchance.
15 *hardily*: firmly.
23 *bearing in hand*: deceiving someone by false promises.
24 *trieth*: sifts out, reveals.
29 *To . . . words*: i.e. a word to a wise man is enough.

Written lifeless at the manner place
Of him that hath no chaff, nor nowhere doth dwell,
But wandering in the wild world, wanting that he has,
And neither hopes nor fears heaven nor hell,
But liveth at adventure, ye know him full well: 40
The twenty day of March he wrote it in his house,
And hath him recommended to the cat and the mouse.

CXXXVII

Tangled I was in love's snare,
Oppressed with pain, torment with care,
Of grief right sure, of joy full bare,
Clean in despair by cruelty:
But ha, ha, ha, full well is me,   5
For I am now at liberty.

The woeful days so full of pain,
The weary night all spent in vain,
The labour lost for so small gain,
To write them all it will not be: 10
But ha, ha, ha, full well is me,
For I am now at liberty.

Everything that fair doth show,
When proof is made it proveth not so,
But turneth mirth to bitter woe,   15

36 *manner place*: kind of place.
37 *that . . . chaff*: that has no livelihood; but cf. *OED* 5.b., proverbial 'An old bird is not caught with chaff' (i.e. tricks).
38 *the wild world*: cf. ML, 40, 'this troublesome world'.
38 *wanting . . . has*: 'desiring what he already has', i.e. 'suffering from an excess of desire'. Cf. XXXVI, 25: 'And that I have, to crave so sore.'
40 *at adventure*: at hazard.
42: The cat is a metaphor for the body, and the mouse for the soul, cf. 8, 35. The idea is that the demands of the body have hurt the soul (cf. 38); hence also the warnings against trusting other people (cf., e.g., 24). There may be a parallel with CVI.

1 *love's*: disyllabic. So in 22.
2 *torment with care*: tormented with grief.
8 *night*: uninflected plural.

Which in this case full well I see:
But ha, ha, ha, full well is me,
For I am now at liberty.

Too great desire was my guide,
And wanton will went by my side;   20
Hope ruled still, and made me bide
Of love's craft the extremity:
But ha, ha, ha, full well is me,
For I am now at liberty.

With feigned words, which were but wind,   25
To long delays I was assigned;
Her wily looks my wits did blind,
Thus as she would, I did agree:
But ha, ha, ha, full well is me,
For I am now at liberty.   30

Was never bird tangled in lime
That broke away in better time
Than I that rotten boughs did climb
And had no hurt, but 'scaped free:
Now ha, ha, ha, full well is me,   35
For I am now at liberty.

CXXXVIII

I abide and abide and better abide
And after the old proverb the happy day,
And ever my lady to me doth say
'Let me alone, and I will provide.'

---

20 *will*: sexual appetite.   25 *words . . . wind*: cf. Tilley, W833.
31: Cf. Tilley, B380.   33: Cf. XIII, 14.

The proverb that underlies 1–2 and 5–6 is 'To him that abides shall betide well'
(Whiting, A8; and cf., e.g., *T & C*, I, 956); *tarry the tide* (5) may also be an ironic
variation on 'Time and tide tarry (stay, wait for) no man' (*ODEP*, p. 822; Tilley,
T323).

I abide and abide and tarry the tide,   5
And with abiding speed well ye may.
Thus do I abide I wot alway,
Neither obtaining, nor yet denied.
Ay me! This long abiding
Seemeth to me as who sayeth   10
A prolonging of a dying death,
Or a refusing of a desired thing.
Much were it better for to be plain
Than to say abide and yet shall not obtain.

CXXXIX

Deem as ye list, upon good cause
I may and think of this or that,
But what or why myself best knows,
Whereby I think and fear not;
But thereunto I may well think   5
The doubtful sentence of this clause:
I would it were not as I think,
I would I thought it were not.

For if I thought it were not so,
Though it were so, it grieved me not: 10
Unto my thought it were as though
I hearkened though I hear not.
At that I see I cannot wink,
Nor from my thought so let it go:
I would it were not as I think,   15
I would I thought it were not.

13–14 *for . . . obtain*: 'For you to refuse me bluntly, than to ask me to wait, and never let me obtain my desires' (MT).

1–2: 'Judge as you please, I may—and do—with good reason think of one thing or another.'
6 *doubtful sentence*: suspicious thought.
7–10: 'I would like my suspicion to be unjustified, or that I had no suspicion—for if I could free my mind from that (even if it were correct), I would not suffer.'

Lo how my thought might make me free
Of that perchance it needeth not!
Perchance none doubt the dread I see,
I shrink at that I bear not.   20
But in my heart this word shall sink
Unto the proof may better be:
I would it were not as I think,
I would I thought it were not.

If it be not, show no cause why   25
I should so think, then care I not;
For I shall so myself apply
To be that I appear not:
That is as one that shall not shrink
To be your own until I die,   30
And if it be not as I think,
Likewise to think it is not.

CXL

Ah! my heart, ah! what aileth thee
To set so light my liberty,
Making me bond when I was free?
Ah! my heart, ah! what aileth thee?

When thou were rid from all distress,   5
Void of all pain and pensiveness,
To choose again a new mistress,
Ah! my heart, ah! what aileth thee?

18: 'From what the situation need not, after all, be.'
19: If *none* (Nott conj.; MS. *no*) is correct, *doubt* means 'fear'.
22: 'Until I get evidence to the contrary.'
25–26 *If . . . think*: 'If it be true that you have not changed your affection, give
me no cause to suppose you have' (Nott, who rightly compares XCIII, 11–12).

'What aileth thee?' was common in refrains, cf. MT, CXII, 1, note.

When thou were well, thou could not hold—
To turn again, thou were too bold!   10
Thus to renew my sorrows old,
Ah! my heart, ah! what aileth thee?

Thou knowest full well that but of late
I was turned out of love's gate:
And now to guide me to this mate,   15
Ah! my heart, ah! what aileth thee?

I hoped full well all had been done,
But now my hope is ta'en and won.
To my torment to yield so soon,
Ah! my heart, ah! what aileth thee?   20

CXLI

I am as I am, and so will I be,
But how that I am none knoweth truly:
Be it evil, be it well, be I bond, be I free,
I am as I am, and so will I be.

I lead my life indifferently,   5
I mean nothing but honestly,
And though folks judge full diversly,
I am as I am, and so will I die.

I do not rejoice, nor yet complain,
Both mirth and sadness I do refrain,   10
And use the mean since folks will feign,
Yet I am as I am, be it pleasure or pain.

9–10; 'When you were well (i.e. not entangled in love), you could not control
yourself—in turning back to love you were all too audacious.'
14 *love's*: disyllabic.
18 *won*: overcome.

---

3 *evil*: wretched. Monosyllabic (*ev'l*).
3 *bond . . . free*: perhaps lit. (cf. Tillyard) 'in prison or not'; or, as often, 'in love
or out'.   6: Cf. CLXXXII, 4.
10 *refrain*: avoid.

Divers do judge as they do trow,
Some of pleasure, and some of woe,
Yet for all that nothing they know,   15
But I am as I am, wheresoever I go.

But since judgers do thus decay,
Let every man his judgement say:
I will it take in sport and play,
For I am as I am, whosoever say nay.   20

Who judgeth well, well God him send,
Who judgeth evil, God them amend:
To judge the best therefore intend,
For I am as I am, and so will I end.

Yet some there be that take delight   25
To judge folks' thought, for envy and spite,
But whether they judge me wrong or right,
I am as I am, and so do I write.

Praying you all that this do read
To trust it as you do your creed,   30
And not to think I change my weed,
For I am as I am, however I speed.

But how that is I leave to you:
Judge as ye list, false or true,
Ye know no more than afore ye knew.   35
Yet I am as I am, whatever ensue.

And from this mind I will not flee,
But to you all that misjudge me
I do protest, as ye may see,
That I am as I am, and so will I be.   40

---

31 *weed*: garb; appearance.

CXLII

That time that mirth did steer my ship
Which now is fraught with heaviness,
And fortune bote not then the lip
But was defence of my distress,
Then in my book wrote my mistress: 5
'I am yours, you may well be sure,
And shall be while my life doth dure.'

But she herself which then wrote that
Is now mine extreme enemy:
Above all men she doth me hate,   10
Rejoicing of my misery.
But though that for her sake I die,
I shall be hers, she may be sure,
As long as my life doth endure.

It is not time that can wear out   15
With me that once is firmly set:
While nature keeps her course about
My love from her no man can let.
Though never so sore they me threat,
Yet am I hers, she may be sure,   20
And shall be while that life doth dure.

And once I trust to see that day,
Renewer of my joy and wealth,
That she to me these words shall say:

Cf. L. It has often been assumed that in 5–6 W refers to the riddle 'am el men',
which ends with 'I ama yowrs an'. Indeed, I suspect that W's original version of
6 was 'I am yours Anne, you may be sure', which fits metrically (cf. 13, 20, etc.),
but that he or someone else prudently revised this into the line that found its
way into D and B.   2 *fraught*: cf. XCVIII, 60.
3 *bote*: i.e. bit. 'When Fortune did not yet show her anger . . .'
5 *book*: i.e. a manuscript which circulated from one person to another, who
might then add poems, comments, etc.
6–7: Cf., e.g., Stevens, 412.   16 *once*: once for all.
18: 'No one can prevent me from loving her.'
23 *wealth*: well-being.

'In faith, welcome to me myself,   25
Welcome, my joy! Welcome, my health!
For I am thine, thou mayst be sure,
And shall be while that life doth dure.'

Ho me! Alas! What words were these?
In covenant I might find them so!   30
I reck not what smart or disease,
Torment or trouble, pain or woe
I suffered so that I might know
That she were mine, I might be sure,
And should be while that life doth dure.   35

26 *health*: welfare.
31 *disease*: distress.
32 *trouble*: affliction.

III

POEMS FROM THE BLAGE MANUSCRIPT

A. Ascribed Poems
B. Unascribed Poems

A. ASCRIBED POEMS

CXLIII

V. Innocentia
Veritas Viat Fides
Circumdederunt me inimici mei

Who list his wealth and ease retain,
Himself let him unknown contain;
Press not too fast in at that gate
Where the return stands by disdain:
    For sure, *circa Regna tonat.*   5

The high mountains are blasted oft
When the low valley is mild and soft;
Fortune with health stands at debate,
The fall is grievous from aloft,
    And sure, *circa Regna tonat.*   10

These bloody days have broken my heart:
My lust, my youth did them depart,
And blind desire of estate.
Who hastes to climb seeks to revert:
    Of truth, *circa Regna tonat.*   15

Probably written during or after W's imprisonment in 1536, when he appears
to have seen Anne Boleyn's execution from his cell in the Tower. He no doubt
also alludes to the execution of Anne's alleged lovers (cf. CXLIX) when
speaking of 'bloody days' (11). The Latin motto has been added by a different
hand. The nouns 'Innocentia', 'Veritas' and 'Fides' are grouped round 'Viat'
as though these qualities must protect him from the enemies who have
besieged him (cf. Psalm 17:9; Psalm 16 in the Vulgate (MT)).
1 *wealth*: well-being.
3–4: 'Do not venture too fast into the gate (i.e. at court) through which you
may return or not only according to the disdain of others.' Cf. *OED press*
v.[1], 16, quotation from Coverdale (1535).
8 *health*: welfare.
8 *debate*: variance.
13 *estate*: high status.

The bell-tower showed me such sight
That in my head sticks day and night:
There did I learn out of a grate,
For all favour, glory or might,
    That yet *circa Regna tonat*.   20

By proof, I say, there did I learn
Wit helpeth not defence to earn,
Of innocency to plead or prate:
Bear low, therefore, give God the stern.
    For sure, *circa Regna tonat*.   25

CXLIV

Live thou gladly if so thou may,
Pine thou not in looking for me,
Since that despair hath shut thy way—
Thou to see me or I to see thee.

Make thou a virtue of a constraint,   5
Deem no fault where none is worthy:
Mine is too much, what needs thy complaint?
God he knoweth who is for me.

Cast upon the Lord thy cure,
Pray unto him thy cause to judge,   10
Believe, and he shall send recure:
Vain is all trust of man's refuge.

---

18 *grate*: the grating of a prison.
24 *Bear low*: i.e. sail with the wind, and humbly.
24 *stern*: cf. XCVIII, 83.

---

3 *thy*: so B, perhaps for *the*.
5: Cf. Tilley, V73.
9–11: Similar to XCIV, 12–14.
11 *recure*: help.
12: 'It is useless to expect shelter from man.' Cf. Psalm 60:11.

CXLV

Accused though I be, without desert,
None can it prove: yet ye believe it true.
Nor never yet since that ye had my heart
Intended I to be false or untrue:
Sooner I would of death sustain the smart   5
Than break one thing of that I promised you.
Accept therefore my service in good part:
None is alive that ill tongues can eschew.
Hold them as false, and let not us depart
Our friendship old in hope of any new.   10
Put not thy trust in such as use to feign,
Except thou mind to put thy friend to pain.

CXLVI

A face that should content me wonders well
Should not be fair, but lovely to behold,
With gladsome cheer all grief for to expel;
With sober looks so would I that it should
Speak without words such words as none can tell.   5
The tress also should be of crisped gold:
With wit and these might chance I might be tied,
And knit again the knot that should not slide.

The first letters form the acrostic ANNI STANHOPE, a reference to Lady Anne
Stanhope, the wife of Henry VIII's Master of the Horse (MT).
9 *depart*: break off.
11 *use to*: are in the habit of.
12: 'Unless you intend to hurt your lover.'

———

1 *wonders*: i.e. wondrously.
2 *lovely*: (P, T, N) loving, kind (cf., e.g., XII, 2). B: *cumley*, a weaker contrast
with *fair*.
3 *cheer*: expression. (Cf. LXII, 15.)
6 *crisped gold*: cf. XCVII, 69. Possibly another ref. to Elizabeth Darrell.
7: 'If she had brains in addition to these qualities, I might be tempted into a
firm relationship.'

CXLVII

Your looks so often cast,
Your eyes so friendly rolled,
Your sight fixed so fast
Always one to behold,
Though hide it fain you would   5
Yet plainly doth declare
Who hath your heart in hold
And where good will ye bear.

Fain would you find a cloak
Your burning fire to hide,   10
Yet both the flame and smoke
Breaks out on every side:
Ye cannot love so guide
That it not issue win,
Abroad needs must it glide   15
That burns so hot within.

For cause yourself doth wink
Ye judge all other blind,
And that secret you think
That every man doth find;   20
In waste oft spend you wind
Yourself from love to quit,
For agues of that kind
Will show who hath the fit.

Causes you fet from far,   25
And all to wrap your woe;
Yet are you never the near,
Men are not blinded so.
Deeply oft swear you no,
But all those oaths are vain,   30
So well your eye doth show
The cause of all your pain.

7 *in hold*: in captivity, cf. I, 10.   9: Cf., e.g., Tilley, F255.
17–18: A variant on 'He who winks isn't blind' (Rollins); cf. Tilley, C169.
21 *wind*: breath.   25 *fet*: i.e. fetch.   27 *near*: nearer.

Think not therefore to hide
That still itself betrays,
Nor seek means to provide   35
To dark the sunny days.
Forget those wonted ways,
Leave off dissembling cheer:
There will be found no stays
To stop a thing so clear.   40

CXLVIII

Pass forth, my wonted cries,
Those cruel ears to pierce
Which in most hateful wise
Doth still my plaints reverse.
Do you, my tears, also   5
So wet her barren heart
That pity there may grow,
And cruelty depart.

For though hard rocks among
She seems to have been bred   10
And with tigers full long
Been nourished and fed,
Yet shall that nature change
If pity once win place,
Whom as unknown and strange   15
She now away doth chase.

38 *cheer*: mien; mood.
39 *stays*: appliances for stopping.

---

4 *reverse*: send back.
9–12: Traditional, cf. Virgil, *Aeneid*, IV, 366–7 (Nott), and other references in
GG, ed. Rollins, 174.

And as the water soft
Without forcing of strength
Where that it falleth oft
Hard stones doth pierce at length,   20
So in her stony heart
My plaints at length shall grave
And, rigour set apart,
Cause her grant that I crave.

Wherefore, my plaints, present   25
Still so to her my suit
As it through her assent
May bring to me some fruit.
And as she shall me prove,
So bid her me regard   30
And render love for love,
Which is an just reward.

B. UNASCRIBED POEMS

CXLIX

In mourning wise since daily I increase,
Thus should I cloak the cause of all my grief;
So pensive mind with tongue to hold his peace
My reason sayeth there can be no relief:

17–20: Cf. LXXXII, 2–4; the idea may have come to W from Petrarch or
Serafino (cf. Nott, Rollins, MT).
21–22: Cf. LXVI, 6–8.
29 *prove*: find to be true through trial (Rollins).

An elegy on Anne Boleyn's supposed lovers (Lord Rochford, Henry Norris,
Francis Weston, William Brereton, Mark Smeaton), executed two days before
her in 1536 (cf. ML, 27–36). W probably did not witness the execution from his
cell in the Tower, for it took place on Tower Hill, but he may well have written
this poem (cf. CXLIII), presumably soon after his release (cf. 28). Lord
Rochford (21) was A. B.'s brother, and like her made himself unpopular by his
arrogance (cf. ML, 26). But his poetry, of which now next to nothing is known,
was held in great esteem.
1: 'As I daily grow more skilled in mourning . . .'

Wherefore give ear, I humbly you require,   5
The affect to know that thus doth make me moan.
The cause is great of all my doleful cheer
For those that were, and now be dead and gone.

What though to death desert be now their call,
As by their faults it doth appear right plain?   10
Of force I must lament that such a fall
Should light on those so wealthily did reign,
Though some perchance will say, of cruel heart,
A traitor's death why should we thus bemoan?
But I alas, set this offence apart,   15
Must needs bewail the death of some be gone.

As for them all I do not thus lament,
But as of right my reason doth me bind;
But as the most doth all their deaths repent,
Even so do I by force of mourning mind.   20
Some say, 'Rochford, haddest thou been not so proud,
For thy great wit each man would thee bemoan,
Since as it is so, many cry aloud
It is great loss that thou art dead and gone.'

Ah! Norris, Norris, my tears begin to run   25
To think what hap did thee so lead or guide
Whereby thou hast both thee and thine undone
That is bewailed in court of every side;
In place also where thou hast never been
Both man and child doth piteously thee moan.   30
They say, 'Alas, thou art far overseen
By thine offences to be thus dead and gone.'

---

5 *require*: implore.   6 *affect*: passion.   9 *desert*: i.e. deserved.
12 *wealthily*: (Maxwell conj.; MS. *welthy*) in such good fortune.
15 *set apart*: i.e. apart from.   19 *the most*: the greatest.
23 *as . . . so*: 'even though you are proud'; *so* is followed by a comma in B.
29 *place*: uninflected plural.
31 *thou . . . overseen*: you have much erred.

Ah! Weston, Weston, that pleasant was and young,
In active things who might with thee compare?
All words accept that thou diddest speak with tongue,   35
So well esteemed with each where thou diddest fare.
And we that now in court doth lead our life
Most part in mind doth thee lament and moan;
But that thy faults we daily hear so rife,
All we should weep that thou art dead and gone.   40

Brereton farewell, as one that least I knew.
Great was thy love with divers as I hear,
But common voice doth not so sore thee rue
As other twain that doth before appear;
But yet no doubt but thy friends thee lament   45
And other hear their piteous cry and moan.
So doth each heart for thee likewise relent
That thou givest cause thus to be dead and gone.

Ah! Mark, what moan should I for thee make more,
Since that thy death thou hast deserved best,   50
Save only that mine eye is forced sore
With piteous plaint to moan thee with the rest?
A time thou haddest above thy poor degree,
The fall whereof thy friends may well bemoan:
A rotten twig upon so high a tree   55
Hath slipped thy hold, and thou art dead and gone.

And thus farewell each one in hearty wise!
The axe is home, your heads be in the street;
The trickling tears doth fall so from my eyes
I scarce may write, my paper is so wet.   60
But what can hope when death hath played his part,
Though nature's course will thus lament and moan?
Leave sobs therefore, and every Christian heart
Pray for the souls of those be dead and gone.

35 *accept*: MT suggestion; MS. *exsept*.
53 *degree*: cf. CXXIII, 28.
55: Cf. XIII, 14.
61 *But . . . hope*: 'But what can hope achieve . . .'

CL

Thou sleepest fast, and I with woeful heart
Stand here alone sighing and cannot flee;
Thou sleepest fast, when cruel Love his dart
On me doth cast alas so painfully;
Thou sleepest fast, and I all full of smart   5
To thee my foe in vain do call and cry:
And yet methinkes thou that sleepest fast,
Thou dreamest still which way my life to waste.

CLI

Dido am I, the founder first of Carthage,
That as thou seest mine own death do procure
To save my faith, and for no new love's rage
To flee Iarbas, and keep my promise sure.
But see fortune, that would in neither age   5
Mine honest will in perfect bliss assure:
For while I lived she made my day short,
And now with lies my shame she doth report.

CLII

Venus in sport to please therewith her dear
Did on the helm of mighty Mars the red.
His spear she took, his targe she might not steer;
She looked as though her foes should all be dead,

---

7 *methinkes*: probably not parenthetical, for cf. It. *Credo*.

---

1 *Dido*: Queen and supposed founder of Carthage, she committed suicide out of loyalty to her dead husband when pressed into a new marriage with Iarbas. Virgil, however, makes her a contemporary of Aeneas (cf. CIV, 1), with whom she falls in love upon his arrival in Africa.
6 *honest*: honourable, chaste.
7 *day*: so MS., perhaps in error for, e.g., *dayes*.   8 *report*: rumour abroad.

Venus (promiscuously in love with Mars) acc. to a traditional conceit conquered best naked, not armed (cf. MEW, 177). The point is here combined with an allusion, also traditional, to the huge phallus of Priapus, by which, as a god of fruitfulness, he was often represented.
2 *mighty . . . red*: cf. *CT*, A1969.

So wantonly she frowneth with her cheer.   5
Priapus can smile and said, 'Do 'way for dread,
Do 'way, madame, these weapons great and grim.
I, I for you am weapon fit and trim.'

CLIII

'Comfort at hand, pluck up thy heart!
Look low, see where it doth stand!
Since the redress of all thy smart
Doth lay so good a hand,
    Pluck up thy heart.   5

Pluck up thy heart! Why droopest thou so?'
So said I, my thought.
And from the hill I looked low
And with mine eye I sought
    Comfort at hand.   10

Comfort at hand mine eye hath found.
My thought, therefore be glad:
If she be there may heal thy wound,
Why shouldest thou then be sad?
    Pluck up thy heart.   15

Pluck up thy heart! A mourning man
Doth get no good by woe.
Be glad alway, for whoso can
Shall find, whereso he go,
    Comfort at hand.   20

Comfort at hand go seek and find,
Look if there be redress!
If not, abide a better wind:
In hope of some release
    Pluck up thy heart.   25

6 *can*: (*OED can* v.²) began, did.

---

4 *hand*: i.e. of cards (?).
7 *my thought*: cf. 12. He addresses his thought. See CLXVI, 19.

CLIV

Do 'way, do 'way, ye little wily prat!
Your slyly slinking cannot ye excuse,
Nor words dissimuled cannot hide that
That will 'pear out if often ye it use.
If ye think other, yourself ye do abuse: 5
For heartly love unspied long to last
If ye essay, your wits sore ye waste.

If it be possible that from a fire great
The black smoke shall not issue out,
Or afore a cripple to halt and counterfeit   10
And be not spied, then quickly go about
Us to beguile: for truly without doubt
We know the craft, the looks and the price,
Wherefore trust me it is hard to blear our eyes.

If that we to you of this do speak   15
For good will, to make ye leave your folly,
Then will ye not stint till ye be wreak,
And ready to swear and still will deny
That that is true, yet will ye never apply
To your own faults, but always ye excuse.   20
Leave, fie, for shame! Ye make men to think and muse!

Ye think to cloak that cloaked cannot be,
And think to hide that open is in sight.
Alas! me thinketh it is a great pity
Yourself to bring in such a plight,   25
That should us cause to think ye light.
Leave off therefore! In faith ye are to blame:
Ye hurt yourself and loseth your good name.

1 *prat*: trickster; or perhaps (MT) prater.
3 *words*: MS. *wordes* (cf. 7 *wyttes*, 13 *Lokys*; also 8 *fyer*)—possibly disyllabic, but the lines vary in length.   3 *dissimuled*: i.e. dissembled.
6 *heartly*: i.e. hearty; heartfelt.   8–9: Cf., e.g., Tilley, F282.
10 ff.: Cf. *T & C*, IV, 1457–8, 'It is ful hard to halten unespied/Before a crepel, for he kan the craft'. Proverbial, cf. Tilley, H6o.
14 *trust . . . eyes*: i.e. 'believe me, it is hard to deceive us'.
28 *loseth*: perhaps 'destroy' rather than 'lose'.

CLV

Defamed guiltiness, by silence unkept,
My name all slanderous, my fault detect
(Guilty: I grant that I have done amiss),
Shall I never do so again, forgive me this.

Betrayed by trust, and so beguiled,   5
By promise unjust my name defiled
(Wherefore I grant that I have done amiss),
Will I never do so again, forgive me this.

Accept mine excuse for this offence,
And spare not to refuse me your presence,   10
Unless ye perceive ye do refrain
From doing amiss, while I live, again.

CLVI

Once in your grace I know I was,
Even as well as now is he.
Though fortune so hath turned my case
That I am down and he full high,
        Yet once I was.   5

Once I was he that did you please
So well that nothing did I doubt,
And though that now ye think it ease
To take him in and throw me out,
        Yet once I was.   10

'Presumably the poet gave away his mistress' name to a friend under pledge of
secrecy' (MT).
2 *slanderous*: shameful.
10: He innocently suggests he does not deserve to be near her, then makes
plain it is the other way round.
11–12: i.e. 'unless you abstain from doing further wrong', with the
implication, 'if you continue to refuse me your presence I will assume that you
have done amiss' (S).

3–4: A reference to the wheel of Fortune.   7 *doubt*: fear; suspect.

Once I was he in times past
That as your own ye did retain,
And though ye have me now outcast,
Showing untruth in you to reign,
     Yet once I was.   15

Once I was he that knit the knot
The which ye swore not to unknit,
And though ye feign it now forgot
In using your newfangled wit,
     Yet once I was.   20

Once I was he to whom ye said:
'Welcome, my joy, my whole delight!'
And though ye are now well apaid
Of me, your own, to claim ye quit,
     Yet once I was.   25

Once I was he to whom ye spake:
'Have here my heart, it is thy own!'
And though these words ye now forsake,
Saying thereof my part is none,
     Yet once I was.   30

Once I was he before rehearsed,
And now am he that needs must die,
And though I die, yet at the least
In your remembrance let it lie
     That once I was.   35

11 *times*: disyllabic.
19 *newfangled*: cf. XXXVII, 19.
19 *wit*: ingenuity.
23 *apaid*: satisfied.
31 *rehearsed*: told of.

CLVII

Quondam was I in my lady's grace
I think as well as now be you,
And when that you have trod the trace
Then shall you know my words be true,
    That quondam was I.   5

Quondam was I. She said 'for ever':
That 'ever' lasted but a short while.
Promise made not to dissever,
I thought she laughed—she did but smile:
    Then quondam was I.   10

Quondam was I: he that full oft lay
In her arms with kisses many one.
It is enough that this I may say:
Though among the mo now I be gone,
    Yet quondam was I.   15

Quondam was I: yet she will you tell
That since the hour she was first born
She never loved none half so well
As you. But what although she had sworn,
    Sure quondam was I.   20

CLVIII

She that should most, perceiveth least
The unfeigned sufferance of my great smart:
It is to her sport to have me oppressed.
But they of such life which be expert
Say that I burn uncertain in my heart.   5
But where judge ye? No more! Ye know not.
Ye are to blame to say I came too late.

---

3 *trod the trace*: gone the same way as the others (lit. 'the common path'). A common phrase.

9 *smile*: deride (me).   14 *the mo*: the majority, i.e. all the others.

---

2 *sufferance*: suffering.

Too late? Nay, too soon methink rather,
Thus to be entreated and have served faithfully.
Lo thus am I rewarded among the other!   10
I thought unvised which was too busy,
For fear of too late I came too hastily.
But thither I came not. Yet came I for all that.
But whithersoever I came, I came too late.

Who hath more cause to plain than I?   15
Thereas I am judged too late I came,
And thereas I came I came too hastily.
Thus may I plain as I that am
Misjudged, misentreated more than any man.
Now judge, let see of this debate,   20
Whether I came too hastily or too late.

CLIX

Spit of their spit which they in vain
Do stick to force my fantasy,
I am professed, for loss or gain,
To be thine own assuredly.
Who list thereat by spit to spurn,   5
My fancy is too hard to turn.

Although that some of busy wit
Do babble still—yea, yea, what though?
I have no fear, nor will not flit
As doth the water to and fro.   10
Spit then their spit that list to spurn,
My fancy is too hard to turn.

9, 19 *entreated*: treated.
11 *unvised*: i.e. ill-advised; imprudent.
13 *But . . . not*: but I did not reach my purpose.
20 *let see*: i.e. 'let us see'; cf. XL, 21.

---

1 *spit*: (1) spite; (2) broach; (3) saliva. (*Spit of* can mean 'in spite of'.)
2 *fantasy* (6 *fancy*): amorous inclination, love.
10: Cf. Tilley, W86.

Who is afraid? Yea, let him flee,
For I full well shall bide the brunt.
May grease their lips that list to lie   15
(Of busy brains as is their wont),
And yet against the prick they spurn:
My fancy is too hard to turn.

For I am set and will not swerve,
Whom faithful speech removeth nought;   20
And well I may thy grace deserve,
I think it is not dearly bought.
And if they both do spit and spurn,
My fancy is too hard to turn.

Who list thereat to list or lour,   25
I am not he that ought doth reche:
There is no pain that hath the power
Out of my breast this thought to seche.
Then though they spit thereat and spurn,
My fancy is too hard to turn.   30

14 *bide the brunt*: cf. ML, 196.
17: 'And yet they kick against the prick'; proverbial, after Acts 9:5, cf. Tilley,
F433.
21 *deserve*: earn.
26 *reche*: i.e. *reck*, but also *reach*, spit.
28 *seche*: i.e. *seek*, drive out by attack.

IV
POEMS FROM
THE ARUNDEL
MANUSCRIPT

A. Ascribed Poems
B. Unascribed Poem

A. ASCRIBED POEMS

CLX

The pillar perished is whereto I leant,
The strongest stay of mine unquiet mind.
The like of it no man again can find
From east to west still seeking though he went.
To mine unhap, for hap away hath rent   5
Of all my joy the very bark and rind,
And I alas by chance am thus assigned
Dearly to mourn till death do it relent.
But since that thus it is by destiny,
What can I more but have a woeful heart,   10
My pen in plaint, my voice in woeful cry,
My mind in woe, my body full of smart,
And I myself myself always to hate
Till dreadful death do cease my doleful state?

Despite T's title ('The louer lamentes the death of his loue'), this has from Nott onwards generally been held to refer to the execution of W's patron Thomas Cromwell, 28 July 1540. For the circumstances, cf. ML, 172–210. W was in tears when he witnessed the event (cf. Mason, 196 ff.). We need not assume that W wrote CLX in prison and in anticipation of his own death. The self-hatred expressed in 13 is probably the result of his restless state (cf., e.g., XXVI, 11), for he was hardly to blame for C.'s fall. But cf. MT.

1 *leant*: cf. Petrarch, *Rime* x, 1–2.
6 *the . . . rind*: i.e. the essence, the whole. Cf., e.g., *T & C*, IV, 1139 (Mason).
8 *Dearly*: earnestly. T *Daily*.   8 *relent*: lessen.
11 *woeful*: T *carefull* (cf. 10).
14 *cease*: conj. (A *cause*; T *ease*).

CLXI

A lady gave me a gift she had not,
And I received her gift I took not.
She gave it me willingly and yet she would not,
And I received it albeit I could not.
If she give it me I force not,   5
And if she take it again she cares not.
Conster what this is and tell not,
For I am fast sworn I may not.

CLXII

The flaming sighs that boil within my breast
Sometime break forth, and they can well declare
The heart's unrest and how that it doth fare,
The pain thereof, the grief, and all the rest.
The watered eyes from whence the tears do fall   5
Do feel some force, or else they would be dry;
The wasted flesh of colour dead can try,
And something tell what sweetness is in gall.
And he that list to see and to discern
How care can force within a wearied mind,   10
Come he to me: I am that place assigned.
But for all this no force, it doth no harm:
The wound alas hap in some other place,
From whence no tool away the scar can race.

For a likely solution to this riddle cf. Peter Motteux's suggestion in Rollins, II,
316.
5 *force*: care.   7 *Conster*: i.e. construe; guess.

---

6 *some force*: i.e. something that causes weeping.
7 *can try of*: 'knows from experience what it is like to have . . .'
10 *care*: grief.
12 *But . . . force*: but all this does not matter.
14 *race*: erase, scratch out. The line is proverbial (Rollins), cf. Tilley, W929; see
also CLXV, 7–8.

But you that of such like have had your part   15
Can best be judge: wherefore, my friend so dear,
I thought it good my state should now appear
To you, and that there is no great desert.
And whereas you in weighty matters great
Of fortune saw the shadow that you know,   20
For tasting things I now am stricken so
That though I feel my heart doth wound and beat
I sit alone—save on the second day
My fever comes, with whom I spend the time
In burning heat while that she list assign.   25
And who hath health and liberty alway,
Let him thank God, and let him not provoke
To have the like of this my painful stroke!

CLXIII

Stand whoso list upon the slipper top
Of court's estates, and let me here rejoice
And use me quiet without let or stop,
Unknown in court, that hath such brackish joys.
In hidden place so let my days forth pass   5
That when my years be done withouten noise,
I may die aged after the common trace.
For him death gripeth right hard by the crop
That is much known of other, and of himself alas
Doth die unknown, dazed with dreadful face.   10

---

21 *For . . . things*: i.e. 'because I have merely been exploring'. (Or *tasting* = 'experiencing'?).

1 *slipper*: slippery. Cf. QM, 457, 'slypper riches'.
2 *estates*: cf. CXLIII, 13.
3 : 'Let unhindered and uninterrupted quiet use me' (cf. *Me dulcis saturet quies*).
7 *after . . . trace*: cf. CLVII, 3. *Common* translates *Plebeius*.
9 *of*: by.
10 *dreadful*: full of fear.

B. UNASCRIBED POEM

CLXIV

The Argument

Sometime the pride of my assured truth
Contemned all help of God and eke of man:
But when I saw man blindly how he goeth
In deeming hearts, which none but God there can,
And His dooms hid, whereby man's malice growth,   5
Mine earl, this doubt my heart did humble then
For error so might murder Innocents.
Then sang I thus in God my confidence.

This follows XCIV in A, and (Nott) would be a fitting proem to it; or else the
gap (fols. 120–7) following in A may have contained one or more other Psalms
meant to accompany CLXIV.
1 *assured truth*: presumptuous confidence.
6 *Mine earl*: Cromwell (S); or possibly Surrey (Nott; cf. CVIII).
6 *this doubt*: the uncertainty (fear?) created by my new awareness.

V

POEMS FROM
HARLEIAN MS. 78

CLXV

Sighs are my food, drink are my tears,
Clinking of fetters such music would crave;
Stink and close air away my life wears,
Innocency is all the hope I have;
Rain, wind, or weather I judge by mine ears;   5
Malice assaulted that righteousness should have:
Sure I am, Brian, this wound shall heal again,
But yet alas the scar shall still remain.

CLXVI

Like as the wind with raging blast
Doth cause each tree to bow and bend,
Even so do I spend my time in waste
My life consuming unto an end.

For as the flame by force doth quench the fire   5
And running streams consume the rain,
Even so do I myself desire
To augment my grief and deadly pain.

Whereas I find that hot is hot
And cold is cold by course of kind,   10
So shall I knit an endless knot:
Such fruit in love alas I find.

Written (Nott) during W's second imprisonment in the Tower, 1541. Not only does the final couplet (cf. CLXII, 14) resemble a sentence in W's Defence (ML, 193), but W's Declaration also contains parallels (cf. ML, 184, *innocence . . . malice . . . let not my life wear away here*). The malice referred to is Bonner's, W's enemy from the time he was in Spain, and his accuser in 1541; cf., e.g., XCI.
2 *crave*: insist on.
6: 'I, who ought to be treated righteously, am assaulted by malice instead.'
7 *Brian*: cf. CVII.

———
5–9: The idea of the stanza is that far from effectively eliminating his grief, he deliberately keeps adding to it.

When I first saw those crystal streams
Whose beauty doth cause my mortal wound,
I little thought within those beams   15
So sweet a venom for to have found.

I feel and see my own decay
As one that beareth flame in his breast,
Forgetful thought to put away,
The thing that breedeth my unrest.   20

Like as the fly doth seek the flame
And afterward playeth in the fire,
Who findeth her woe and seeketh her game,
Whose grief doth grow of her own desire;

Like as the spider doth draw her line   25
With labour lost, so is my suit.
The gain is hers, the loss is mine:
Of evil sown seed such is the fruit.

---

13 *streams*: the rays darting from the lady's eyes.
19 *thought*: mental anxiety (?). Cf. CLIII, 7.
21 ff.: Cf. XXIV, and Tilley, F394.
26 *With*: P. H: *as*.
28: Cf. Tilley, G405, and XXIX, 14.

VI

POEM FROM
PARKER MS. 168

CLXVII

Like as the bird in the cage enclosed,
The door unsparred and the hawk without,
'Twixt death and prison piteously oppressed
Whether for to choose standeth in doubt,
Certes so do I, which do seek to bring about   5
Which should be best by determination,
By loss of life liberty, or life by prison.

O mischief by mischief to be redressed!
Where pain is the best there lieth little pleasure:
By short death out of danger yet to be delivered   10
Rather than with painful life thraldom and dolour,
For small pleasure much pain to suffer.
Sooner therefore to choose me thinketh it wisdom
By loss of life liberty than life by prison.

By length of life yet should I suffer   15
Awaiting time and fortune's chance.
Many things happen within an hour:
That which me oppressed may me advance.
In time is trust, which by death's grievance
Is utterly lost. Then were it not reason   20
By death to choose liberty, and not life by prison.

A debate on a conventional model (cf. Nott; Rollins, II, 317), this presents the poet as lover (cf. 25), metaphorically imprisoned as a bird, discussing the traditional question whether he must continue in his stifling state, or prefer death instead. The first stanza poses the problem; the second argues in favour of death; the third against it; the final one submits the unresolved question to the judgement of others.

2 *unsparred*: unbolted.
4 *Whether*: which of the two, i.e. death or prison.
6 *determination*: deliberation.
8: The misfortune of imprisonment would be cured only by that of death.
9–10: 'Where pain is in either case the best I can possibly expect, there is but some pleasure: namely, that by a quick death I can set myself free from subjection.'
17: Cf. Tilley, H741. The idea here is that time may bring disaster, but equally well an upward turn of Fortune's wheel.
20–21: i.e. 'Then it would be unwise to prefer death to life in prison.'

But death were deliverance, and life length of pain.
Of two ills, let see now, choose the best
This bird to deliver, you that hear her plain.
Your advice, you lovers, which shall be best: 25
In cage in thraldom, or by the hawk to be oppressed?
And which for to choose make plain conclusion:
By loss of life liberty, or life by prison.

23: An ironic variation on the proverb (cf. Tilley, E207): instead of the least of
the two evils, we must choose that which will best succeed in delivering the
lover from his plight. Nott and others emend *best* to *lest*, but cf. 6, 9, and 25.
The rhyme *best-best* is normal W practice.

23 *let see*: i.e. 'let us see' (cf. CLVIII, 20).

VII

POEM FROM
HILL MS. ADD. 36529

CLXVIII

Lux, my fair falcon, and your fellows all,
How well pleasant it were your liberty!
Ye not forsake me that fair might ye befall,
But they that sometime liked my company,
Like lice away from dead bodies they crawl: 5
Lo what a proof in light adversity!
But ye, my birds, I swear by all your bells
Ye be my friends, and so be but few else.

Probably written after Cromwell's fall (July 1540; cf. CLX), and before W's imprisonment in 1541. He seems to complain that his friends desert him before the blow; though in 2 he may say 'How I would enjoy your liberty' rather than 'How nice it would be for you to be free'. Or perhaps the poem was written in May 1536, at the time when W, Anne Boleyn and her 'fellows' (cf. 1) were all in prison; Anne was represented in her Coronation pageants by a white ('fair') falcon. If so, 2 might mean 'How nice it would be if you were free and if I shared your freedom'. Cf. also SCM, 174–5.

1 *Lux*: the name may pun on *lux* (light) and *luck*.

6: 'How effective a test of character is contained in even a little adversity' (Tillyard). Cf. LIII, 8.

VIII

POEMS FROM
TOTTEL'S *SONGES AND*
SONETTES

CLXIX

Within my breast I never thought it gain
Of gentle mind the freedom for to lose.
Nor in my heart sank never such disdain
To be a forger, faults for to disclose.
Nor I cannot endure the truth to gloze,   5
To set a gloze upon an earnest pain.
Nor I am not in number one of those
That list to blow retreat to every train.

CLXX

For want of will, in woe I plain,
Under colour of soberness,
Renewing with my suit my pain,
My wanhope with your steadfastness.
Awake therefore, of gentleness!   5
Regard at length, I you require,
The swelting pains of my desire.

Betimes who giveth willingly
Redoubled thanks aye doth deserve;
And I that sue unfeignedly   10
In fruitless hope alas do starve.
How great my cause is for to swerve
And yet how steadfast is my suit,
Lo, here ye see: where is the fruit?

Some of this could easily refer to, e.g., Bonner's treatment of W; cf. XCI.
2 *lose*: destroy.   4 *forger*: 'fabricator of lies' (Rollins).
4 *faults*: i.e. non-existing faults.
5 *gloze*: disguise, hide with false talk. T's *gloss* in 6 may represent *OED gloss* sb.[2]
rather than *gloss* sb.[1] or *gloze*, but cf., e.g., CVIII, 498.
8 *blow . . . train*: 'withdraw from every enterprise' (MT; *train*=military train,
army).

---

1 ff. *will*: satisfaction of sexual desire.   4 *wanhope*: despair.
6–9: For a possible source, cf. Rollins, II, 186.
6 *require*: implore.   7 *swelting*: swooning.
8–9: Cf. *LGW*, G 441–2; Tilley, G125.
11 *starve*: die (for lack of satisfaction).

As hound that hath his keeper lost   15
Seek I your presence to obtain,
In which my heart delighteth most,
And shall delight though I be slain.
You may release my band of pain:
Loose then the care that makes me cry,   20
For want of help or else I die.

I die: though not incontinent,
By process yet consumingly
As waste of fire, which doth relent
If you as wilful will deny.   25
Wherefore cease of such cruelty,
And take me wholly in your grace
Which lacketh will to change his place.

CLXXI

If ever man might him avaunt
Of fortune's friendly cheer,
It was myself, I must it grant,
For I have bought it dear.
And dearly have I held also   5
The glory of her name,
In yielding her such tribute, lo,
As did set forth her fame.

15 *hound*: dog. Cf. *ODEP*, p. 517.   20 *care*: grief.
21: 'Or else I shall die for lack of help.'
23 *By process*: i.e. of time.   24 *relent*: melt away.
28: Either 'Who does not want to change his (i.e. my) place', or 'Who would
change his place if his craving were satisfied'. Or perhaps *Which* refers to *grace*,
i.e. 'Your favour would be forthcoming, if only you had desire enough.'

———

Music for one voice going with this song can be found in a copy of Nott's
edition of Tottel (1814?) held at Arundel Castle. Nott found this, written 'in
the characters of the times', in the copy of the 1557 edition of T belonging to
Sir W. W. Wynne which has now disappeared. Cf. Stevens, 136; and Hughey,
The Library, 1935–6, 395.

1 *avaunt*: i.e. vaunt.   2 *fortune*: probably in fact a woman;
if so, *fancy* (14) means 'amorous inclination'.   3 *grant*: confess.

Sometime I stood so in her grace
That as I would require   10
Each joy I thought did me embrace
That furthered my desire.
And all those pleasures lo had I
That fancy might support,
And nothing she did me deny   15
That was to my comfort.

I had (what would you more, perdie?)
Each grace that I did crave.
Thus fortune's will was unto me
All thing that I would have.   20
But all too rathe, alas the while,
She built on such a ground:
In little space too great a guile
In her now have I found.

For she hath turned so her wheel   25
That I, unhappy man,
May wail the time that I did feel
Wherewith she fed me then.
For broken now are her behests
And pleasant looks she gave,   30
And therefore now all my requests
From peril cannot save.

Yet would I well it might appear
To her my chief regard,
Though my deserts have been too dear   35
To merit such reward.

9: Cf. LXXI, 15.   10 *require*: implore (cf. 18).   21 *rathe*: quickly.
22: Cf. LXXI, 18.   27 *feel*: taste.   29 *behests*: promises.
33–36: 'Yet I should much like Fortune to see that my chief concern just now is that at least my requests be saved from peril, though my deservings have been of too great a worth to merit nothing better.'

Sith fortune's will is now so bent
To plague me thus, poor man,
I must myself therewith content,
And bear it as I can.   40

CLXXII

Such is the course that nature's kind hath wrought
That snakes have time to cast away their stings.
Ainst chained prisoners what need defence be sought?
The fierce lion will hurt no yielden things:
Why should such spite be nursed then in thy thought,   5
Sith all these powers are pressed under thy wings,
And eke thou seest, and reason hath thee taught
What mischief malice many ways it brings?
Consider eke that spite availeth nought!
Therefore this song thy fault to thee it sings.   10
Displease thee not for saying thus my thought,
Nor hate thou him from whom no hate forth springs:
For furies that in hell be execrable
For that they hate are made most miserable.

CLXXIII

Sufficed not, madame, that you did tear
My woeful heart, but thus also to rent
The weeping paper that to you I sent,
Whereof each letter was written with a tear?

3: Traditional (Rollins). *Ainst*: against.
4: Cf. LI, 25 ff. *Yielden*: i.e. that have yielded.
6 *these powers*: the mistress is like a snake, jailer, and lion.
13–14: W means that the lady, who behaves like an infernal spirit, will herself be accursed in hell and made miserable because she hates him. The Roman *Furiae* by contrast avenged crimes, as infernal deities.

1–4: The question mark (Nott's, not in T) would give the sense: 'Didn't the destruction of my heart, but did tearing up my letter satisfy your greed?' If declarative, the sentence means: 'The destruction of my heart did not, but tearing up my letter did satisfy your greed'; which, though possible, seems to fit in less well with what follows.

Could not my present pains alas suffice   5
Your greedy heart, and that my heart doth feel
Torments that prick more sharper than the steel,
But new and new must to my lot arise?

Use then my death. So shall your cruelty,
Spite of your spite, rid me from all my smart,   10
And I no more such torments of the heart
Feel as I do. This shalt thou gain thereby.

CLXXIV

When first mine eyes did view and mark
Thy fair beauty to behold,
And when mine ears listened to hark
The pleasant words that thou me told,
I would as then I had been free   5
From ears to hear and eyes to see.

And when my lips gan first to move,
Whereby my heart to thee was known,
And when my tongue did talk of love
To thee that hast true love down thrown,   10
I would my lips and tongue also
Had then been dumb, no deal to go.

And when my hands have handled ought
That thee hath kept in memory,
And when my feet have gone and sought   15
To find and get thy company,
I would each hand a foot had been
And I each foot a hand had seen.

12 *This*: though the lady would seek satisfaction by killing the lover, ironically
he (not she) would be relieved.

---

7 *gan*: began, did.
12 *no . . . go*: not to move at all (Nott).

And when in mind I did consent
To follow this my fancy's will,   20
And when my heart did first relent
To taste such bait, my life to spill,
I would my heart had been as thine
Or else thy heart had been as mine.

CLXXV

Since love will needs that I shall love,
Of very force I must agree;
And since no chance may it remove,
In wealth and in adversity
I shall alway myself apply   5
To serve and suffer patiently.

Though for good will I find but hate
And cruelty my life to waste,
And though that still a wretched state
Should pine my days unto the last,   10
Yet I profess it willingly
To serve and suffer patiently.

For since my heart is bound to serve,
And I not ruler of mine own,
Whatso befall, till that I starve   15
By proof full well it shall be known:
That I shall still myself apply
To serve and suffer patiently.

Yea though my grief find no redress,
But still increase before mine eyes,   20
Though my reward be cruelness,
With all the harm hap can devise,
Yet I profess it willingly
To serve and suffer patiently.

20 *fancy*: amorous inclination.   22 *spill*: destroy.

4, 27 *wealth*: well-being.   10 *pine*: inflict torment on.   15 *starve*: die.

Yea though fortune her pleasant face   25
Should show to set me up aloft,
And straight my wealth for to deface
Should writhe away as she doth oft,
Yet would I still myself apply
To serve and suffer patiently.   30

There is no grief, no smart, no woe
That yet I feel or after shall,
That from this mind may make me go;
And whatsoever me befall,
I do profess it willingly   35
To serve and suffer patiently.

CLXXVI

Mistrustful minds be moved
To have me in suspect:
The truth it shall be proved,
Which time shall once detect.

Though falsehood go about   5
Of crime me to accuse,
At length I do not doubt
But truth shall me excuse.

Such sauce as they have served
To me without desert,   10
Even as they have deserved,
Thereof God send them part!

---

27 *deface*: destroy.

No doubt written, as MT suggests, when W was in danger from his enemies in
1536, 1538, or 1540.   2 *suspect*: suspicion.   3 *proved*: found out.
4 *once detect*: one day reveal. Cf. Tilley, T333; also CXXXVI, 24.
7 *doubt*: (also) fear.
9 ff.: An expansion of the proverb 'To be served with the same sauce' (i.e. 'to
be subjected to the same treatment'); cf. Tilley, S99.

CLXXVII

Lover:	It burneth yet alas, my heart's desire.
Lady:	What is the thing that hath enflamed thy heart?
Lo.:	A certain point, as fervent as the fire.
La.:	The heat shall cease if that thou wilt convert.
Lo.:	I cannot stop the fervent raging ire. 5
La.:	What may I do if thyself cause thy smart?
Lo.:	Hear my request alas with weeping cheer.
La.:	With right good will, say on: lo I thee hear.
Lo.:	That thing would I that maketh two content.
La.:	Thou seekest perchance of me that I may not. 10
Lo.:	Would God thou wouldst as thou mayst well assent.
La.:	That I may not the grief is mine, God wot.
Lo.:	But I it feel, whatso thy words have meant.
La.:	Suspect me not: my words be not forgot.
Lo.:	Then say, alas: shall I have help, or no? 15
La.:	I see no time to answer yea, but no.
Lo.:	Say yea, dear heart, and stand no more in doubt.
La.:	I may not grant a thing that is so dear.
Lo.:	Lo with delays thou drives me still about.
La.:	Thou wouldest my death, it plainly doth appear. 20
Lo.:	First may my heart his blood and life bleed out.
La.:	Then for my sake alas thy will forbear.
Lo.:	From day to day thus wastes my life away.
La.:	Yet, for the best, suffer some small delay.
Lo.:	Now, good, say yea: do once so good a deed. 25
La.:	If I said yea, what should thereof ensue?
Lo.:	An heart in pain of succour so should speed;
	'Twixt yea and nay, my doubt shall still renew:
	My sweet, say yea, and do away this dread.

7 *cheer*: face.   12 *the*: T2. T1: *thy*.
16 *yea*: makes sense, but perhaps W wrote *ye but no*.
25 *good*: sweetheart.
28 *doubt*: cf. CLXXVI, 7.

La.:   Thou wilt needs so: be it so, but then be true.   30
Lo.:   Nought would I else, nor other treasure none.

Thus hearts be won by love, request, and moan.

CLXXVIII

I see that chance hath chosen me
Thus secretly to live in pain,
And to another given the fee
Of all my loss to have the gain.
By chance assigned thus do I serve,   5
And other have that I deserve.

Unto myself sometime alone
I do lament my woeful case.
But what availeth me to moan,
Since truth and pity hath no place   10
In them to whom I sue and serve,
And other have that I deserve?

To seek by mean to change this mind
Alas I prove it will not be,
For in my heart I cannot find   15
Once to refrain, but still agree
As bound by force alway to serve.
And other have that I deserve.

Such is the fortune that I have
To love them most that love me least,   20
And to my pain to seek and crave
The thing that other have possessed.
So thus in vain alway I serve:
And other have that I deserve.

32: This may be the lover's comment, but more likely it is W's (Foxwell, Rollins).

---

3 *fee*: reward.   4: Cf. Tilley, M337, R136.
6: Cf., e.g., 'One sows and another reaps' (*ODEP*, p. 597; Tilley, S691).
13 *mean*: lament.   14 *prove*: cf. CXLVIII, 29.

And till I may appease the heat,   25
If that my hap will hap so well,
To wail my woe my heart shall fret,
Whose pensive pain my tongue can tell.
Yet thus unhappy must I serve,
And other have that I deserve.   30

CLXXIX

For shamefast harm of great and hateful need
In deep despair as did a wretch go
With ready cord out of his life to speed,
His stumbling foot did find an hoard, lo,
Of gold, I say, where he prepared this deed,   5
And in exchange he left the cord tho.
He that had hid the gold and found it not,
Of that he found he shaped his neck a knot.

CLXXX

Throughout the world, if it were sought,
Fair words enough a man shall find:
They be good cheap, they cost right nought,
Their substance is but only wind.
But well to say and so to mean,   5
That sweet accord is seldom seen.

1–2 *For . . . despair*: 'In deep despair because of the shame and grief which the great and hateful need to commit suicide brought upon him . . .'
6 *tho*: then.

Cf. Tilley, W808 and W804 (3), and W833 (4). 3 *Good cheap*: i.e. a bargain (Nott).

CLXXXI

In court to serve, decked with fresh array,
Of sugared meats feeling the sweet repast,
The life in banquets and sundry kinds of play
Amid the press of lordly looks to waste,
Hath with it joined ofttimes such bitter taste,   5
That whoso joys such kind of life to hold
In prison joys, fettered with chains of gold.

CLXXXII

Disdain me not without desert,
Nor leave me not so suddenly;
Since well ye wot that in my heart
I mean ye not but honestly,
    Disdain me not.   5

Refuse me not without cause why,
Nor think me not to be unjust;
Since that by lot of fantasy
This careful knot needs knit I must,
    Refuse me not.   10

Mistrust me not, though some there be
That fain would spot my steadfastness;
Believe them not, since that ye see
The proof is not as they express:
    Mistrust me not.   15

2: 'Enjoying the sweet consumption of sugared foods'; cf. *sweetmeat* = 'sweet food, as sugared cakes or pastry, confectionery' (*OED*, 1).
4 *press*: crowd; pressure, distress. Cf. CV, 3–5.

---

4 *not but*: nothing else than, only. 'My intentions towards you are purely honourable'; cf. CXLI, 6.
8 *fantasy*: cf. XLIII, 1.
9 *careful*: full of grief.
12 *spot*: vilify.

Forsake me not till I deserve,
Nor hate me not till I offend,
Destroy me not till that I swerve:
But since ye wot what I intend,
    Forsake me not.   20

Disdain me not that am your own,
Refuse me not that am so true,
Mistrust me not till all be known,
Forsake me not, ne for no new,
    Disdain me not.   25

CLXXXIII

Speak thou and speed where will or power ought helpth,
Where power doth want will must be won by wealth.
For need will speed where will works not his kind,
And gain: thy foes thy friends shall cause thee find.
For suit and gold, what do not they obtain?   5
Of good and bad the triers are these twain.

24 *ne*: not.

---

1 *Speak and speed*: proverbial (Rollins), cf. Tilley, S719. It means 'Speak and
you shall prosper'; cf. 'Ask and have' (XXXVI, 27), which is sometimes added
to it.
3–4: 'For where your will cannot have its way, the need of others will bring
you success and profit; your enemies, once bribed, will make you find your
friends.' Cf., e.g., Whiting, M637 and 638.
5: Cf. Tilley, M1102.

CLXXXIV

If thou wilt mighty be, flee from the rage
Of cruel will, and see thou keep thee free
From the foul yoke of sensual bondage.
For though thy empire stretch to Indian sea
And for thy fear trembleth the farthest Thylee,   5
If thy desire have over thee the power,
Subject then art thou, and no governor.

If to be noble and high thy mind be moved,
Consider well thy ground and thy beginning:
For He that hath each star in heaven fixed,   10
And gives the moon her horns and her eclipsing,
Alike hath made thee noble in His working,
So that wretched no way thou may be
Except foul lust and vice do conquer thee.

All were it so thou had a flood of gold,   15
Unto thy thirst yet should it not suffice.
And though with Indian stones a thousandfold
More precious than can thyself devise
Ycharged were thy back, thy covetise
And busy biting yet should never let   20
Thy wretched life, ne do thy death profit.

---

2 *will*: sexual desire.   4 *Indian*: cf. LXXXV, 3.
5 *Thylee*: (so T) Thule. 'Even if the remotest part of the world trembles for fear of you . . .'
9: A reference to 'the origin of man. The argument of the stanza is that as God created the glory of the moon and stars, so He created each man to fulfil as noble a function, if man will but keep his nature free' (Tillyard). Cf. ML, 42.
15 ff.: Cf. CVI, 77 ff.
15 *All*: even if.   18 *devise*: imagine.   19 *Ycharged*: cf. IX, 6.
19–21 *thy covetise . . . profit*: 'Your inordinate desire, and the anxious gnawing of which you would be the victim, would never leave your miserable life, nor be of profit to you when you die.' *Busy biting* virtually means 'gnawing anxiety', as does Boethius' *cura mordax* and Chaucer's *bytynge bysynesse*. It was common to speak of the biting of conscience. Cf. also, e.g., CVI, 112, and QM, 461, '*busely* prickyng . . . one that *byteth* and gnaweth hym self'.

APPENDIX

Where necessary, the Appendix aims to give chiefly the following information:

1   The most important primary sources in which the poem appears (cf. the Note on the Text).
2   Non-stylistic indications of W's authorship (i.e. ascriptions; the presence of W's hand).
3   The metrical form.
4   The first line of the likely or possible source underlying W's poem as a whole. (For practical convenience, I refer to the sources as they are printed in MT, which also offers useful discussions of them, but I have not been able to record MT's textual inaccuracies.)

I. D, T. 'Tho' in margin of E; in W section of T. Rondeau. Petrarch, *Rime*, 'Or vedi, Amor, che giovenetta donna.'

II. T; in the W section. Rondeau.

III. D, T, N. In W section of T. Sonnet. Petrarch, *Rime*, 'Cesare, poi che 'l traditor d'Egitto.' E's heading is 'oute of Petrarch, a Sonett' (similar headings are provided for XXVI and XCVIII). As Rollins shows, the story of Caesar's shedding tears when receiving Pompey's head from Ptolemy had become commonplace. Cf. also F, II, 28, about W's admiration for Caesar.

IV. A, T. In W section of T. Sonnet. Petrarch, *Rime*, 'Amor, che nel penser mio vive e regna.'

V. D, B.

VI. A leaf is missing with the earlier part of this poem, which is followed by these lines:

> I plede, and reason my selffe emonge
> agaynst reason, howe I suffer
> but, she that doethe me all the wronge
> I plede and reason my sealffe emonge

This incoherent fragment seems unconnected with VI, and is perhaps written in a different hand.

VII. B, A. 'Wyat' in margin. W may have revised *Sithens* (8) into *Sins* (cf. Padelford; ST). Sonnet. Petrarch, *Rime*, 'Una candida cerva sopra l'erba'; but cf. also Romanello's fifteenth-century imitation 'Vna cerva gentil' (see MT).

VIII. A, T. In E lines 1–21 are missing; they are taken from A. In W section of T. Rhyme royal. Petrarch, *Rime*, 'Quell 'antiquo mio dolce empio signore.'

IX. A, T. 'Wyat' in margin; in W section of T. Sonnet. Petrarch, *Rime*, 'Io non fu' d'amar voi lassato unqu'anco.'

X. D, A, T. 'Tho' in margin; in W section of T. Sonnet.

XI. T; in the W section. SCM (142) draws attention to the internal rhymes, creating the scheme *ababcbcb*.

XII. A, T. 'Wyat' in margin; in W section of T. Sonnet. Petrarch, *Rime*, 'S'una fede amorosa, un cor non finto.'

XIII. D, A, T. 'Tho' in margin; in W section of T. Sonnet.

XIV. D, A, T. 'Wyat' in margin; in W section of T. The first half of line 14 is supplied from D. Sonnet. Serafino, *Opere*, 'El cor ti diedi non che el tormentassi' (with the next strambotto).

XV. D. 'Wyat' in margin. Rondeau. Perhaps influenced by Jean Marot's 'S'il est ainsi', cf. XVIII.

XVI. D, B, A, T. 'Tho' in margin; in W section of T. Sonnet.

XVII. 'Wyat' in margin. Rondeau. The conceit of the heart leaving the body was traditional (cf. F and MT).

XVIII. 'Wyat' in margin. Rondeau. Jean Marot, 'S'il est ainsi que ce corps t'abandonne', in its turn an imitation of Serafino's 'Se questo miser corpo t'abandona.' Cf. MT.

XIX. D. 'Tho' in margin. Rondeau.

XX. D, T. 'Wyat' in margin; in W section of T. Rondeau. Petrarch, *Rime*, 'Ite, caldi sospiri, al freddo core'; but W's poem may be derived from a French rondeau based on P.'s poem.

XXI. B, T. 'Wyat' in margin; in W section of T. Rhyme royal.

XXII. D, T. 'Wyat' in margin; in W section of T. Rhyme royal. Cf. Serafino, *Opere*, 'Laer che sente el mesto e gran clamore.'

XXIII. T. 'Tho' in margin; in W section of T. Rhyme royal.

XXIV. A, T. 'Wyat' in margin; in W section of T. Sonnet. Petrarch, *Rime*, 'Sono animali al mondo di sí altera.'

XXV. A, T. 'Wyat' in margin; in W section of T. Sonnet. Petrarch, *Rime*, 'Perch'io t'abbia guardato di menzogna.'

XXVI. D, P, T, N. 'Wyat' in margin; in W section of T. Sonnet. Petrarch, *Rime*, 'Pace non trovo e non ho da far guerra.' P mentions this source, as does N; and cf. III.

XXVII. A. 'Tho' in margin. Sonnet. Petrarch, *Rime*, 'Orso; al vostro destrier si po ben porre.'

XXVIII. A, T. 'Wyat' in margin; in W section of T. Sonnet. Petrarch, *Rime*, 'Passa la nave mia colma d'oblio.' The conceit used was frequent both in Italian and in English verse (cf. F and SCM, 33 and 56 ff.).

XXIX. A, T. 'Wyat' in margin; in W section of T. Sonnet. Cf. Petrarch, *Rime*, 'Mirando 'l sol de'begli occhi sereno'; but SCM (33–35) cites Chaucer, *RR* and *T & C*, for native parallels to much in this poem.

XXX. A, T. 'Wyat' in margin; in W section of T. Sonnet. Petrarch, *Rime*, 'Mie venture al venir son tarde e pigre.'

XXXI. A, T. 'Wyat' in margin; in W section of T. Sonnet. Petrarch, *Rime*, 'Amor, fortuna e la mia mente schiva.'

XXXII. A, T. 'Wyat' in margin; in W section of T. Sonnet. Petrarch, *Rime*, 'Mille fïate, o dolce mia guerrera.'

XXXIII. A, T. 'Tho' in margin; in W section of T. Sonnet. Sannazaro, *Le Rime*, 1531 (but Sannazaro's authorship is uncertain), 'Simile a questi smisurati monti.' Cf. MT.

XXXIV. B, T. 'Tho' in margin; in W section of T. Dragonetto Bonifacio, 'Madonna non so dir tante parole' (printed with Verdelot's music *c.* 1535; cf. MT). The poem is followed in E (and B) by a reply in a different hand (the same hand in B); this is probably not by W, but interesting for such light as it throws on what happened to this and similar MSS. It is printed in MT with some minor errors and one major one, *giue* for *griue* in 10.

XXXV. 'Tho' in margin. Rondeau. Analogue: Pierre Sala of Lyons, 'Vielle mulle du temps passé.' (Cf. MT.)

XXXVI. 'Tho' in margin.

XXXVII. D, T. 'Tho' in margin; in W section of T. Rhyme royal.

XXXVIII. 'Tho' in margin.

XXXIX. D, B, A. 'Tho' in margin; 'fynys q^d Wyat' in D. The stanza form may owe something to the Italian sestina. (Cf. Ivy Mumford, *EM*, 1963, 12–15, about W's 'patience' poems and their possible relation to Italian musical forms.) In MT, there are four poems related formally and to a lesser extent thematically which may be conceived of as a group: XXXIX, XL, CXC, and CCXXIX. The first is the only one ascribed to W; the last two can be found in MT, F, etc. XL is here printed because it occurs in E and clearly relates to its predecessor. Cf. also MT's CCLIII (here CLXXV). The poems are possibly indebted to Serafino, 'Canzona de la Patientia' (cf. MT), but the theme was always dear to W's heart, and cf. his interest in Plutarch, Seneca, Boethius.

XL. D, B, A.

XLI. D; which supplies lines 1–23 (missing from E). In D the stanza form is consistent throughout.

XLII. D, A, T. 'Tho' in margin; corrected by W; in W section of T. Strambotto (one ottava rima stanza used as an epigram).

XLIII. D, A, V.

XLIV. A, T. 'Tho' in margin; corrected by W; in W section of T. Strambotto. Serafino, *Opere*, 'Incolpa donna amor se troppo io uolsi.'

XLV. D. 'Tho' in margin; possibly corrected by W; 'fynys q^d Wyatt' in D. Rondeau.

XLVI. D, P, T, N. 'Tho' in margin; corrected by W; 'W' in D; in W section of T. Strambotto.

XLVII. D, A, T. 'Tho' in margin; in W section of T. Sonnet. Petrarch, *Rime*, 'Vive faville uscian de'duo bei lumi.'

XLVIII. A, T. 'Tho' in margin; in W section of T. Strambotto. Serafino, *Opere*, 'À che minacci, à che tanta ira e orgoglio.'

XLIX. A, T. 'Tho' in margin; in W section of T.

L. A, T. 'Tho' in margin; in W section of T. Rhyme royal. Headed 'anna' in E.

LI. D, B. 'Tho' in margin; corrected by W; 'ffynys q^d Wyatt' in D. D supplies lines 41–48. For the form cf., e.g., Robbins, poems 137 and 173.

LII. D, T, V, N. 'Tho' in margin; 'ffynys q^d Wyatt' in D; in W section of T.

LIII. A, T. 'Tho' in margin; corrected by W; in W section of T. Cf. Giusto de'Conti, *Rime &c*, Venice, 1531, 'Chi dara a gliocchi miei si larga vena.' (See MT.)

LIV. D, A, T. 'Tho' in margin; corrected by W; in W section of T. Strambotto.

LV. D; lines 17–20 are absent from E, 'with consequent dislocation of speech-headings' (MT). 'Wyat' in the margin of E; but cf. SCM, 4, about D. In the carol tradition. Another version, with music by Thomas Cornish, consisting of 1–12 only, appears in B.M. Add. MS. 31922, 'Henry VIII's MS.', a courtly songbook (*c.* 1515) with poems by the King and others; cf. the transcription in F (the text is also in MT, and in Stevens). W may have been reworking a popular song (LV is more sophisticated in 9–12); it is not known whether there was a version, not by W, including the stanzas beyond 1–12.

LVI. D, A, T. 'Wyat' in margin; corrected by W; 'TW' in D; in W section of T. Sonnet. Petrarch, *Rime*, 'Pien d'un vago penser, che mi desvia.'

LVII. D, A. 'Tho' in margin; corrected by W.

LVIII. D, A. 'Tho' in margin.

LIX. D, H, A, T. 'Tho' in margin; corrected by W; 'Wiat' in D; 'Tho. W.' in H; in W section of T. Strambotto.

LX. D, P, T, N. 'Tho' in margin; corrected by W; in W section of T. Strambotto. Serafino, *Opere*, 'Sio con caduto interra inon son morto.'

LXI. A, T. 'Tho' in margin; corrected by W; in W section of T. Strambotto. Serafino, *Opere*, 'Se una bombarda è dal gran foco mossa.'

LXII. D, A. 'Tho' in margin. Rhyme royal.

LXIII. D. 'Tho' in margin; corrected by W.

LXIV. T. 'Tho' in margin; corrected by W; in W section of T. Strambotto. About sources, cf. Rollins.

LXV. D, T, N. 'Tho' in margin; in W section of T.

LXVI. D, B, T, V, N. 'Tho' in margin; corrected by W; ascribed 'fynys q^d Wyatt' in D; in W section of T. N ascribes LXVI to Rochford (Anne Boleyn's brother, cf. CXLIX). The ascription may have been taken over from A (cf. Hughey, I, 25), and is of dubious authority anyhow.

LXVII. D, B. 'Tho' in margin.

LXVIII. D, H, B, T. 'Tho' in margin; corrected by W; 'Tho. W.' in H; in W section of T. Strambotto.

LXIX. D. 'Tho' in margin; corrected by W.

LXX. D, B. E provides only the beginnings of the lines (the leaf is torn); the remainder is supplied from D. 'Tho' in margin.

LXXI. D. Since the leaf in E is torn (cf. LXX), the beginnings of the lines are supplied from D.

LXXII. D, B. 'Tho' in margin.

LXXIII. D. 'Tho' in margin; ascribed 'ffynys q^d Wyatt' in D. For a discussion of possible sources, cf. MT.

LXXIV. D. 'Tho' in margin. Followed in E by a gap, then part of the first satire (CV).

LXXV. D, T. In W's hand; 'Tho' in margin; in W section of T. Strambotto.

LXXVI. D, H, P, T, N, CC. In W's hand; 'Tho' in margin; 'T.W.' in H; in W section of T. Strambotto. Serafino, *Opere*, 'Ogni pungente & uenenosa spina.' In E, the poem is followed by the second satire (CVI).

LXXVII. D. 'Tho' in margin.

LXXVIII. B. Rhyme royal.

LXXIX. A, T. In W section of T. Sonnet. Cf. Filosseno, *Sylve*, Venice, 1507, 'Pareami in questa nocte esser contente' (in MT); but erotic dreams are common in Petrarchan and medieval English literature.

LXXX. T. In W's hand; 'Tho' in margin; in W section of T. Strambotto. Biblioteca Nacional, Madrid, MS. 4117, f. 227^v, 'Mentre nel duro petto e dispietato.' (Cf. MT.)

LXXXI. T. In W's hand; 'Tho' in margin; in W section of T. Strambotto. Source, perhaps indirectly: Petrarch, *Rime*, 'Vinse Anibàl, e non seppe usar poi.'

LXXXII. A. 'Tho' in margin. Perhaps corrected by W. For a discussion of possible sources, cf. MT.

LXXXIII. A. In E, this is followed by the third satire (CVII).

LXXXIV. 'Tho' in margin.

LXXXV. 'Tho' in margin; corrected by W. For probable sources, cf. MT.

LXXXVI. H. 'Tho' in margin; 'T.W.' in H. Petrarch, *Rime*, 'O bella man che mi destringi 'l core.'

LXXXVII. B. 'Tho' in margin; corrected by W. A poem somewhat similar to this ascribed to Alexander Scott is probably, as F and others argue, an imitation of W's, but cf. John MacQueen, *FMLS*, 1967, 219–20.

LXXXVIII. 'Tho' in margin; corrected by W. Strambotto.

LXXXIX. D. 'Tho' in margin. MT suggests the form may have been influenced by Italian *canzoni*.

XC. T. 'T.W.' in margin; in W section of T.

XCI. 'Tho' in margin.

XCII. A, T. 'Tho' in margin; in W section of T. Sonnet.

XCIII. The two E versions have been conflated. Rhyme royal.

XCIV. E, 1–37 (corrected by W); A, which supplies the remainder. Terza rima. The best discussions of the sources are those by Mason (cf. CVIII, below), who is undoubtedly right in claiming that the

Campensis–Zwingli *Enchiridion Psalmorum* is the main source for XCIV (its influence on CVIII is also clear, but less conspicuous). W may have consulted the English translation of Campensis, *A Paraphrasis upon all the Psalmes of Dauid* (1535), but there is no clear evidence of this.

XCV. B, T. In W's hand; 'Tho' in margin; ascribed 'W' in B; in W section of T. Strambotto. Cf. MT for a discussion of possible sources.

XCVI. In W's hand.

XCVII. A, T. 'Tho' in margin; corrected by W; in W section of T. Sonnet. Probably partly derived from Petrarch, *Rime* ccxxiv (cf. XII).

XCVIII. D, A, T. In W's hand; in W section of T. Poulter's measure. Petrarch, *Rime*, 'Sí è debile il filo a cui s'attene.' (Cf. III.) W in his own way follows the stanzaic divisions of his original, as Nott noted, and the poem can be seen to consist of seven sections (14 + 14 + 14 + 12 + 14 + 12 + 14), followed by a coda of six lines.

XCIX. T. In W's hand; in W section of T. Strambotto.

C. T. In W's hand; in W section of T. Strambotto.

CI. T. In W's hand; in W section of T.

CII. In W's hand. Poulter's measure. Petrarch, *Rime*, 'Di pensier in pensier, di monte in monte.'

CIII. H, T. 'A Ridell. Tho. W.' in H; in W section of T. Strambotto. The source is provided by H:

> Vulcanus genuit, peperit natura, Minerua
> Edocuit, genitrix ars fuit atque dies.
> Vis mea de nihilo est, tria dant mihi corpora pastum.
> Sunt nati strages, ira, ruina, fragor.
> Dic hospes quid sim, num terrae, an bellua ponti?
> An neutrum, an prosint facta uel orta modo?

accompanied by 'Idem latine ex Pandulpho' (i.e. Pandolfo Collinutio, fl. *c.* 1500). Acc. to Nott the Latin poem is part of a dialogue by P. C., governor of the state at Siena, in which he probably tried to persuade 'his fellow citizens to purchase artillery for the defence of the town'.

T's explanatory title is 'Discripcion of a gonne'. Its text may have been copied into E, and I therefore chiefly follow H. The next E poem is Surrey's 'The great Macedon', followed by the Penitential Psalms (cf. CVIII).

CIV. A, T. In W's hand; in W section of T. Poulter's measure. Cf. David Scott, 'Wyatt's Worst Poem', *TLS*, 13 September 1963, 696, about W's debt to Joannes de Sacrobosco's *De Sphaera* (Paris, 1527 ff.), with commentary by J. Faber Stapulensis. After l. 52, but well apart from it, there are two more lines in W's hand, which seem to read: 'Nor is it lyk that man may think thes steres all/streys ther path as thei do passe within that hevinly hall.' CIV is the last W poem in E.

CV. D, C, A, P, T, CC. Since lines 1–51 are absent from E, D must serve as the copy text for them (cf. Hughey), though C is used for ll. 28–30, and in some places provides a better or clearer reading. In W section of T. Terza rima. Alamanni, *Opere Toscane* (Lyons and Florence, 1532), Satira X, 'À Thomaso Sertini'. Cf. MT.

CVI. D, A, T. In W section of T. Terza rima. Cf. the second half of Horace, Satire II, vi; Henryson's 'Taill of the Uponlondis Mous and the Burges Mous'; and Denton Fox, *N & Q*, 1971, 203–7. W may have known several versions of the story; cf. Thomson, 259–67. Chaucer's pervasive influence on W's language has been noted by Nott and others; the footnotes merely record some of the more striking examples.

CVII. A, T. Corrected by W; in W section of T. Terza rima. Probably suggested by Horace, Satire II, v.

CVIII. R, A, Q. Lines 100–53 are missing from E. I have supplied them from R and A, using the printed text (Q) as a check. MEW (140–54) seems right in regarding R as superior in some places; but the text constructed (153–4) includes unwarranted readings. I nevertheless owe one or two suggestions to it. CVIII is in W's hand, with many corrections; it is not always clear which reading should be preferred. The poem was printed, with W's name on the title page, in 1549 (Q).

The Prologues are in ottava rima, and heavily indebted to Pietro Aretino's paraphrase of the Penitential Psalms, in Italian (1534), which also influences to some extent W's version of the Psalms themselves. These are in terza rima. While it seems likely enough that W consulted several versions of the Bible (amongst them the Latin Vulgate of 1525), it is hardly possible to understand the degree of his originality (or sometimes his meaning) without reference to other important sources: Harold Mason, in *TLS*, 27 February and 6 March 1953, *Humanism and Poetry in the Early Tudor Period* (London, 1959), 204–21, and MEW, 178–93, discusses W's handling of material derived from Ioannis Campensis' *Enchiridion Psalmorum* (1532; and 1533, with Zwingli's paraphrase), George Joye's translation of Zwingli (1534), Luther, Tyndale, Fisher. MT's Commentary should be approached with caution, since it presses the claims of doubtful sources, and too often pays no attention to significant ones (cf. XCIV). See also Donald M. Friedman's 'The "Thing" in Wyatt's Mind', *EinC*, 1966, 375–81, and Robert G. Twombly's 'Thomas Wyatt's Paraphrase of the Penitential Psalms of David', *TSSL*, 1970, 345–80, both of which provide further information on the relation between W and his sources.

CIX. Signed 'Th W'.

CX. Ascribed 'fynys qd Wyatt'. Perhaps partly suggested by Ovid, *Amores*, I.2, 1–4.

CXI. Ascribed 'fynys qd Wyatt'.

CXII. Ascribed 'fynys qd W.'.

CXIII. Lines 1–7 appear in E, in Grimald's hand, and were probably 'edited' by him. T. Ascribed 'ffynys qd Wyatt' in D; in W section of T. Rhyme royal. Source (Nott), perhaps indirectly, Petrarch, *Rime*, 'O cameretta che già fusti un porto'. But SCM (152) compares Lydgate's 'The Complaint of the Black Knight', 218–24, and Chaucer's 'A Complaint to His Lady'.

CXIV. T. Ascribed 'W'; in W section of T.

CXV. 'W' at foot of third stanza.

CXVI. T; in the W section. Strambotto. Serafino, *Opere*, 'Viuo sol di mirarti hai dura impresa.'

CXVII. T; in the W section. Sonnet.

CXVIII. B, T. In W section of T. Petrarch, *Rime*, 'S'i'l dissi mai, ch'i'vegna in odio a quella.' Cf. further MT (for 'Cecchini' read 'Nott').

CXIX. B, T. In W section of T. Rhyme royal.

CXX. V.

CXXII. Perhaps written by a woman.

CXXV. Rhyme royal.

CXXXI. Sonnet.

CXXXII. An introductory couplet was commonly provided as the burden of carols. The stanzas are in rhyme royal.

CXXXIII. Ottava rima. This may owe something to Petrarch, *Rime*, 'Voi ch'ascoltate in rime sparse il suono', but cf. MT.

CXXXIV. Sonnet.

CXXXVI. Rhyme royal. This need not be W's, but there are some marked parallels with words and phrases in his letters, e.g. *advertise* (3); *bruit and . . . fame* (11; cf. ML, 149); *And thus of this letter making an end* (34) . . . *commend* (35) . . . *recommended* (42)—cf. ML, 133; *But says as he thinks* (6; cf. ML, 146). Cf. also CV, 46; and CVI. But such parallels are not conclusive.

CXXXVII. Cf. Serafino, *Opere*, 'Fvi serrato nel dolore.'

CXXXVIII. Sonnet.

CXXXIX. GG.

CXL. B.

CXLI. B. Also in the Bannatyne MS. (cf. John MacQueen, ed., *Ballatis of Luve*, Edinburgh, 1970); and, in a much shorter carol form (with the burden provided at the beginning as 'I ham as I ham and so will I be/but howe I ham none knowithe truly') in MS. Latin 35 (University of Pennsylvania Library; discussed by R. L. Greene, *RES*, 1964, 175–80, and in MEW). It looks as though the shorter poem might underlie the other versions, among which D appears to be the most authoritative.

CXLII. B, which provides l. 32. Rhyme royal.

CXLIII. Cf. Seneca's *Phaedra*, 1125 ff. (ML, 32 and 234); the refrain *circa Regna tonat* is taken over literally. Authorship: see motto.

CXLIV. Signed 'T W' in B.

CXLV. T; in the W section.

CXLVI. P, T, N; which are preferred to the (miscorrected?) B version where they agree and give better sense. In W section of T. Strambotto.

CXLVII. T; in the W section.

CXLVIII. T; in the W section. Possibly inspired by Petrarch's 'Ite, calde sospiri' (cf. XX).

CL. Strambotto. Serafino, *Opere*, 'Ahime tu dormi, & io con alta uoce', and 'Tu dormi, io ueglio, & uó perdendo ipassi' (cf. MT).

CLI. Strambotto. The ancestor of this is a Greek epigram, which W may have known in a Latin version by Ausonius or someone else (cf. MT). However, the poem in Ausonius is not particularly close to CLI, and MEW (176–7) rightly argues that it need not be W's source. Cf. CLXXIX.

CLII. Strambotto. Possible source (cf. MEW, 177):

> De Venere, et Priapo
> Tractabat clypeum Marti placitura Dione:
> Saeuaque foeminea sumpserat arma manu.
> Pone, Dea, exclamat petulanti uoce Priapus;
> Pone, decent istas haec magis arma manus.

Sannazaro, *Opere Omnia Latine Scripta* (1535), Epigrams, Book II, 13.

CLIV. Rhyme royal.

CLVIII. Rhyme royal.

CLX. T; in the W section. The T variants seem preferable, but T is apt to be even more unreliable than A. Sonnet. Petrarch, *Rime*, 'Rotta è l' alta colonna e 'l verde lauro.'

CLXI. T; in the W section. Also in MS. Rawlinson Poet. 172, fol. 3ᵛ. 'Poems with a like termination throughout were called *like loose* (*i.e.* like end), from a term in archery' (F, II, 164).

CLXII. T; in the W section. A double sonnet. Cf. CLXXII.

CLXIII. T; in the W section. Source (Chalmers, cf. Rollins, II, 211): Seneca, *Thyestes*, 391–403. Rollins and Hughey print the Latin correctly; Nott, F, and MT incorrectly.

CLXIV. Strambotto.

CLXV. T. Headed in H: 'Tho. W. to Bryan'; in W section of T; referred to as W's by Surrey (cf. ed. Emrys Jones, poem 34, 6). Strambotto.

CLXVI. Ascribed in H: 'T Wyat of Love'. Comparison with E shows that H is generally reliable, and we may therefore probably assume that its text is reasonably trustworthy and that the poem is indeed W's. If so, a poem by Surrey in P, which shares some of its stanzas with W's, is perhaps a reworking of CLXVI. (A version in N is almost identical to P's; cf. Hughey, I, 375–6.) T, which is often even further removed from E than P, produces yet another version as Surrey's; significantly, it is closer to P than to H. The P version appears in MT's Commentary, with several minor errors, and one major one, *name* for *harme* (st. 6). Padelford's text is more accurate.

CLXVII. T; in the W section. Rhyme royal.

CLXVIII. T, N. In W section of T. Strambotto.

CLXIX. This and all the following poems are ascribed to W by T.

CLXX. Rhyme royal.

CLXXII. Sonnet, rhyming *abababababababcc*. This form, unique in W, but sometimes used by Surrey, is often seen as intermediate between the Petrarchan one, with a marked division between octave and sestet, and the 'Shakespearean' scheme of three quatrains followed by a couplet. It seems closer to the latter than to the former. W's common form, *abbaabbacddcee*, is itself a compromise between the two schemes. Probably W's use of the final couplet logically led to his invention of the scheme established firmly in the language by Surrey, and made famous by Shakespeare. Cf. CLXII, which has the form *abbacddceffegg*, i.e. three quatrains followed by a couplet.

CLXXIV. There is a version in the *Paradise of Dainty Devices* (1576; ed. H. E. Rollins, Cambridge, Mass., 1927) with the signature W. H. (William Hunnis); it is very different from W's poem, and in any case T's ascription is probably more reliable. The probable source is Tebaldeo, *Opere* (Venice, *c.* 1500), 'Deh per che non mi fur suelti de testa.' (Cf. MT.)

CLXXV. Cf. XXXIX and XL.

CLXXVII. Ottava rima. Cf., e.g., 'La Belle Dame sans Merci' as an example of a dialogue poem (F), a genre which also occurs (Nott) in, e.g., *The Paradise* (cf. CLXXIV) and *England's Helicon* (1600; ed. Hugh Macdonald, London, 1949).

CLXXIX. Strambotto. Ultimately this goes back to an epigram probably written by Plato (text in Nott, F, and Rollins). This was translated twice by Ausonius (*Epigrammata*, xxii, xxiii). The first version appears in Nott, F, and MT. W may derive his version from Ausonius, or from another paraphrase. The claim that Ausonius' first (or second) version necessarily underlies W's is as dubious as in the case of CLI.

CLXXXI. Rhyme royal.

CLXXXII. V2 (Folger fragment), Z. T, as elsewhere, is without a refrain in l. 5, etc.; this deficiency is made up from V2. Though V's text, as often, is poor and here uses the internal rhyme *not-not-wot*, etc., less consistently than T, the conflation creates a poem with a systematic structure. Z is even more eccentric than V2, but it supplies *wote* in l. 19, where T has *know*.

CLXXXIV. Rhyme royal. Cf. Chaucer, *Boece*, III, metres 5, 6, and 3. W may have consulted Boethius' *De Consolatione Philosophiae*, or a paraphrase other than Chaucer's; nonetheless, there are so many linguistic resemblances between the *Boece* passages and W's poem (several of which were not dictated by the Latin, cf. particularly Chaucer's rendering of metre 3), that W's debt to Chaucer seems certain. MT prints the relevant passages from Boethius, and from Thynne's edition of Chaucer (1532), with several errors (cf. MEW, 173). Patricia Thomson's suggestion (*RES*, 1964, 262–7) that CLXXXIV is a 'formal imitation' of Chaucer's 'Truth' (*Balade de Bon Conseyl*)) is unnecessary and does not seem to be strongly supported by the evidence.

SELECTED TEXTUAL NOTES

I	14	*entreateth*: MS. *entreath*. (T *entreateth*, but D *entreathe*.)
VIII	19, 23, 25, 42	*hath*: MS. *have*. (23, 42: A, T *hath*: and cf. XXII, 4.)
	26	*araced*: MS. *ataced*. (A, T *araced*.)
	55	*this*: MS. *this his*. (Cf. metre; It. *questo tiranno*; and, e.g., XXIII, *wot not*.)
XII	1	*in*: A, T *an* (cf. It. *un*).
XXII	4	*hath*: MS. *have*. D *hathe*. (But T *haue*.)
	21	*rewarded*: D, T *reward*.
XXV	7	*toward*: A *a worde*, T *one word*. (Cf. It. *parole fai*—Maxwell.)
XXVI	13	*death and life*: so D, P, T. E *lyff & deth*.
XXXI	8	*at*: MS. *and*; later *in* (so A, T).
XXXII	8	*no*: later addition in MS. (So A, T.)
XXXIII	9	*boistous*: so A, T. Cf. *OED boistous*. E *boyseus*.
XXXIX	5	*can*: MS. first had *not*. (D, B, A *can*.)
XLI	32	*hard*: F conj.; gap in E.
XLIII	28	*steadfast*: from D. E *stedfastnes*. (So A.)
LII	29	*such*: later insertion in E. T (*Souch*). D *& yf suche chance do chaunce* (so V).
LIII	14	*rue*: later insertion in E. (So A, T.)
LVIII	5	*day*: later insertion in E. So D.
	27	*entreat*: so D, A. E *trete*. Cf. metre.
LXII	20	*my*: so D, A. E *me*; but cf. 6.
LXV	8	*to*: so D, T, N. Omitted in E.
LXVII	7	*only*: so D; omitted in E.
LXX	19	*weary*: Nott. conj.; B *wery*, D *verye*. Cf. CXXXVII, 8.
LXXI	22	*determed*: D *determind*. But in line 1 E has *rmed*.
LXXII	19	*yslain*: D *I slayne*. E *slain*, but cf. metre.
LXXIII	29	*my tears*: *my* from D; not in E.
LXXVIII	1	*thy port*: *thy* from B; not in E.
LXXXII	18	*boot*: Nott conj.; absent from E and A.
LXXXVII	5	*grounded*: from B. E *ground is*.
	28	*hath*: MS. *have*. Cf. XXII, 4.
LXXXVIII	3	*me*: uncertain reading.
LXXXIX	5	*For*: so D; E *from*.
XC	22	*doth*: from T; not in E.
XCI	2, 3	*thy*: MS. *the*.
	15	*it*: Flügel conj.; not in MS.
XCIII	38	*that that*: E *that*. Nott conj. *Truth*. This fits eminently, but the copyist may easily have omitted a second *that* (i.e. *truth*).

XCIV   16 *Bright as*: E *Vpright all*. A: *Vprighte as*. Nott conj. *Bright*; proved correct by Campensis.
    52 *men's*: A *mans*. Cf. Campensis *iustorum*.
XCVIII   70 *streams*: W *strenes*, almost certainly for *stremes* (thus D, A, T).
CV   45 *coward*: so C, A, P. D *cowardes* (= *cowardous?*).
    54 *he* (2): D etc.; omitted in E.
CVI   14 *when her*: D, A, T. E *wher*.
    25 *delicates*: A, T. E *the delicates*.
    52 *looked*: from A, T. E *loke*.
    55 *for though the unwise*: E *for tho*; A, T *for the vnwise*.
    89 *set*: from A, T. E *se*.
    107 *them*: A, T. E *then*. Cf. XCVIII, 70.
CVII   37 *nowadays*: E *nowadaye se* (possibly *nowadaye so*). A, T *now adayes*.
CVIII   4 *David's*: W *david*; but cf. 'syght'.
    56 *worldly*: W *wordly*.
    311 *descends*: possibly (but probably not) *distendes*.
    464 *not*: W *no*; but cf. 'the'.
    469 *do*: possibly *to*.
    536 *so much*: *so* possibly rejected.
CX   4, 8, 12, 16, 24, 28, 32 *meaneth*: MS. *menys*. But cf. 1, 20 *menythe*.
CXIV   8 *face*: T. D *place*.
    11 *upon*: from T. D *on*.
CXV   20 *Do*: Nott conj.; MS. *to*.
CXVIII   14 *of*: B, T *on*.
    16 *word*: B, T *wordes*.
    17 *If I said so*: B. T *And yff I dyd*.
    24 *this*: B, T *hys*.
    32 *by*: B *my*.
    33 *for*: B, T *from*.
CXXVII   3 *no*: Nott conj.; not in MS.
CXXXV   15 *setst*: M conj.; MS. *seiste*.
    22 *that thou*: MS. *thou*. Cf. metre.
CXXXVII   8 *weary*: Nott conj.; MS. *verye*. Cf. LXX, 19.
CXLI   16 *But I*: B, etc., include *I*; D omits it.
CXLII   35 *be*: B; not in D.
CXLIV   8 *who is for me*: MS. *who ys me for me*; but *me* (1) appears to be deleted.
CXLV   6 *promised*: B *promace*, changed to *promast*, perhaps by a later hand. T *promised*.
    12 *friend*: B *frynd*, changed to *frynds*, perhaps by a later hand. T *frend*.
CXLVIII   18 *of*: T *or*.
    32 *an*: MS. reading obscure, but *an* rather than MT's *my*. T *a*.

CXLIX	45	*thee lament*: Maxwell conj.; MS. has *lament* followed by *y* and two (?) indecipherable letters, possibly *ne*, though one would expect *ee*.
CLIII	24	*In hope*: MT; MS. *in soo hope*.
CLVIII	11	*thought*: MS. *thoughe*. But cf. XXIX, 10, where MS. *though* clearly represents *thought*.
CLIX	1	*they*: MT conj.; MS. *y*ᵗ.
CLXII	21	*tasting*: T *trifling*.
CLXIII	8	*For*: T; A *ffrom*.
CLXVI	13	*first saw*: from P, T. H *forsaw*.
CLXXVII	7	*alas with*: T1; T2 *and rew my*.

INDEX OF FIRST LINES

page